CW01475819

# FROM ARRIAN TO ALEXANDER

# FROM ARRIAN TO ALEXANDER

## Studies in
## Historical Interpretation

✤

A. B. BOSWORTH

CLARENDON PRESS · OXFORD
1988

Oxford University Press, Walton Street, Oxford OX2 6DP

Oxford New York Toronto
Delhi Bombay Calcutta Madras Karachi
Petaling Jaya Singapore Hong Kong Tokyo
Nairobi Dar es Salaam Cape Town
Melbourne Auckland

and associated companies in
Beirut Berlin Ibadan Nicosia

Oxford is a trade mark of Oxford University Press

Published in the United States
by Oxford University Press, New York

British Library Cataloguing in Publication Data
Bosworth, A. B.
From Arrian to Alexander: studies in
historical interpretation.
1. Arrian, Anabasis  2. Alexander III,
King of Macedonia  3. Iran—History
—To 640
I. Title
938'.07'0924—DF234.A773
ISBN 0-19-814863-1

Library of Congress Cataloging in Publication Data
Bosworth, A. B.
From Arrian to Alexander.
Bibliography: p.
Includes index.
1. Alexander, the Great, 359–323 BC.  2. Arrian.
3. Greece—History—Macedonian Expansion, 359–323 BC—
Historiography. I. Title.
DF234.2.B67  1988  938'.07'072  87–7039
ISBN 0-19-814863-1

Set by Eta Services (Typesetters) Ltd, Beccles, Suffolk
Printed and bound in Great Britain by
Biddles Ltd, Guildford and King's Lynn

# PREFACE

This book has two aims, as its title implies. In the first place it is designed as a contribution to Arrian scholarship, enlarging on important general issues which could only be tackled briefly or peripherally in my *Historical Commentary on Arrian*. In some ways it can be regarded as an extended *prolegomenon* to the second volume of that work, which has already been unduly delayed and threatens to be delayed still further (ὅμως δὲ λῦσαι δυνατὸς ὀξεῖαν ἐπιμομφὰν | τόκος). The focus is the literary techniques and historical method of Arrian and the subject matter is deliberately chosen from the latter books of the Alexander history. The study, I think, has wide implications. Much of the extant historical writing that survives from antiquity is secondary, a reworking of material already familiar to its readers; and the primary objective of the authors was not the discovery of new facts but the literary presentation of a known tradition. Arrian saw himself as the definitive historian of Alexander who would provide the classic account of the king's exploits, and he used every device of rhetoric and literary allusion at his disposal, reshaping and embellishing the source material that he chose as the basis for his narrative. His sources are known and his techniques respond well to analysis. For that reason the results of this study (I hope) will be found generally useful in assessing the Greek historians of the Roman Empire.

There is also a more philosophical intention. The study of ancient historiography is all too often divorced from the writing of history proper. Much labour is devoted to illustrating the methods, biases, and deficiencies of extant and non-extant historians, only to be neglected when it is a question of establishing hard fact. The period of Alexander the Great is a particularly good example. The peculiar nature of the historical sources is well known, all late, derivative, and fallible, but it is rare that full attention is paid to the process of transmission. All too often it is assumed that Arrian *is* simply transcribed Ptolemy (or Aristobulus), or Diodorus an echo, albeit a crude one, of Cleitarchus. That leads at worst to a simple balancing of Arrian and the so-called vulgate tradition. One accepts what fits one's conceptual scheme and rejects what is inconsistent, on largely subjective grounds. I make no apologies for advocating a more complicated method. In the first place one needs to examine the general context of an attested tradition and evaluate the literary and, where relevant, the rhetorical techniques at work, separating the presumed original material from its secondary embellishment. Only then can one pit the variant traditions against each other and determine the range of agreement and contradiction. Not every problem responds to the technique, for one requires controls, cases where the same source material is used by two or more derivative writers, and often the basic material for comparison does not exist. Fortunately the historical tradition of Alexander's reign is rich enough for the methods of the extant writers to be at least partially elucidated. The last chapters of the book are an attempt to put these principles into practice and approach fundamental questions of fact from a historiographical perspective.

The book originated as a series of seminars given at Oxford University under the Faculty of Literae Humaniores (in Hilary Term, 1984). There seemed to be a unity of theme which justified publication in revised form as a monograph and I am grateful to the Oxford University Press for accepting the work. I have a deep obligation to all members of my Oxford audience, who both challenged and refined my views, and in particular to George Forrest who hosted the seminars and to Peter Brunt, George Cawkwell, Simon Hornblower, and John Atkinson who asked the hard questions. I must also express my gratitude to my own university for the leave which made the work possible and specifically to Neil O'Sullivan who criticized the typescript, Ian Sharples who helped with proof reading and indexing, and my secretaries, Carol Freele and Kay Sanders who processed a difficult manuscript with skill and understanding. Lastly I should pay tribute to the courtesy and efficiency of En Kho and the Inter Library Loans section at the Reid Library without whose assistance there could be no serious work in the Humanities in this state.

A.B.B.

*July 1987*

# CONTENTS

# LIST OF FIGURES

# TABLE

# ABBREVIATIONS

References to ancient sources and modern literature follow standard conventions. In each chapter the footnotes are interrelated to provide direction to full bibliographical information. The following list has two functions: it gives special abbreviations of works frequently used and also explains abbreviations which might be considered abstruse.

| | |
|---|---|
| *AAA* | Ἀρχαιολογικὰ Ἀνάλεκτα ἐξ Ἀθηνῶν: *Athens Annals of Archaeology* |
| *AE* | *L'Année Épigraphique* |
| *ANRW* | *Aufstieg und Niedergang der römischen Welt*, ed. H. Temporini and W. Haase (Berlin/New York, 1972– ) |
| Avenarius | G. Avenarius, *Lukians Schrift zur Geschichtsschreibung* (Meisenheim/Glan, 1956) |
| *BE* | *Bulletin Épigraphique*, ed. J. and L. Robert (epigraphical reviews, published initially in *REG* and reprinted as a series with indices; Paris, 1972– ) |
| Berve | H. Berve, *Das Alexanderreich auf prosopographischer Grundlage* i–ii (Munich, 1926) |
| Brunt, *Arrian* | P. A. Brunt, *Arrian* i–ii (Loeb Classical Library; Cambridge, Mass., 1976–83) |
| *CHIran* ii | *The Cambridge History of Iran* ii, ed. I. Gershevitch (Cambridge, 1985) |
| *CIL* | *Corpus inscriptionum Latinarum* |
| *FGrH* | F. Jacoby, *Die Fragmente der griechischen Historiker* (Berlin/Leiden 1923– , rev. edn. 1957). (References to the text are given by the number of the author in the collection [e.g. 'Duris, *FGrH* 76 F 1'], references to the commentary by the volume number [e.g. '*FGrH* ii.D 563'].) |
| *Greece & the E. Mediterranean* | *Greece and the Eastern Mediterranean in History and Prehistory: Studies Presented to Fritz Schachermeyr*, ed. K. H. Kinzl (Berlin, 1977) |
| Halfmann | H. Halfmann, *Die Senatoren aus dem östlichen Teil des Imperium Romanum* (Göttingen, 1979) |
| Hamilton *Plut. Al.* | J. R. Hamilton, *Plutarch Alexander: A Commentary* (Oxford, 1969) |
| Hammond, KCS | N. G. L. Hammond, *Alexander the Great: King, Commander and Statesman* (Park Ridge, NJ, 1980) |
| Hammond, *Three Historians* | N. G. L. Hammond, *Three Historians of Alexander the Great* (Cambridge, 1983) |
| *HCArr.* | A. B. Bosworth, *A Historical Commentary on Arrian's History of Alexander* (Oxford, 1980– ) |
| *IGR* | *Inscriptiones graecae ad res romanas pertinentes* |

| | |
|---|---|
| *ILS* | *Inscriptiones latinae selectae*, ed. H. Dessau (Berlin, 1892–1916) |
| Kornemann | E. Kornemann, *Die Alexandergeschichte des Königs Ptolemaios I. von Aegypten* (Leipzig, 1935) |
| *PACA* | *Proceedings of the African Classical Association* |
| *PIR*[2] | *Prosopographia imperii Romani, saec. I, II, III*, 2nd edn., eds. E. Groag, A. Stein, L. Petersen (Berlin/Leipzig, 1933– ) |
| Pearson, *LHA* | L. Pearson, *The Lost Histories of Alexander the Great* (Philological Monographs XX; Am. Phil. Ass. 1960) |
| *RE* | *Realencyclopädie der classichen Altertumswissenschaft*, ed. Pauly, Wissowa, Kroll (Stuttgart, 1893– ) |
| Schachermeyr, *Alexander der Grosse* | F. Schachermeyr, *Alexander der Grosse: Das Problem seiner Persönlichkeit und seines Wirkens* (SB. Wien 285; Vienna, 1973) |
| *SEG* | *Supplementum epigraphicum Graecum* |
| Stadter | P. A. Stadter, *Arrian of Nicomedia* (Chapel Hill, 1980) |
| Strasburger, *Studien* | H. Strasburger, *Studien zur alten Geschichte* i–ii (Hildesheim, 1982) |
| *SVF* | *Stoicorum veterum fragmenta* i–iv, ed. H. von Arnim (Leipzig, 1903–24) |
| Tarn, *Alexander* | W. W. Tarn, *Alexander the Great* i–ii (Cambridge, 1948) |
| Walbank, *HCP* | F. W. Walbank, *A Historical Commentary on Polybius* i–iii (Oxford, 1957–79) |
| Wilcken, *UPZ* | U. Wilcken, *Urkunden der Ptolemäerzeit* i–ii (Berlin, 1922–37) |
| Wilcken, *Berliner Akademieschriften* | U. Wilcken, *Berliner Akademieschriften zur alten Geschichte und Papyruskunde (1883–1942)* i–ii (Leipzig, 1970) |
| Wirth, *Studien* | G. Wirth, *Studien zur Alexandergeschichte* (Darmstadt, 1985) |

# INTRODUCTION
## SOME BASIC PRINCIPLES

THE period of Alexander the Great is at first sight well attested.[1] There is an apparent abundance of narrative material: full-length histories of the reign by Arrian and Curtius Rufus, a formal biography by Plutarch, a whole book of Diodorus Siculus' *Bibliotheca*, two books of Justin's epitome of Pompeius Trogus, and substantial passages in the latter books of Strabo's *Geography*. This wealth of documentation is misleading, for all the primary sources are late. The earliest of our extant authorities, Diodorus, composed his work in the third quarter of the first century BC. Strabo wrote in the late Augustan period, Curtius at a still undefined date in the early Empire,[2] Plutarch and Arrian in the second century AD, and Trogus' work, composed under Augustus, is known through the third-century epitome of Justin. There is, then, a hiatus of close to three centuries between the death of Alexander in June 323 and the first connected narrative of the reign. The problem of transmission therefore becomes acute. What sources did our extant authorities use and how faithfully did they report the substance of what they read? Both questions are clearly important. A careless and perfunctory epitome by a secondary author

[1] For modern bibliography the two surveys by Jakob Seibert are indispensable: *Alexander der Grosse* (Erträge der Forschung 10; Darmstadt, 1972); *Das Zeitalter der Diadochen* (Erträge der Forschung 185; Darmstadt, 1983). Both volumes present an exhaustive survey of modern literature from the middle of the nineteenth century and obviate the need for extensive references to secondary works. I shall attempt to limit my annotations to what is most important or most recent.

[2] The controversy about the date is unresolved and continuing. J. E. Atkinson, *A Commentary on Q. Curtius Rufus' Historiae Alexandri Magni Books 3 and 4* (Amsterdam, 1980) 19–57, has presented the strongest case yet for the reign of Claudius (see further, Syme, *HSCP* 86 [1982] 197 f.), and there are more arguments in support of the Claudian dating in H. Bodefeld's dissertation, *Untersuchungen zur Datierung der Alexandergeschichte des Q. Curtius Rufus* (Düsseldorf, 1982). The problem is far from settled (for some counter-arguments see *CP* 78 [1983] 151–4), but it is largely irrelevant to the study of Alexander. Most scholars would concede that Curtius was later than Diodorus and earlier than Plutarch or Arrian.

can be as rich a source of historical error as conscious mendacity and distortion in a contemporary historian. On the other hand a derivative history based on reliable authorities, carefully selected and meticulously reported, may be more trustworthy than any single first-generation source.

The main thrust of modern scholarship has been to attempt to isolate the contemporary or near-contemporary historians of Alexander and to reconstruct as far as possible the outline and characteristics of each work. This approach has had major and permanent results. Its most tangible product is the two hundred pages of fragments of lost Alexander historians which Felix Jacoby compiled in his monumental *Fragmente der griechischen Historiker*.[3] We have a fair knowledge of the names and the general sequence of the primary historians and a sample, largely random, of the content of their work. Contemporary history began in the king's lifetime, with Anaximenes' work *On Alexander*[4] and, more importantly, the *Deeds of Alexander* by Callisthenes of Olynthus, who lived at court from the beginning of the campaign in Asia until his dramatic death in 327 and gave a first-hand narrative of events down to 330 at least.[5] Callisthenes' work was the only history known to be exactly contemporaneous with the events, but after the king's death there was a great efflorescence of memoirs by senior and not-so-senior members of his staff. Onesicritus and Nearchus wrote early in the period of the Successors, and at some indeterminate date before his own death (in 283 BC) came the work of Ptolemy.[6] Some time after the battle of Ipsus (301) the ageing Aristobulus of Cassandreia composed his history of the reign, and during the first generation after Alexander (so it is now

---

[3] Jacoby, *FGrH* ii.в 618–828 (nos. 117–53; commentary ii.d 403–542). A few additional fragments, mostly insignificant, are printed at *FGrH* iii.в 742–3 and in H. J. Mette, *Lustrum* 21 (1978) 18–20. For a sensible and readable appraisal of the principal fragments see L. Pearson, *The Lost Histories of Alexander the Great*. There is also a recent compendium by P. Pédech, *Historiens campagnons d'Alexandre* (Paris, 1984), which deals extensively with Callisthenes, Onesicritus, Nearchus, Ptolemy, and Aristobulus.

[4] *FGrH* 72 F 15–17, 29. The work is too scantily attested to support any conclusions on its nature or purpose.

[5] *FGrH* 124. The last datable fragments (F 36–7) deal with Gaugamela, late in 331. See further Jacoby, *RE* x. 1674–1707 (still fundamental); Pearson, *LHA* 22–49 (cf. Badian, *Studies in Greek and Roman History* 251–2); Pédech (above, n. 3) 14–69. See below, pp. 4 ff.

[6] The date is elusive. For a sceptical survey of arguments for both early (post 320) and late (*c.*285) dates see J. Roisman, *CQ* 34 (1984) 373–85.

generally agreed[7]) Cleitarchus of Alexandria wrote what was probably the most widely read of the early histories of the reign. There was also less formal material: pamphlets of differing political persuasions, such as the treatises on the deaths of Alexander and Hephaestion by Ephippus of Olynthus, and works of a documentary or pseudo-documentary nature like the *stathmoi* of the Royal surveyors and the Royal *Ephemerides* which Eumenes allegedly compiled.[8] These sources, contemporary or near-contemporary, provided a rich field for the historian of antiquity, and it is tempting to trace their effect on the extant tradition, using the preserved fragments as a basis. The method is to examine the texts and testimonia and extrapolate characteristic attitudes and biases which can then be identified in the secondary tradition. It is an approach which can be fertile when one has some external evidence for the sources used,[9] as is the case with Arrian, but there are major drawbacks when the identification is merely speculative.

The principal and besetting problem is that the majority of Alexander's early historians are only known through brief citations, and it is rare that one can examine any single author *in extenso*. Nearchus is the chief exception to the rule. His account of his voyage from South India to Susa is the narrative base for the second half of Arrian's *Indike*, and we have a fair idea of the content of his work in outline and detail. For some passages Strabo acts as a control source and provides an independent record of the original.[10] As a result portions of Nearchus' work are well attested and capable of analysis. The same is true, to a more limited degree, of Aristobulus,[11] but there is no extended extract which can compare with Arrian's digest of Nearchus. Most often the lost histories are known from a scattering of citations, usually short, indirect, and uncharacteristic. The vast majority of the verbatim quotations come from the *Deipnoso-*

---

[7] Cf. Schachermeyr, *Alexander in Babylon* 211–24; Badian, *PACA* 8 (1965) 1–8. See further pp. 88 ff. below.

[8] Cf. *FGrH* 126 (Ephippus), 119–23 (surveyors [βηματισταί]), 117 (*Ephemerides*). On the latter see below, ch. 7.

[9] The best example of the genre is probably Hermann Strasburger's early monograph, *Ptolemaios und Alexander* (Leipzig, 1934 = *Studien zur alten Geschichte* [Hildesheim, 1982] 83–147).

[10] Arr. *Ind.* 18–42 = *FGrH* 133 F 1 (Jacoby interweaves seven extracts from Strabo).

[11] See below. ch. 2.

*phistae* of Athenaeus of Naucratis, but their value is largely impaired by the content, which, thanks to Athenaeus' avowed interests, is concentrated upon the pleasures of the flesh and the table and cannot be expected to give a representative sample of the authors cited. In some cases, such as the pamphlets of Ephippus and Nicobule, the rather lurid passages quoted by Athenaeus may indeed be characteristic of those productions, but it is hard to think that his excerpts from the works of Alexander's surveyors (a comment on the Tapurians' addiction to wine and descriptions of the natural produce of the East) are in any sense typical of their general tenor.[12] Other authors are no less selective in their citation, and usually they are not concerned to reproduce the wording of their original. In any case the sources are usually named because there is something suspect in what is recorded. Ancient writers tend to refer to their authorities by name primarily to criticize—to point out falsehood or to indicate information the veracity of which they are not prepared to guarantee. As a result the preserved citations naturally highlight the colourful and the erroneous. Material which was sober and informative would be exploited without comment.

Callisthenes of Olynthus makes an interesting case study. One would naturally expect him, as Alexander's first historian, to have been widely used and cited, but there are no more than a dozen identifiable references to his *Deeds of Alexander*. Those references are a scattered bunch. Observations on the mythology of Asia Minor, reported by Strabo, comprise the majority.[13] Otherwise there is a Homeric scholion citing his description of the Pamphylian Sea doing obeisance before Alexander (F 31), two vignettes from his account of Gaugamela, retailed by Plutarch (F 36–7), and finally the two major fragments. Both these fragments are critical. Polybius examines his description of the battle of Issus, concentrating on the figures he gives for both sides and proving their incompatibility with the terrain as described.[14] The passage is designed to

---

[12] Athen. x. 442B = Baeton, *FGrH* 119 F 1; ii. 67A, xi. 500D = Amyntas, *FGrH* 122 F 4, 1. See also Brunt, *CQ* 30 (1980) 485–6 on the extant fragments of Chares of Mytilene (*FGrH* 125).

[13] *FGrH* 124 F 28–30, 32–3, 38(?).

[14] Polyb. xii. 17. 1–22. 7 = *FGrH* 124 F 35. There are detailed commentaries by P. Pédech, *Polybe xii* (Budé 1961), 104 ff. and Walbank, *HCP* ii. 364 ff.

prove Callisthenes' incompetence, and indeed Polybius does isolate real faults in his account—gross exaggeration of Persian numbers and a eulogistic bias towards Alexander and his Macedonians.[15] But on the other hand much of Polybius' criticism is demonstrably wrong-headed, vitiated by the false assumption that all Alexander's infantry was contained in his phalanx and by the equally false conviction that the phalanx at Issus was as clumsy and inflexible as the phalanx of his own day.[16] Polybius' attempt to convict Callisthenes of ignorance and military incompetence largely fails, and most of the details he singles out have been taken as axioms for modern reconstructions of the battle-site.[17] We should be grateful for Polybius' minuteness of criticism, for all its petty-mindedness. Had he merely stigmatized the description as false without argument, his statement would have been unhesitatingly accepted, and had he quoted the Persian numbers out of context Callisthenes would surely have been dismissed as worthless. As it is, the detail given helps rectify the criticism and allows a broad, if sketchy, reconstruction of Callisthenes' narrative. In most cases we have a single detail, isolated from its context, and there is no way of telling whether or not it is characteristic of the author, or even correctly reported.

The other major fragment concerns the journey to Siwah. Once again the context of the citation is critical. Strabo refers to Callisthenes' narrative as a classic example of historical flattery. The motif of adulation first occurs with the story of the two ravens acting as guides to the oasis, and Strabo states that it persists throughout the consultation of the oracle. There was an equally suspect sequel in the report of the formal delivery at Memphis of oracles from Branchidae and Erythrae.[18] Now Strabo is not pretending to give a full reproduction of Callis-

---

[15] On the exaggerated numbers (of cavalry and mercenaries) see Polyb. xii. 18. 2 ff., and for exaggeration of the difficulties of the terrain to enhance the Macedonian achievement, see particularly 18. 11–12.

[16] Cf. xii. 19. 1–4, 21. 2–10 (calculation of phalanx numbers); 20. 6–8, 22. 4 (criticism of phalanx movements).

[17] xii. 17. 4–5. For the modern literature see Seibert, *Alexander der Grosse* 98–102; *HCArr.* i. 198 ff. For the adaptation and embellishment of Callisthenes in the later tradition see *Entretiens Hardt* 22 (1976) 25–32.

[18] Strabo xvii. 1. 43 (814) = *FGrH* 124 F 14a. For some of the specific problems of the passage see Pearson, *LHA* 33–6 and my own observations in *Greece & the E. Mediterranean* 68–75.

thenes' narrative. He is emphasizing details which he considered biased to flatter Alexander, and there is every indication that he was retailing standard criticisms. Plutarch also singled out the episode of the guidance by ravens,[19] and long before, early in the third century, Timaeus of Tauromenium had arraigned Callisthenes as an example of unphilosophical adulation for his concentration on ravens and frenzied women (i.e. the Sibyl of Erythrae).[20]

Callisthenes' account of the consultation of Ammon was clearly a well-known passage and regularly cited as an illustration of partial and interested writing. It fell within the wider context of his general picture of the king, which was widely denounced as flattery. Both Timaeus and Philodemus[21] stated that his historical work amounted to an apotheosis of Alexander, and several of the fragments illustrate the theme. Plutarch highlights his prayer to Zeus at Gaugamela.[22] The Homeric scholia depict the Pamphylian sea offering *proskynesis* to its new lord (F 31). Most importantly, Strabo's passage on the visit to Siwah is an extended essay on the subject, culminating in the priest's statement that Alexander was son of Zeus and appending the oracles from Asia Minor which also declared his divine sonship. This was a genuine and undeniably important feature of Callisthenes' work,[23] but it was only one feature. Polybius' critique of his description of Issus reveals that he gave quite detailed statements of numbers and movements which, coming from a contemporary and eyewitness, have every likelihood of being correct.[24] But this is not the material for which Callisthenes is quoted. Such facts were absorbed into the secondary historical tradition without acknowledgement, and the named citations concentrate upon the eulogistic and the bizarre.

As a result Callisthenes' work is totally lost for us. His style, like that of most of the prose writers of his day, was reprobated by later generations as inflated and clumsy, and he had no

[19] Plut. *Al.* 27. 4 = *FGrH* 124 F 14b.

[20] Polyb. xii. 12b. 2 = *FGrH* 566 F 155.

[21] Philod. π. κολακ. i².4 = *FGrH* 124 T 21.

[22] Plut. *Al.* 33. 1 = *FGrH* 124 F 36. See further *Greece & the E. Mediterranean* 57–60.

[23] For Callisthenes' view of his own importance (which was not unlike Arrian's own) see Arr. iv. 10. 2. On his panegyric tendencies see Jacoby, *RE* x. 1701–4.

[24] Polyb. xii. 19. 1–2, 5–6, 20. 1.

chance of survival as a literary model. But he certainly influenced the early tradition of Alexander history. The main lines of his description both of Issus and of the Siwah visit were repeated and developed by later writers. Even the exaggerations were echoed and embellished.[25] The same must have been true of his narrative as a whole, but the vast bulk of his work is irretrievable. One facet alone is preserved for us in a sharp and lurid light.

The problem is especially acute in the case of Cleitarchus. It is clear that he was a popular author in the Roman period, the only historian between Ephorus and Timagenes to be included in Quintilian's canon.[26] He is cited by a wide range of authorities, and he may have been the most generally read of all the Alexander historians. Unfortunately, the thirty-six fragments which Jacoby accepts as authentic deal exclusively with trivialities. The most extensive come from Aelian of Praeneste, who excerpted several of Cleitarchus' descriptions of the animal curiosities of India,[27] and Strabo (probably echoing the strictures of Eratosthenes) comments critically on the geographical errors in his description of Central Asia.[28] Indeed most of the citations are critical. Demetrius focuses on his stylistic impropriety (F 14), Curtius Rufus on exaggeration and invention (F 24–5), Cicero on rhetorical mendacity (F 34). The general impression conveyed by the fragments alone is therefore far from favourable. It suggests a taste for the tawdry and colourful, a predilection for sensationalism, a preoccupation for rhetoric which encouraged exaggeration and preferred imaginative fiction to sober truth.[29] Unfortunately we have no easy way of testing these criticisms. The handful of verbatim quotations that survive amounts to five lines in all and can scarcely be representative. There is no extensive appreciation of any part of his work, nothing comparable to Polybius' detailed critique of Callisthenes.

---

[25] For details see *Entretiens Hardt* 22 (1976) 26 f.; *HCArr* i. 31, 212, 217, 272–3.

[26] Quint. *Inst.* x. 1. 74 = *FGrH* 137 T 7. Cf. Jacoby, *RE* xi. 654: 'In Rom war er … im 1. Jhdt. v. Chr. die grosse Mode.'

[27] *FGrH* 137 F 18–19, 21–2.

[28] F 13, 16.

[29] For thoroughgoing condemnation see Tarn, *Alexander* ii. 54–5; Hammond, *Three Historians*, esp. 25–7. Jacoby, *RE* xi. 645, was (typically) more measured and judicious.

The general impression conveyed by the fragments may be correct, as far as it goes, but it is unlikely to be the whole story. If, for instance, our knowledge of Herodotus were limited to the citations in Athenaeus and Plutarch's essay *On the Malice of Herodotus*, we should have a much larger body of testimony than exists for Cleitarchus and it would give the same general impression, a sensational and trivial concentration on curiosities and a penchant for bias and historical deformation. The extant criticisms of Cleitarchus may be similarly misleading. It would certainly be erroneous to conclude that everything he wrote was sensational, biased, or fictional. What is needed is a more extensive sample of Cleitarchus' work than that provided by the named fragments.

That sample is probably provided by the so-called 'vulgate tradition'. One of the few established results of the source-criticism of the Alexander period has been the extrapolation of a common tradition at the root of several of the extant sources. It is undeniable that large segments of Diodorus and Curtius Rufus run parallel, retailing the same information and supplementing each other to a degree that is only explicable if both authors were ultimately working from the same source.[30] The same material is detectable in Justin's epitome of Trogus and in the *Metz Epitome* (a late compilation following roughly the same tradition as Curtius but extant only for the campaign between Hyrcania and South India). There is obviously a common tradition, and the term 'vulgate', despite a certain clumsiness, is a useful shorthand. It is sometimes misunderstood,[31] and for the reader's convenience I should state that when I refer to the 'vulgate tradition' I am referring to the body of material which is multiply attested (in Diodorus and Curtius and often in Justin and the *Metz Epitome*) and can reasonably be attributed to a common source. 'Vulgate sources' is perhaps a more questionable expression, but once again it can be useful shorthand to denote the sources which *on a given occasion* reflect the common tradition. There is no implication that these sources use the vulgate and nothing else.

---

[30] A list of parallels, far from complete, was compiled by Eduard Schwartz (*RE* iv. 1873 f.). For a survey of modern literature see Seibert, *Alexander der Grosse* 26–8 and J. R. Hamilton, *Greece & the E. Mediterranean* 126–46 (additional parallels 127 n. 7).
[31] For criticisms of the use of the term see Hammond, *Three Historians*, esp. 2.

Plutarch, for instance, is eclectic.[32] He may follow the common tradition of Diodorus and Curtius but more often he uses material that is quite distinct. What is denoted as the vulgate may come from different sources at different times, but the nucleus is usually agreement in Diodorus and Curtius, corroborated, as the case may be, by one or more other sources. 'Vulgate' nicely encapsulates the idea of a shared tradition without begging the question of its authorship.

But there is a very strong probability that the vulgate tradition is based ultimately on Cleitarchus. The key passage is provided by Curtius (ix. 8. 15), who refers to Cleitarchus as his source for the number of Indians killed during Alexander's campaign in the kingdom of Sambus. The information is no variant. It is a figure taken out of the general narrative and comes in a context that is exactly paralleled in Diodorus.[33] We therefore have an instance of a common tradition with a direct attribution to Cleitarchus. That establishes a strong probability that the rest of the shared tradition goes back ultimately to the same source. The other alternative, that Diodorus and Curtius used two or more common sources independently, is far less plausible and founders on what is known of Diodorus' approach to historical composition. Where cross-comparison is possible, it is demonstrable that Diodorus followed a single source for chapters on end, transferring only when he came to the end of his subject-matter.[34] There are occasional inserts from other sources, but such inserts are largely digressions,

[32] See the excellent appreciation by Hamilton, *Plut. Al.* xlix–lii. Hammond, *Three Historians* 170 n. 5, has taken me to task for inconsistency in references to Plutarch, including him sometimes in the vulgate, sometimes not. All the references which include him as a vulgate source are instances where he corroborates the shared tradition of Diodorus and Curtius. Where he stands apart from that shared tradition, he cannot be classed as part of the vulgate. The same is of course true of Curtius. He is to a great extent dependent on the common tradition, but he undeniably uses a multiplicity of other sources.

[33] Diod. xvii. 102. 5–7. Diodorus gives 80,000 as the number of victims, whereas the manuscripts of Curtius vary between 800 and 800,000. Given the general concordance, it is usually assumed that the numerals in Curtius are (as so often) corrupt. The common source is not in doubt.

[34] The most illuminating segment of narrative is Diod. iii. 12–48, where the source is Agatharchides of Cnidus (cf. iii. 11. 2). The same material is digested by Photius (*Bibl.* cod. 250), and there is impressive agreement both in economy and vocabulary. For parallel texts see Müller, *GGM* i. 123–93 and, for discussion, D. Woelk, *Agatharchides von Knidos: Über das Rote Meer* (diss. Bamberg, 1966); J. Hornblower, *Hieronymus of Cardia* 27–32. See further, Seibert, *Das Zeitalter der Diadochen* 30–2.

short and limited in scope. Within each book Diodorus tends to change sources as he moves from area to area, particularly when he reverts to the history of his native Sicily, and he adds chronographic material from a separate date-table.[35] But Book xvii is unusually homogeneous. The narrative focus is exclusively on Alexander and there is no material on the history of the Greek west, nor is there any chronographic information.[36] It is overwhelmingly probable that his material derives from a single major source and that there is a single source for the tradition shared with Curtius.

Now Diodorus himself takes us back to Cleitarchus. In a digression in Book ii he gives Cleitarchus' figures for the dimensions of the walls of Babylon and presents them as a variant, contrasting with the description of his main source, Ctesias.[37] This information is paralleled in Curtius' description of Babylon, which otherwise corresponds to Diodorus' narrative in Book xvii.[38] It looks as though Diodorus extrapolated the material relating to the city walls and used it in his mythological exordium, to set off the information in Ctesias. There may well be a similar digression later. After describing the death of Themistocles, following his main source for Greek affairs in Book xi, Diodorus adds a variant from an unnamed source (ἔνιοι ... τῶν συγγραφέων).[39] That variant is the story of Themistocles drinking bull's blood, an episode which we know was rhetorically treated by Cleitarchus.[40] Once more, it looks as though Diodorus has drawn upon his general knowledge of Cleitarchus to embellish his earlier historical narrative.[41]

---

[35] These passages are usefully listed by Schwartz, *RE* v. 666–9.

[36] The same is true of Book xviii, which is largely (if not wholly) based on Hieronymus of Cardia. Sicilian history resumes emphatically at xix. 1 with the tyranny of Agathocles (cf. xviii. 1. 6, 75. 3); notes on Roman history continue from xix. 10. 1, and the chronographic information emerges again in Book xx.

[37] Diod. ii. 7.3 = *FGrH* 137 F 10.

[38] Curt. v. 1. 10–45 (esp. 26); cf. Diod. xvii. 64. 3–6. Hammond (*Three Historians* 190 n. 25) mentions only the figure of 365 stades for the circuit of the walls, which he suggests might have been reported by sources other than Cleitarchus. He omits the rest of the correspondences which make the hypothesis of a common source compelling. See, however, Hamilton, in *Greece & the E. Mediterranean* 138–40.

[39] Diod. xi. 58. 2–3.

[40] Cic. *Brut.* 42–3 = *FGrH* 137 F 34.

[41] This was suggested by Schwartz, *RE* v. 684 and accepted by Jacoby, *FGrH* ii.D

In that case it can hardly be doubted that Cleitarchus provided the narrative base for his account of Alexander, and that Cleitarchus is the ultimate source of the vulgate tradition. The attribution has, of course, been challenged, largely on the ground that several of the extant fragments of Cleitarchus are not found in any of the so-called vulgate sources. In fact the points of detail contained in the fragments are in general so trivial that their omission is only to be expected. The two most striking absences (the Roman embassy and the story of Ptolemy's presence at the Malli town) are more difficult to explain,[42] but given Diodorus' extreme selectiveness it is not too surprising that he passed over both incidents. On the other hand there is a reasonably strong correlation between many of the preserved fragments and the common tradition of Diodorus and Curtius; and it remains the strongest probability that the vulgate tradition in general and Diodorus' account in particular is derived ultimately from the single source, Cleitarchus.

In that case there is a large corpus of material which can be traced back to Cleitarchus, and in theory the broad characteristics of his work should be capable of reconstruction. That is easier said than done. The material in the vulgate covers a wide spectrum, from wild and colourful zoological fantasy to sober and apparently well-informed campaign reports. A recent analysis has concluded that there is not a single common source for Diodorus and Curtius but two, a baroque and sensation-hungry author, hostile to Alexander and his Macedonians (Cleitarchus), and a better-informed, more impartial historian, not prone to sensationalism and fiction (Diyllus?).[43] It is perhaps more profitable to ask whether the same source cannot be both Jekyll and Hyde, capable both of objective reporting and emotional bathos (one need only reflect on the almost infinite variety of material in Herodotus).

A more pertinent question is the amount of distortion that has taken place in transmission. All the extant sources of the vulgate tradition are highly erratic and second-rate authors, and they may be assumed to have altered their material for the

---

[42] See below, ch. 4.
[43] Hammond, *Three Historians*, esp. 12–51. See now the critical observations of Badian, *EMC* n. s. 4 (1985) 461–3.

worse. Contraction is a serious problem. Cleitarchus' work was fairly voluminous. In Book xii he described the Indian ascetics and their disregard for death.[44] That presumably came in the context of Calanus' self-immolation in Persis late in 325. The period to Alexander's death, one assumes, would have required several more books. By contrast Diodorus covers the entire reign in a single book (admittedly of unusual length) and Justin is even more grossly abridged. Given such a drastic précis it is not surprising that some episodes in Diodorus are abbreviated to near gibberish, and the distortion in Justin is such that one often needs other texts to infer even what was in his immediate exemplar, Trogus.[45] There is also the problem of embellishment and exaggeration in the immediate source. That is a particular danger with Curtius Rufus, whose work is deeply infused with rhetoric.[46] His narrative is punctuated by a running commentary, with highly subjective attributions of motive, and there is no doubt that his source material is reworked, often a mere vehicle for descriptive rhetoric or moralizing comment. Even Diodorus is prone to impose his own personality. The style of his original is watered down and reduced to flat monotony. More seriously, he has an eye for the sensational and has favourite themes, usually banalities such as epic pictures of slaughter and fighting in relays.[47] That accounts for the unbalanced nature of such episodes as the battle of the Granicus. Diodorus' interest is attracted by the single combat between Alexander and the Persian commanders and he spends a disproportionate amount of his battle narrative expatiating upon it. The remaining details are scattered and drastically abbreviated, so as to obscure the strategy and defy any rational re-

---

[44] Diog. Laert. i. 6 = *FGrH* 137 F 6. The other book numbers are unhelpful. The sack of Thebes came (as we would expect) in Book i (F 1), the Sardanapalus saga (perhaps a digression based on Alexander's visit to Anchiale in 333) in Book iv (F 2), the Adonis cult at Byblus (332?) in Book v, and a dissertation on the upright tiara in Book x (F 5). The book number in F 4 is contracted and possibly corrupt. One can hardly reconstruct the outlines of Cleitarchus' history, but its volume is not in doubt.

[45] For some examples see *HCArr.* i. 358 (on Justin xii. 4. 12); *Antichthon* 17 (1983) 42 (on Justin xiii. 4. 20).

[46] Cf. Atkinson (above, n. 2) 67–73, with my comments in *CP* 78 (1983) 157–9. W. Rutz, *Hermes* 93 (1965) 370–82.

[47] On this, see R. K. Sinclair, *CQ* 16 (1966) 249–55. For a general appreciation of Diodorus see Hornblower (above, n. 34) 22 ff.

construction of the engagement.[48] There is no control source, and we cannot assume that Diodorus' original was as unbalanced as his epitome of it.

Cleitarchus, then, is elusive. Is he also irretrievable? My feeling is that it *is* possible to reconstruct something of his work, but the exercise of doing so is particularly arduous. One must begin with an appreciation of the methods of the major extant sources. In the case of Diodorus this is not too difficult, for there is an abundance of material for comparison outside Book xvii. Curtius is far more difficult, for his work is confined to the Alexander period, the text is lacunose and often corrupt, and there are no extant sources to provide a direct check on his methods of excerpting. One can only rely on cross-comparison, where the material is attested in other contexts. That is the crux. The starting-point should be examination of extended passages which are reported by Diodorus and Curtius (preferably other sources as well).[49] Then one can build up a composite narrative and gain some idea of what is omitted or distorted in each individual writer. The more focuses that can be brought to bear on the vulgate, the more illumination of the common base will accrue. But the illumination will come from the continuous narrative of the extant works, not from the scattered and unrepresentative 'fragments' to which Cleitarchus' name is explicitly attached.

The importance of Arrian is now clear. His work is the most complete and the most sober account of Alexander's reign and at the same time it provides explicit information about the sources used. The seven-book *History of Alexander* was based on Ptolemy son of Lagus and Aristobulus son of Aristobulus. That is stated explicitly in the Preface and confirmed by the narrative which refers repeatedly to the authority of both men.[50] From Book vi the narrative range is expanded by the inclusion of Nearchus and there are explicit borrowings from the geographical work of Eratosthenes. The companion work, the *Indike*,

---

[48] The *aristeia* monopolizes the narrative from xvii. 20. 1 to 21. 3. The rest of the narrative is a series of commonplaces, the opening sentence (19. 3) a celebrated historical crux. For a mordant critique of the tradition see Badian, in *Ancient Macedonia* ii. 272–4. See also Hammond, *JHS* 100 (1980) 73 f., *Three Historians* 16f.

[49] The method has been well employed by Hamilton, in *Greece & the E. Mediterranean* 129–35, comparing Curtius ix with Diod. xvii. 89–104.

[50] See the exposition in *HCArr.* i. 16–34 for details.

dealing with the natural curiosities of India and the voyage of Alexander's fleet in the southern Ocean, is equally candid about its use of sources: the material comes from Eratosthenes, Megasthenes, and Nearchus.[51] In the case of Arrian we have the entire range of primary sources spelt out for us, and they are exciting and contemporary. Ptolemy, Nearchus, and Aristobulus were all eyewitnesses of the campaigns, and the first two at least were major actors in the great events they described. It is not surprising that the primary sources have occupied the centre stage of research. The text of Arrian is often read as though it were practically the same as Ptolemy, and Ptolemy/ Arrian is a traditional shorthand used to characterize that part of Arrian's narrative that is commonly believed to be based on Ptolemy. Ernst Kornemann even subjected Arrian's text to a detailed stylistic analysis, extrapolating what he thought were distinctive thumb-prints of Ptolemaic phraseology.[52] The assumption, usually implicit, is that one may go direct from Arrian to his sources and that Arrian himself may be disregarded, a simple soldier who paid his tribute to the memory of Alexander by selecting the best possible sources and reproducing them with patient fidelity.

The object of this exercise is wholly commendable. Arrian's sources *are* of fundamental importance, far more so for the modern historian than Arrian himself. In particular Ptolemy's picture of Alexander is of consuming interest, an account of the reign by one of its great architects and beneficiaries. But whatever results are obtained, they are necessarily distorted unless they are based on a careful study of Arrian as a writer. It is obvious from the most perfunctory reading of Arrian and the most superficial study of his career that he was a sophisticated and experienced writer, with the highest claims to stylistic excellence. To put it mildly, he is unlikely to have transcribed his sources without reshaping them and adding his own comments. The methodology outlined for approaching Cleitarchus will therefore hold good for Arrian's sources also. Arrian's preten-

---

[51] See below, ch. 2.

[52] E. Kornemann, *Die Alexandergeschichte des Königs Ptolemaios I. von Aegypten* (Leipzig, 1934). The method is here at its most extreme and was rightly criticized from the outset (see Strasburger's review in *Gnomon* 13 [1937] 483–92); but its basic assumptions are pervasive in modern scholarship.

sions as a historian need to be elucidated, in particular his aims in composing a history of Alexander. His modes of citing sources should also be studied and, where possible, his version should be contrasted with other writers' use of the same source material. Finally his own contribution should be delineated, the degree to which he comments on his material, whether par-enthetically or in formal digressions and set speeches. That is the object of this book and explains its somewhat pretentious title. One cannot examine the history of Alexander without a study of the primary sources and the primary sources them-selves are embedded in secondary and derivative works like those of Arrian.

In the following chapters I deal first with Arrian's ambitions and methodology and attempt to establish a foundation for evaluating his sources, particularly Aristobulus, who is particu-larly prominent in the last two books and used by authors other than Arrian. The discussion will focus incidentally on episodes which are of considerable interest and lead to two issues of fundamental importance, the nature of the Royal *Ephemerides* and the tradition of Alexander's Last Plans. The details are often extremely controversial, and it would be over-sanguine to expect my conclusions to command universal assent. I hope, however, that there will be some support for the methodology and the general proposition that one should approach the unknown from a thorough study of what is known.

# ARRIAN AND HIS HISTORICAL
# PRODUCTION

THE study of Alexander, as we have seen, is in large part the study of Arrian, who provides the constant thread against which the rest of the tradition must be assessed. But that narrative should never be read without awareness of its author. Arrian, in the Alexander history at least, was no Thucydides, bent on chronicling his own age. He was an intensely active member of the Graeco-Roman aristocracy of the second century AD, who chose to write about a man dead for more than four centuries and a man who had become less a historical figure than a rhetorical *exemplum*, invoked as an illustration of every conceivable virtue and vice. Arrian's book was a self-confessed reworking of extant material, selected and arranged according to his own predilections. It acts as a filter. The relatively vast spectrum of literature in his day was trimmed by deliberate limitation of sources, and those chosen sources were selectively deployed to present the picture which Arrian thought did most justice to his hero. His methods will be examined later. What concerns us first is the man himself.[1] How did Arrian come to the history of Alexander and how important was that history in relation to his other works?

---

[1] A relative spate of monographs and articles in recent years has rendered obsolete Eduard Schwartz's classic treatment in Pauly–Wissowa (*RE* ii. 1230–47 = *Griechische Geschichtsschreiber* [Leipzig, 1959] 130–55). See in particular the monograph of P. A. Stadter, *Arrian of Nicomedia* (Chapel Hill, 1980) and the doctoral dissertation of Everett L. Wheeler, 'Flavius Arrianus: A Political and Military Biography' (diss. Duke University, 1974). There is also a major article by Sir Ronald Syme, 'The Career of Arrian', *HSCP* 86 (1982) 181–211 and some very valuable comments may be found in the Loeb edition prepared by P. A. Brunt (I, ix–xxiv; II, 534–41). My own contributions, which have evoked some controversy, may be found in *CQ* 22 (1972) 163–85 and *HCArr.* i. 1–7. See also G. Wirth, 'Anmerkungen zur Arrianbiographie', *Historia* 13 (1964) 209–45 = *Studien zur Alexandergeschichte* (Darmstadt, 1985) 14 ff.; 'Arrian und Traian—Versuch einer Gegenwartsdeutung', *Studi Clasice* 16 (1974) 169–209 = *Studien* 210 ff; W. Ameling, 'L. Flavius Arrianus Neos Xenophon', *Epigraphica Anatolica* 4 (1984) 119–22.

Arrian was a native of Nicomedia (Izmit) in the province of Bithynia. He was a Greek-speaker and of Greek stock but a Roman citizen, his full name now attested as L. Flavius Arrianus. In all probability the citizenship had been in the family for several generations. Syme plausibly suggests that an ancestor was a beneficiary of L. Flavius, suffect in 33 BC and an adherent of Antony in the east (Dio xlix. 44. 3).[2] At all events Arrian's family belonged to the provincial aristocracy of Bithynia. He reports that he occupied the priesthood of Demeter and Kore, the patron deities of his city (*Bithyn.* F 1. 1), and in all probability he held civic office in Nicomedia.[3] It was there that he received his primary education and developed a taste for hunting in the rural hinterland. However, his studies in due course took him to Greece. Like many of the *jeunesse dorée* of the provinces, he made his way to Epirus and Nicopolis, where the Stoic sage, Epictetus, held court; and around 108, when he was in his early or mid-twenties, he took copious notes on the impromptu lectures given there, which he admits affected him deeply at the time.[4] How deep and lasting the effect was we shall examine later, but it is unquestionable that the experience was formative. It was also socially profitable. Not only was Nicopolis visited by procurators and a *corrector* of consular status during Arrian's stay;[5] it was also graced by the presence of the young Hadrian, who cultivated Epictetus.[6] He may not have met Arrian there, but at least the two had a common dilettante interest in moral philosophy, which provided some basis for later friendship.

At this time Arrian also served in the Roman army. He himself claims that he had practised soldiery (στρατηγία) and literature since his youth (*Cyneget.* 1. 4), and his military experience, which explicitly involved command,[7] obviously entailed

---

[2] Syme (above, n. 1) 184; cf. *PIR*[2] F. 188; Broughton, *MRR* ii. 414.

[3] Cf. Arr. i. 12. 5, with the interpretation advocated in *HCArr.* i. 106. See also W. Ameling, *Epigraphica Anatolica* 4 (1984) 130, who suggests that Arrian held the office of πρῶτος ἄρχων.

[4] Arr. *Ep. ad Gell.* 7–8.

[5] Epict. *Diss*, iii. 4, 7. For possible identifications see F. Millar, *JRS* 55 (1965) 142, 147; Syme (above, n. 1) 184–5.

[6] HA *Hadr.* 16. 10. Syme 185 hints at a dating during 112, when Hadrian was honorary archon in Athens.

[7] For Arrian's other uses of στρατηγία see vi. 26. 3; *Tact.* 5. 2.

much more than the paramilitary exercises of the Nicomedian *ephebeia*. There happens to be some strong, if indirect, evidence in the *Indike* (4. 15–16). Arrian mentions that he had seen two of the navigable tributaries of the Danube, the Inn and the Save. He adds that the confluence of the Inn and Danube marked the frontier between the provinces of Rhaetia and Noricum and that the Save joined the Danube at Taurunum. Both statements suggest personal acquaintance. In the first place it stands beyond doubt that the lower reaches of the Inn formed the common border of Rhaetia and Noricum, but it is a somewhat recondite piece of information, recorded elsewhere only by Tacitus (*Hist.* iii. 5) and Claudius Ptolemaeus.[8] The confluence was a military area. By the mid second century AD auxiliary forts existed to the east and west, that on the Norican side (Boiodurum) dating back to the Flavian period.[9] It was an obvious region for a young equestrian *praefectus cohortis* to see service. Taurunum on the Danube (modern Zemun) is far more obscure. Pliny (*NH* iii. 148) had also named it as the meeting point of the Save and the Danube, but he was not claiming autopsy and his sources were not contemporary. In Arrian's day it was not a particularly important place, nor was it exactly on the confluence. That position, according to the itineraries, was occupied by Singidunum (Belgrade), some three or four Roman miles distant.[10] Singidunum apparently enjoyed its greatest prosperity under the Antonines, and from the reign of Hadrian it formed the permanent headquarters of IV Flavia. Even in Trajan's reign it must have eclipsed Taurunum. For Arrian to have named Taurunum in preference he must have had some specific association with the place, and the association can only have been military. Taurunum was one of the harbours of the Pannonian fleet, and also the temporary

---

[8] Cf. G. Ulbert, 'Zur Grenze zwischen den römischen Provinzen Noricum und Raetien', *Bayerische Vorgeschichtsblätter* 36 (1971) 101–23; G. Alföldy, *Noricum* (London, 1974) 57–8.

[9] A *cohors quingenaria* was based at Boidurum. Cf. L. Eckhart, *Roman Frontier Studies 1967* (Tel Aviv, 1971) 143; Alföldy, *Noricum* 146–7.

[10] *Itin. Ant.* Singiduno castra: IIII Tauruno classis; *Peuting.* Confluentibus co. Singiduno III Tauruno. Cf. J. Klemenc, in *Quintus Congressus Internationalis Limitis Romani Studiosorum* (Zagreb, 1963) 67: On the relative importance of Taurunum and Singidunum see Syme (above, n. 1) 196 f; Grassl, *Chiron* 12 (1982) 249.

home of detachments of VII Claudia during Trajan's Dacian Wars.[11] That would make a suitable posting for an equestrian officer. Arrian could easily have followed his service by the Inn with a spell as *tribunus angusticlavius*,[12] spending time in lower Pannonia around Taurunum.

Arrian's military service need not have been protracted— and it probably was not (he seems to think that there were relatively few navigable tributaries along the Danube, and he obviously did not have acquaintance with the entire course of the river). There was plenty of time for interludes of relaxation in the more civilized world of the south. Accordingly we find Arrian in the entourage of the Trajanic favourite, C. Avidius Nigrinus, probably in the years immediately after Nigrinus' consulate (110).[13] The young and cultured Greek naturally attached himself to distinguished patrons, and it was surely in these middle years of Trajan's reign that his friendship with Hadrian blossomed. In 112/13 the prince was eponymous archon at Athens, and it is tempting to suppose that Arrian was with him. He was an Eleusinian initiate (iii. 16. 10) and a regular visitor to the city. If he was in Greece at the time, he must surely have paid his respects. The friendship cannot have come out of nothing. It was certainly of palmary importance, amply attested by Arrian himself, most notably in the *Periplus*, the literary report of his tour of inspection in the Black Sea (131/2). There he addresses the emperor in surprisingly intimate terms. Take for instance his sacrifice near Trapezus: 'you must know for whose welfare we prayed for first, for you are well acquainted with our ways and are yourself conscious that you deserve to have your welfare the object of prayer from all mankind, even those who have enjoyed less benefit than us at your

[11] J. Szilágyi, *Inscriptiones Tegularum Pannonicarum* 84; A. and J. Sisel, *Inscriptiones Latinae quae in Jugoslavia inter annos 1940 et 1960 repertae et editae sunt* (Ljubljana, 1963) no. 278.

[12] See, however, H. Grassl, 'Arrian im Donauraum', *Chiron* 12 (1982) 245–52, esp. 248 f., who argues for two different visits: a military tribunate under Trajan gave him experience of Taurunum, whereas he saw the Inn much later, as a *comes* of Hadrian.

[13] A Plassart, *Fouilles de Delphes* iii. 4 (1970), nos. 290, 294. Nigrinus is attested *leg. Aug. pr. pr.* and was presumably a special representative of the emperor, replacing the proconsul of Achaea. In that case he was probably a consular, as was Pliny in Bithynia (cf. Syme 185; *Roman Papers* ii. 781 f.). For the other view, that he was a (praetorian?) *corrector*, operating alongside the proconsul, see W. Eck, *Chiron* 13 (1983) 187 n. 479.

hands' (*Peripl.* 2. 4).[14] There is a world of difference between this and the stilted, deferential terms in which Pliny addressed Trajan. The language itself supports the claims its writer makes. The emperor knew Arrian personally and had showered his favour upon him. Promotion was the direct result of the friendship, and we may assume with some confidence a fairly deep acquaintance before Hadrian's accession.

During Trajan's Parthian Wars there is little evidence for either man. The report that Arrian held a command near the Caspian Gates is certainly without foundation, the product of Byzantine carelessness or inventiveness.[15] Like so many of his contemporaries he may have played some role in the legionary or auxiliary command, but there is no way of telling. The fact that he later reported Trajan's campaigns in his *Parthica* proves interest, not participation, and the theory that he devoted ten out of seventeen books to the years 114–17 is based on the merest speculation.[16] As regards Arrian our ignorance is complete, and we are not much better served for Hadrian. At the time of Trajan's death he was legate of Syria (newly appointed, it seems),[17] but there is no record of his earlier activity. Nothing excludes the two having served together, Arrian as an equestrian protégé of the prince, and they may even have been together in Syria at the time of Trajan's death. But there is no proof and no basis for conjecture.

Hadrian's accession brought quick promotion, as Arrian attests. The downfall of Nigrinus in the sensational affair of the four consulars did not affect him.[18] Evidently the patronage of Hadrian had long since eclipsed that of Nigrinus, and Arrian's association with the discredited man was not close enough to impair his prospects. He now, if not before, entered the senate.

---

[14] For other personal references see *Peripl.* 1–2 *passim*, 5. 2, 11. 2–3, 12.2, 16. 6, 17. 2. Compare the casual imperatives which Arrian uses to request replacement statues of Hermes and the emperor himself (*Peripl.* 1. 4, 2. 1) with the studied and cumbersome mode of request in Pliny (*Ep.* x. 17b. 2; 37. 3, 41. 4, 61. 5).

[15] Joh. Lyd. *de mag.* iii. 48 (p. 142. 6 Wuensch) = *FGrH* 156 F 37. On the context and the general reliability of its author see my observations in *CQ* 33 (1983) 265–70.

[16] Against the theory, axiomatic for Roos, Jacoby, and most modern studies, see *CQ* 33 (1983) 271–6. There is no doubt that Trajan's exploits were treated in considerable detail, but we have no reason to think that they monopolized two-thirds of the work.

[17] HA *Hadr.* 4. 6: Dio lxviii. 33. 1; lxix. 1. 2, 2. 1. His successor (autumn 117) was L. Catilius Severus (HA *Hadr.* 5. 10; *ILAfr.* 43; Eck, *Chiron* 13 [1983] 148 f.).

[18] HA *Hadr.* 7. 1–2; Dio lxix. 2. 5; cf. Syme, *Roman Papers* 327–8.

The time and method of entrance are both obscure, but there is
much to be said for Syme's recent suggestion that he was directly adlected *inter praetorios.*[19] That would be one of Hadrian's
early actions on reaching the purple. His friend from Nicomedia became a Roman senator of some seniority and proceeded
up the ladder of promotion. The rungs of that ladder are beyond reconstruction. Syme has argued very tentatively for a
legionary legateship, followed in due course by one of the
twelve imperial provinces of praetorian status, but there is no
unequivocal evidence and the case is built upon general career
patterns.[20] Between AD 117 and 161 all but four of the thirty-
one known consular legates held legionary commands. That is
a strong point admittedly, but it is unwise to force Arrian's
career into any matrix. His promotion, thanks to Hadrian's
personal interest and friendship, may have been quite unusual.
Byzantine literary tradition has it that he was promoted to the
consulate on the strength of his cultural eminence,[21] and his
appointment to Cappadocia need not have been preceded by
specifically military posts. It is known that Hadrian appointed
the sophist, Avidius Heliodorus, to govern Egypt on the
strength of his rhetorical reputation;[22] and, as is also well
known, the great jurist, Salvius Julianus, held no post outside
Rome between praetorship and consulate but proceeded to
govern Lower Germany and Spain.[23] Arrian was arguably as
celebrated a man of letters as Salvius in the sphere of law, and

[19] Syme (above, n. 1) 187, 190. The closest parallel would be the magnate of
Ancyra, C. Iulius Severus, who occupied all the local offices in his native Galatia, gave
hospitality to the units of Trajan's army passing to the Parthian front, and was adlected
*inter tribunicios* by Hadrian. He moved on to a legateship of IV Scythica (132/3) and
subsequently, in quick succession, to the proconsulate of Achaea and a posting as *corrector* in Bithynia (*IGR* iii. 173–5; cf. *PIR²* I. 573; Halfmann 151 f., no. 62).
[20] Syme (above, n. 1) 192–6, improving on the catalogue of B. Campbell, *JRS* 65
(1975) 28–31.
[21] Phot. *Bibl.* cod. 58. 4; 'Suda' s.v. Ἀρριανός (T2 Roos). Cf. Wirth, *Studien* 3 ff.; 231–
2; *Historia* 13 (1964) 506–9; Bosworth, *CQ* 22 (1972) 164–5; *HCArr.* i. 2. It has been
argued repeatedly (cf. Wirth 232; Stadter 13–14) that Cappadocia was too important
not to be entrusted to a man of sound military background. One should note, however,
that Catilius Severus, Hadrian's first governor of Syria and legate of Cappadocia during Trajan's Parthian Wars, had only a single legionary legateship and came to the
consulate not through any imperial province but by way of the two treasuries at Rome
(*ILAfr.* 43). Not a military man in any sense in his early years.
[22] ἐξ ἐμπειρίας ῥητορικῆς (Dio lxxi. 22. 2). Cf. Pflaum, *Carrières* no. 106; E. Bowie,
*YCS* 27 (1982) 58.
[23] *ILS* 8973. He is cited as an exception by Syme (above, n. 1) 193.

he might have been dispensed from the more arduous forms of service. But he does hint that his experience of command, like his taste for hunting, was consistent,[24] and one would expect some military involvement between his youthful service and his tenure of Cappadocia.

The one probable post we know of before Arrian's consulate was not military—the proconsulate of the unarmed province of Baetica. A Greek metrical epigram, now notorious, was found at Corduba.[25] It is a dedication to Artemis by the proconsul Arrianus. The second couplet is lacunose and has been proof against restoration, but its general sense is clear: Arrian offers the goddess his poem, the gift of the Muses, in preference to trophies from the hunt. The poetic conceit, the hunting context, the use of Greek[26] all combine to suggest that the author of the epigram was the historian Arrian (though it must be confessed that the quality of his verse is far inferior to that of his prose!).[27] In that case his governorship must be assigned to the years around 125. Its location, Baetica, was a congenial and civilized place for a Greek senator of a literary bent to pass a season. It is also reasonable to suppose that he joined Hadrian's entourage for some of the provincial journeys. One passage in the extant writings is striking and suggestive. Arrian writes of the nomad horsemen of Africa with evident admiration, and the details he gives (eight-year-old boys riding bareback to overhaul and lasso wild asses[28]) suggest personal experience of hunting in that province, introduced as a vivid illustration of

[24] *Cyneget.* 1. 4: ἀπὸ νέου ἐσπουδακώς. For the use of the perfect to denote continuous activity compare *Cyneget.* 35. 3 (τοὺς ἐπὶ θηρᾷ ἐσπουδακότας).

[25] *AE* 1974. 370 = *SEG* xxvi. 1215. For the extensive bibliography see Stadter 195–6 n. 61, to which may now be added Eck, *Chiron* 13 (1983) 192, Syme (above, n. 1) 190–2 (tending to discount the evidence—'Let Corduba recede') and J. H. Oliver, *The Civic Tradition and Roman Athens* (Baltimore, 1983) 66–9.

[26] For the extreme rarity of Greek inscriptions in Spain see Eck, *RE* Suppl. xiv. 120. The author of our dedication was almost certainly of Greek extraction.

[27] It perhaps has a counterpart in the epigram which Hadrian wrote to celebrate Trajan's dedication on Mt. Casius of spoils from Dacia and which Arrian apparently considered worth mentioning in his *Parthica* (*Anth. Pal.* vi. 332: 'Suda' s.v. Κάσιον ὄρος = Arr. *Parth.* F. 36 [Roos]—the attribution to Arrian is conjectural but probable).

[28] *Cyneget.* 24. 3. Arrian contrasts their expertise with the relative incompetence of the royal huntsmen of Cyrus the Younger (24. 2: cf. Xen. *Anab.* 1. 5. 2) and, as Stadter 59 notes, he is inspired to a rhetorical cadenza. He was most probably writing from personal experience. Syme's suggestion (n. 1, above, 197) that Arrian had somewhere viewed the exercises of the Moorish cavalry of Lusius Quietus is best discarded (Lusius hardly recruited boys).

the virtues of the chase pure and simple, not debased by the use of snares and unseemly trickery. If Arrian did observe these exploits in person, it is hard to resist the conclusion that he was with Hadrian during his tour of Africa in 128. He will have returned as consul designate and held the *fasces* as one of the suffects of 129 or 130.[29]

For a short time the clouds of uncertainty dissipate. Virtually the sole securely dated item of Arrian's career is his stay in Cappadocia, which he governed as imperial legate for at least six years, arriving around 131 and remaining until at least 137. It was a busy and successful period, culminating in 135 when he countered a threat of invasion by the nomad Alani and drove them north through the Caucasus by an effective show of force.[30] A rather curious record of that transaction survives in the Ἔκταξις κατὰ ’Αλανῶν, a brief, highly stylized adaptation of Arrian's battle plans, written as a literary display piece.[31] Two other small monographs also document his activities as legate. The *Periplus* reports on a voyage of inspection in the Black Sea which Arrian carried out in 131/2, while the *Tactica* begins with a rehash of hellenistic theory on infantry tactics and continues with an invaluable appendix documenting the parade exercises of the contemporary auxiliary cavalry.[32] Both works are curious uneven collages, blending vivid eyewitness descriptions with routine reworking and embellishment of obsolete material from literary sources, but they are works of considerable sophistication, the work of an assured prose stylist. *Strategia* and *sophia* have rarely been so closely integrated.

Arrian left Cappadocia shortly before Hadrian's death and did not apparently continue in public life after his friend and

---

[29] He was consul with an unidentified Severus (*CIL* xv. 244, 532). Either 129 or 130 (after the spring in both cases) is a possibility (the *fasti* for 127 and 128 are complete). If one could be sure that Arrian was in Cappadocia before the end of 130 (cf. Eck, *Chiron* 13 [1983] 169), then the earlier date would be confirmed. But one cannot exclude Arrian's arriving in Cappadocia in the summer of 131 after a consulate the previous year (Syme 199–200).

[30] Dio lxix. 15. 1. On these events see *HSCP* 81 (1977) 217–32 with Syme, *Roman Papers* 1439–43.

[31] *HSCP* 81 (1977) 233–55; Wheeler (above, n. 1) 260–328; Stadter 45–9.

[32] See now Stadter 32–45. On the *Periplus* see the edition by G. Marenghi, *Arriano, Periplo del Ponte Eusino* (Naples, 1958) and on the *Tactica* F. Kiechle, 'Die Taktik des Flavius Arrianus', *Bericht der röm.-germ. Kommission* 45 (1964) 87–129, with Stadter, *CP* 73 (1978) 117–28 and Wheeler, *GRBS* 19 (1978) 351–65.

patron was gone. There is a possibility that he governed other provinces,[33] but no epigraphical or literary record subsists, and after a six-year term in Cappadocia Arrian might have been thought to have had his fair share of command. At all events he retired to Athens, where he received honorary citizenship and in 145/6 became eponymous archon,[34] like Hadrian more than thirty years before. There he lived out an apparently contented old age, a passionate huntsman to the end: the *Cynegeticus*, his latest datable work, gives a most endearing picture of his love of the chase and his even greater love of his dogs. He may have survived until the reign of Marcus, dying rich in years and reputation, to be commemorated by Lucian as a man belonging to the first circle of the Romans and a lifelong friend of culture.[35]

Lucian's tribute is interesting. He places Arrian's public status and literary achievement side by side and implies that they were of equal importance. Clearly they were. Nothing is more misleading than to regard senatorial posts as exclusive demands upon their incumbents' time.[36] Let us consider the case of a younger contemporary of Arrian, A. Claudius Charax.[37] Like Arrian he held a priesthood in his native Pergamum,[38]

[33] Lucian mentioned an Antonine governor of Syria with an enthusiasm for philosophy (*Peregr.* 14) and the identification with Arrian has been found attractive (cf. G. Alföldy, *Konsulat und Senatorenstand unter den Antoninen* [Bonn, 1977] 238–9). A recent reconstruction of the *fasti* of Syria has Sex. Julius Maior in office between 137 and 140/1, to be followed by Barbuleius Ligarianus (previously Arrian's successor in Cappadocia). See Syme, *Roman Papers* 1390–10; *Romanitas–Christianitas* (ed. G. Wirth; Berlin/New York, 1982) 239–43 with Eck, *Chiron* 13 (1983) 179 f., no. 448. The sequence is conjectural, based on a difficult and fragmentary inscription (*AE* 1937. 137), but it is consistent with the known facts. One can hardly infer that Arrian was the only friend of philosophy to govern provinces.

[34] *IG* ii². 2055; 'Ἀρχ. Δελτ. 30Α (1975) 121; S. Follet, *Athènes aux II' et III' siècles* (Paris, 1976) 34–6. For his residence in Athens and purported family see *HCArr.* 3–4; Stadter 16–17. J. H. Oliver, *The Civic Tradition and Roman Athens* 69–72, suggests that he had a quasi-official position, acting as Pius' representative in dealings with the philosophical schools. That is sheer fantasy.

[35] Luc. *Alex.* 2: ἀνὴρ Ῥωμαίων ἐν τοῖς πρώτοις καὶ παιδείᾳ παρ᾽ ὅλον τὸν βίον συγγενόμενος. The language is reminiscent of Lucian's characterization of Herodes Atticus (*Peregr.* 19): ἀνδρα παιδείᾳ καὶ ἀξιώματι προὔχοντα.

[36] Cf. Syme (above, n. 1) 195: 'Some students of the Principate are prone to set a high value on administration. The Romans did very little of it.'

[37] *SEG* xviii. 557 = *AE* 1961. 320. Cf. C. Habicht, *Istanbuler Mitteilungen* 9/10 (1959/60) 109–25; Halfmann 161 f., no. 73. There is now a monograph by O. Andrei: *A. Claudius Charax di Pergamo* (Bologna, 1984).

[38] 'Suda' s.v. Χάραξ = *FGrH* 103 T 1.

2. *Arrian and his Historical Production*

and he was a philosopher of repute—not wholly to the taste of Marcus Aurelius, who found him harsh and bombastic.[39] Again like Arrian, he was prominent in his home city, honoured for his benefactions, and was widely known abroad, receiving an honorary magistracy at Sparta.[40] From the latter years of Hadrian's reign he followed a senatorial career. Adlected to aedilician rank, he served with II Augusta in Britain and governed Cilicia before his suffect consulship in 147. At the same time he was active as a historian and achieved fame in that field of study. The citizens of Patrae honoured him for his history while he was consul designate and his work was widely known by that date.[41] Much of his writing must have been concomitant with his posts in the Roman *cursus*.

Arrian likewise began writing at an early age. To us he is exclusively a historian, but in his own time he was known more as a philosopher. That is what two contemporary inscriptions (from Corinth and Athens) explicitly name him.[42] Some of that reputation will have derived from the publication of his notes of Epictetus' lectures, but it seems that he also wrote philosophy of his own.[43] Fragments of a meteorological treatise have survived in excerpt,[44] and there is every possibility that there were other works of the same nature. Many of his writings were no longer extant in Photius' day,[45] and the lost works may well have included philosophy. Posterity remembered him as the mouthpiece of Epictetus and disregarded his own ventures in the field.

Associated with his philosophical ambitions was a conscious imitation of Xenophon, who was more famous in later antiquity as a philosopher than a historian.[46] The Byzantine biographical tradition, based on Heliconius of Byzantium,

---

[39] M. Ant. viii. 25. 2; cf. Habicht (above, n. 37) 120.

[40] *IG* v. 1. 71, col. iii. 5, 8, 25: πατρόνομος in Sparta.

[41] *SEG* xviii. 557; cf. *CQ* 22 (1972) 170.

[42] *AE* 1968. 473 (Corinth): cf. Bowersock, *GRBS* 8 (1967) 279 f.; *AAA* 3 (1970) 377–80 = *AE* 1971. 437 (Athens).

[43] *HCArr.* 5–6; cf. Stadter 19–31.

[44] Roos, *Arriani Scripta Minora* 186–95 (surviving mostly as excerpts in Stobaeus). On the history of the attribution to Arrian the historian see Stadter 202 n. 19.

[45] φασὶ δὲ αὐτὸν καὶ ἕτερα γράψαι, ἃ οὔπω εἰς ἡμετέραν ἀφίκετο γνῶσιν (Phot. *Bibl.* cod. 58. 5).

[46] Cf. Quint. x. 1. 75 (cf. 82): *Xenophon non excidit mihi, sed inter philosophos reddendus est.*

maintains that he was actually named the new Xenophon.[47]
Arrian describes himself as a homonym of Xenophon in the late
*Cynegeticus* and, a few years before, in his *Order of Battle against
the Alani*, he had named himself Xenophon.[48] Works of the
same period refer to 'the elder Xenophon',[49] and there is an
implicit contrast with the younger aspirant to the name. The
mannerism cannot be traced in the *History of Alexander*, which is
deeply indebted to Xenophon in style and content but displays
no direct imitation. The very title *Anabasis of Alexander* is first
attested in Stephanus of Byzantium and need not be Arrian's
own.[50] It could be a name first conferred upon the work in late
antiquity to give the second Xenophon a second *Anabasis*. This
is not a vital detail. What matters is the relative importance of
Xenophon. In the Alexander history he is an undeniable source
of inspiration, his account of the deeds of the Ten Thousand a
standing challenge to make the achievements of Alexander
equally famous,[51] but there is no hint that Arrian is parading
himself as a second Xenophon. The imitation is explicit and
unmistakable in the *Periplus* and *Cynegeticus*, and it probably
came late in life as Arrian's own career took on the lineaments
of Xenophon.[52] Philosopher, biographer of Epictetus (his personal Socrates), historian, general, and huntsman, his life
assumed a progressively greater overlap, and his relations with
Hadrian were not unlike those of Xenophon with King Agesilaus.[53] The adoption of the name was a fairly late development
and it may originally have been conferred upon him as a title of

[47] Phot. *Bibl.* cod. 58. 4; 'Suda' s.v. Ἀρριανός. A double herm, found at Athens, has
been attributed to Xenophon and Arrian (J. H. Oliver, *AJA* 76 [1972] 327–8).

[48] *Cyneget.* 1. 4; 16. 6; 22. 1. *Ect.* 10, 22.

[49] *Peripl.* 12. 5, 25. 1. For the comparable expression ἐκεῖνος ὁ Ξενοφῶν see *Peripl.* 1. 1,
2. 3; *Cyneget.* 16. 7, 21. 2; 25. 4, 30. 2.

[50] Steph. Byz. s.v. Ἀσσακηνοί. The title also occurs in the archetype of Arrian, the
twelfth-century *codex Vindobonensis*, in the Byzantine excerpts *de legationibus*, and in the
'Suda' s.v. περὶ Πινδάρου. Arrian himself gives no indication of a title, and the Alexander history is most often cited as his 'work about Alexander' (cf. *HCArr*. i. 7–8).

[51] i. 12. 3 (see below, pp. 32ff.). See also ii. 7. 8–9; vii. 13. 4. For Xenophon's stylistic
influence, modest compared with that of Herodotus, see *HCArr*. i. 36 and the discussion
below, ch. 6.

[52] So *HCArr*. i. 7; Ameling, *Epigraphica Anatolica* 4 (1984) 119–22. Stadter 2–3 adheres to his earlier hypothesis (*GRBS* 8 [1967] 155–61) that the name Xenophon was
an actual *cognomen*, not in any sense an assumed title.

[53] Arrian may well have been directly influenced by Xenophon's *Agesilaus*. See
below, ch. 6.

honour, as were the accolades of 'new Homer' and 'new Themistocles' which were conferred by the Athenians upon the Syrian magnate, C. Julius Nicanor.[54] It symbolized the unique blend of political achievement and literary eminence which Lucian singles out for comment.

It was as a historian that Arrian was known to subsequent generations. For us his work on Alexander is of paramount importance. Two texts are involved, which Arrian clearly regarded as inseparable. The major work, explicitly described as such,[55] was the formal narrative of the exploits of the king, the seven-book history known since Byzantine times as the *Anabasis of Alexander*. This was supplemented by a monograph on India, which Arrian describes as his 'Indian' composition ($\dot{\eta}$ $\text{'}I\nu\delta\iota\kappa\dot{\eta}$ $\xi\upsilon\gamma\gamma\rho\alpha\phi\dot{\eta}$).[56] That is a relatively short work devoted to the geography, customs, and natural curiosities of the subcontinent,[57] which culminates in a detailed description of Nearchus' voyage from Patala in southern India to the Persian Gulf and Susa. It is also written in Ionic, in conscious imitation of the Ionian ethnographic tradition. In the formal history Arrian speaks of the Indian monograph as a work for the future, to be completed when inclination and inspiration lead him to do so,[58] but it is evident that the two works were planned together. The major work foreshadows the minor one, giving an outline of its contents, and each work contains cross-references to the other.[59] More seriously, the thumb-nail sketch of Indian geography in Book v of the Alexander history is carefully designed to supplement the fuller exposition in the *Indike*, enlarging on Eratosthenes' geographical framework of Asia (which is simply mentioned in passing in the specialist monograph)[60] and concentrating on the alluvial nature of the great Indian plains, a feature not mentioned in the minor work

---

[54] *IG* ii². 3786–9. For other examples see Ameling (above, n. 1) 120–1.

[55] ἐν τῇ μέζονι ξυγγραφῇ (*Ind.* 21. 8, 26. 1).

[56] v. 6. 8; vi. 16. 5. 'Ινδική is the title unanimously attested by Photius, Stephanus of Byzantium (s.v. *Μάσσακα*), and the *codex Vindobonensis*. Cf. Stadter 116 with n. 4.

[57] Arrian's own description of contents (v. 5. 1).

[58] ταῦτα (sc. Nearchus' voyage) μὲν δὴ ἐν ὑστέρῳ ἔσται τυχόν (vi. 28. 6). For other references to the *Indike* as a work for the future see v. 5. 1, 6. 8; vi. 16. 5.

[59] See preceding note for references in the main work. In the *Indike* see 19. 8, 21. 8, 23. 6, 26. 1, 32. 1, 40. 1.

[60] v. 5. 2–6. 8 (cf. *Ind.* 3. 2–3).

(which deals primarily with the volume of the Indian rivers).[61] The same sources are used in both works but the material is deliberately divided between them. Arrian may have published his *Indike* after the Alexander history, but he obviously composed them both at roughly the same time, if not *pari passu*,[62] and they can legitimately be studied together.

Other works were known in antiquity. The history of Alexander was certainly not the most voluminous, nor was it necessarily the most celebrated. In his *Bibliotheca* (composed towards the middle of the ninth century AD) Photius saw fit to summarize four of Arrian's major works,[63] and he lets us know incidentally of more. The most informative passage is the beginning of his discussion of the *Bithyniaca*, Arrian's eight-book history of his native province. There Photius summarizes the preface in which Arrian apologized for his delay in writing the work, claiming that he needed preparation in the art of history. The *Bithyniaca*, says Photius, was Arrian's fourth historical work, appearing after earlier treatises on Dion, Timoleon, and Alexander.[64] Just how much of this information comes from Arrian himself is debatable. Photius states that Arrian mentioned explicitly the works on Dion and Timoleon and gave some hint of their content. The reference to the history of Alexander may conceivably be Photius' own addition,[65] but there is no reason to think so. It is admittedly mentioned very cursorily, but Photius was under no obligation to reproduce everything Arrian said about his work. After all, he had given a summary of the Alexander history only a few pages earlier (cod. 91: the

---

[61] v. 6. 3–6. Compare *Ind.* 4. 6–12. At v. 6. 8 he refers cursorily to the fifteen tributaries of the Indus, which are all named in the *Indike* (4. 8–12; cf. Strabo xv. 1. 32 [700]). Similarly Alexander's passage of Gedrosia, fully described in the larger work, is merely mentioned in passing in the *Indike* (26. 1, 32. 1).

[62] Cf. F. F. Schwarz, *East & West* 25 (1975) 192–4; Stadter 116.

[63] The *Parthica* (cod. 58), the Alexander history and *Indike* (cod. 91), the history of the Successors (cod. 92), the *Bithyniaca* (cod. 93).

[64] Phot. *Bibl.* cod. 93. 3 = Arr. *Bithyn.* F 1. 3 (Roos); *FGrH* 156 T 4: μετὰ γὰρ τὰ περὶ 'Αλέξανδρον καὶ Τιμολέοντα καὶ Δίωνα, μετὰ τὰς περὶ αὐτοὺς ἱστορίας, ἥδε αὐτῷ ἡ συγγραφὴ ἐξεπονήθη.

[65] Argued by Stadter 181–2, expanding Jacoby, *FGrH* ii.D 552. Wirth, *Studien* 32, 240 f., suggested that the entire phrase τὰ περὶ 'Αλέξανδρον ... Δίωνα is a scribal gloss. See, however, *CQ* 22 (1972) 178–82, where it is argued that the reference to the Alexander history goes back to Arrian himself (so already Schwartz, *RE* ii. 1235). For a more idiosyncratic view of the evidence of Photius see the recent discussion by G. Zecchini, *Critica storica* 20 (1983) 13–15.

*Bithyniaca* is cod. 93) and would be justified in assuming that his readers could dispense with an additional description. The fact remains that Photius had some reason for placing the Alexander history before the *Bithyniaca*, and the most economical hypothesis is that he took the information directly from Arrian. Indeed the sequence Dion, Timoleon, Alexander is paralleled in Plutarch's work. Plutarch clearly wrote the three biographies as an interrelated whole,[66] connected by cross-references. He may well have provided Arrian with a model to surpass.

The Alexander history, then, came early in the sequence of Arrian's historical writings. It was followed by longer and more ambitious works: the *Bithyniaca*, the seventeen-book history of Parthia from the establishment of the monarch to Trajan's conquests,[67] and finally (most curious of all) the *History of the Successors*, which devoted ten books of narrative to the brief period between Alexander's death and the end of the campaigning season of 320.[68] If the sequence is fairly clear, the exact dating is most mysterious, and the Alexander history has been placed both early and late in Arrian's career.[69] I must state at the outset that there is no scrap of positive evidence for a late dating, in the reign of Antoninus Pius. Most scholars who have propounded it have been influenced by Schwartz's fallacy that Arrian's literary career could only begin after his public life had ended.[70] The evidence for the earlier date is certainly nebulous, but it does exist and has some cumulative force.

In the first place there is an argument from silence, which I

---

[66] Argued by J. Mewaldt, *Hermes* 42 (1907) 564–78 (cf. C. P. Jones, *JRS* 56 [1966] 66–7; J. R. Hamilton, *Plut. Al.* xxxv–vii). The case for simultaneous composition of the Roman lives has been expanded by C. B. R. Pelling, *JHS* 99 (1979) 75–83.

[67] Stadter 135–44 gives a brief characterization. See, however, *CQ* 33 (1983) 265–76.

[68] Stadter 144–52. A new fragment from Book x, preserved on palimpsest, has been published by J. Noret, *AC* 52 (1983) 235–42.

[69] For a summary of the controversy see *CQ* 22 (1972) 163 f.; Stadter 179–87 (the main champion of the late dating had been Schwartz, *RE* ii. 1230–6, of the earlier F. Reuss, *Rh. Mus.* 45 [1899] 455–61). For recent statements see *HCArr.* i. 8–11; Brunt, *Arrian* ii. 534–9; P. Vidal-Naquet, in *Arrien: Histoire d'Alexandre*, trans. P. Savinel (Paris, 1984) 319–22.

[70] More recently there has been a general acknowledgement that Arrian's political and literary activities were concomitant. The argument for a later dating (after Arrian became a Roman senator) now rests entirely upon the interpretation of i. 12. 5 (on which see below, pp. 32 ff.).

think establishes a terminus. Arrian is prone to draw on his personal experience to add colour and corroborative argumentation to his historical narrative. We have noted his eyewitness description of the Danubian tributaries, and I would add the precise (deceptively precise[71]) location of the statue-group of the tyrannicides in Athens (iii. 16. 8) and the praise of the high quality of Epirote cattle (ii. 16. 5). Now, if there was one area where Arrian had acquired detailed knowledge, it was in Cappadocia, where he served for six years and more.[72] Yet the Alexander history gives no hint of eyewitness knowledge, and there are passages where such knowledge would have been directly relevant. The most informative is the description of Heracleides' voyage of discovery in the Caspian (vii. 16. 1–4). Here Arrian is patently dependent on his primary sources (principally Aristobulus) for his geographical information.[73] He retails the statement that the 'origins' (ἀρχαί) of the sea have not yet been discovered. There is no reference to the later discoveries of Patrocles which determined Eratosthenes' concept of the Caspian as a gulf of Ocean, a concept which Arrian himself knew and employed in his rhetoric.[74] Nor is there any hint of anything other than literary knowledge of the subject. Yet his legateship of Cappadocia took him into Lesser Armenia

---

[71] The location by reference to the Metroon is difficult to reconcile with the rest of the literary tradition and the actual topography of the *agora*. For the problems see *HCArr.* i. 317–18. See also vii. 13. 5, where Arrian refers to Micon's celebrated paintings in the *stoa poikile*, another of the great sights of the *agora*. This again suggests (but does not prove) autopsy.

[72] I would no longer insist on Reuss's argument (*Rh. Mus.* 45 [1899] 459) that Arrian's apparent ignorance of the transfer of Lysippus' commemorative statue-group from Dium to Rome (i. 16. 4; cf. *HCArr.* i. 125 f.) indicates that the passage was written before he knew the capital at first hand. Arrian certainly writes as though the monument were still in Macedonia (ἐν Δίῳ ἑστᾶσιν). Recent attempts to save his credit by interpreting the tense as aorist or historic present (Stadter 184; Hammond, *CQ* 30 [1980] 461) founder against his own usage. At vii. 10. 4 he echoes the passage (οἴκοι ἑστᾶσιν) and there is no doubt that the tense is a true perfect and denotes the present condition of the statues (so too *Peripl.* 1. 3: ὁ μὲν γὰρ ἀνδριὰς ἔστηκεν ὁ σός). But, even so, Arrian's knowledge of the monuments of Rome need not have been comprehensive and he may not have observed Lysippus' masterpiece in the *campus Martius*. Ignorance of its contemporary location is compatible with any period in his career. On the other hand it is certainly easiest to explain if he did not as yet know Rome.

[73] See ch. 5, n. 156.

[74] For the testimonia and fragments of Patrocles see *FGrH* 712 (esp. F 5–7). For Arrian's use of the theory of the gulf of Ocean see v. 5. 4, 26. 1–2 (see below, p. 130).

and brought him into contact with the Alani.[75] The geography of the Caspian must have been reasonably familiar to him then, and it was reported, correctly or not, that the Alani had made a circuit of the sea during their earlier invasion of AD 72.[76] By the second century enough accurate information had become available for Marinus of Tyre and Claudius Ptolemaeus to reject the framework of Eratosthenes and describe the Caspian correctly as an inland sea.[77] It is hard to believe that none of the new knowledge percolated to Arrian while he was in Cappadocia or that he deliberately ignored it in his writing.

That is particularly pertinent to the description of the navigable rivers discharging into the Caspian. Arrian (following Aristobulus?) states that the Oxus and Iaxartes flow into the Caspian and adds that majority opinion (ὁ πλείων λόγος[78]) reports the same of the Armenian Araxes (vii. 16. 3). This reflects the state of knowledge at the time of Alexander. Writers like Medeius of Larisa alleged that the Araxes cut through a gorge similar to Tempe to discharge into the Caspian, whereas Callisthenes had followed Herodotus, claiming that the river split into forty tributaries.[79] Alexander's men had never seen the Araxes and there was a good deal of uncertainty about its course. By Arrian's day the uncertainty was long past. The Araxes and its course had been familiar since the campaigns of Lucullus and Pompey. It was long established that it first made a confluence with the Cyrus (R. Kur) and then flowed directly

---

[75] In the encounter with the Alani *XV Apollinaris*, unlike *XII Fulminata*, was at full strength (*Ect.* 5–6, 15). The legion was presumably near its headquarters at Satala, close to the head waters of the Araxes (cf. *HCSP* 81 [1977] 233–4).

[76] Jos. *BJ* vii. 245–6. The details have been contested, notably by von Gutschmid and Mommsen (cf. *Antichthon* 10 [1976] 68 f.), but, even if Josephus' account is garbled, it is reasonable to assume that the military activity around the Caspian generated more interest in the geography of the region.

[77] Ptol. *Geogr.* v. 9. 12; vi. 14. 1–2. Cf. Herrmann, *RE* x. 2280; J. O. Thomson, *A History of Ancient Geography* 293–4. It is at least possible that the trading activities of entrepreneurs like Maes Titianus (on whom see Cary, *CQ* 6 [1956] 130–4; M. Raschke, *ANRW* ix. 2. 846 nn. 795–6) made information about central Asia more accessible. Marinus acknowledged his debt to Maes (Ptol. i. 11. 6), and it is hard to believe that Arrian as legate of Cappadocia was wholly indifferent to the eastern trade and the geographical information that accrued from it.

[78] Arrian elsewhere (i. 11. 6; iii. 3. 6) uses the expression to refer to the consensus of his historical sources.

[79] Strabo xi. 14. 13 (531) = Medeius, *FGrH* 129 F 1; Callisthenes, *FGrH* 124 F 38 (cf. Hdt. i. 202. 3).

into the Caspian.[80] The lower reaches of the river in fact passed through the territory of the Albani, who were directly affected by the Alan invasion of 135. Even if Arrian did not intervene in person,[81] he was surely familiar with the terrain. None the less he claims no personal knowledge (in direct contrast to his procedure with the Inn and Save), and it is a fair assumption that, when he wrote, he had no experience of Cappadocia. The same applies to his discussion of Eratosthenes' critique of the Alexander historians who located Prometheus' cave in the Hindu Kush (v. 3. 2). While in Cappadocia Arrian had been shown Mt. Strobilus in the Caucasus, Prometheus' alleged place of punishment (*Peripl.* 11. 5). He was able to corroborate Eratosthenes' argument from autopsy, yet he refrained from doing so. Elsewhere he is ready enough to draw on his knowledge of Epirus to support the rationalizing argument of Hecataeus,[82] but here he gives no hint of relevant experience.

The dating before the governorship of Cappadocia gives a very wide scope. There is only one text[83] which gives a more positive indication, the celebrated delayed introduction at i. 12. 5.[84] That passage is the culmination of an excursus and Arrian's language is very carefully chosen. He begins with the story that Alexander while honouring the tomb of Achilles expressed his envy that the hero had his exploits chronicled by Homer. That leads him to the observation that Alexander's achievements have never been adequately commemorated in prose or verse, despite their overwhelming magnitude. For that reason he was inspired to embark on the history, considering himself fully equal to the task (i. 12. 4). In future he will be the

---

[80] Plut. *Pomp.* 34. 4; App. *Mithr.* 103. 480 (cf. Strabo xi. 4. 2 [501]). Stadter's argument (187 n. 19) that Arrian qualified his expression because he knew that the Araxes did not flow directly into the Caspian is very weak.

[81] As stated by Themistius (*Or.* 34. 8). Accepted in *HSCP* (1977) 229–32, but Syme, *Roman Papers* 1440, remains sceptical.

[82] ii. 16. 6. Compare *Ind.* 41. 2 for a description of the strait between Leucas and Acarnania, expanding on Nearchus' description of the Persian Gulf (autopsy is not explicitly claimed).

[83] The oracles issued to the Macedonians are described as recent events (vii. 30. 2), but they cannot, to my knowledge, be dated.

[84] See, in general, G. Schepens, *Ancient Society* 2 (1971) 254–68; Stadter 60–4 (cf. also *Illinois Classical Studies* 6 [1981] 157–71); *HCArr.* i. 104–6; Brunt, *Arrian* ii. 538–40; J. R. Moles, *JHS* 105 (1985) 162–8.

approved historian of Alexander, the Homer of the Macedonian Achilles. Arrian now proceeds to an elaborate *recusatio*. He has no need to give his name (which is celebrated) nor to report his native land, his family or any offices he has held in his country. What he sets on record is this, that in his eyes country, family, and offices are these works of his (οἶδε οἱ λόγοι), and have been since his youth.

Arrian is deliberately underscoring his literary reputation. He has no need to give credentials, for his works speak for themselves. There is deliberate allusiveness, a play on what had become a convention of historical writing. In the imperial period historians might delay introducing themselves for some considerable space. Dionysius of Halicarnassus, for instance, writes six chapters of introduction before giving biographical details about himself (*AR* i. 7. 2) and only states his name and birthplace in the sentence before the narrative proper.[85] Appian does the same in a passage which might be a commentary on Arrian: 'as for the author, many men know of me and I have prefaced my name. But, to put it more plainly, I am Appian of Alexandria, a man of the first rank in my country and advocate at Rome before the emperors until they deigned to make me their procurator.'[86] Arrian, however, dispenses with any *explicit* self-advertisement. Indeed he says that he has no need to supply any biographical material. Everything is indifferent except his writings. This he states with the maximum possible force, using a familiar rhetorical trope. His writings, he says, mean everything to him—they are his country, family, offices. The expression is indebted ultimately to Andromache's impassioned invocation of Hector: Ἕκτορ, ἀτὰρ σύ μοί ἐσσι πατὴρ καὶ πότνια μήτηρ / ἠδὲ κασίγνητος (*Il.* vi. 429–30). There are also direct parallels in material familiar to Arrian. Xenophon's Clearchus invokes his men as his country, friends, and allies (*Anab.* i. 3. 6) and, even more strikingly, Epictetus defined self-interest as man's highest love: 'this to him is father, brother, kinsman, country, and god' (*Diss.* ii. 22. 16).

---

[85] For other examples see *HCArr.* i. 106 and, on Arrian's choice of context, see Moles 167.

[86] App. *Prooem.* 15. 62. Arrian's delayed preface has been taken as a stinging riposte to Appian (Moles 168). Given Appian's almost demonstrable use of Arrian's work elsewhere, (*CQ* 22 [1972] 177 ff.; see below ch. 3, n. 65), the similarity is best taken as an echo of Arrian, the sincere, if clumsy, flattery of imitation.

Arrian in fact fuses together two conventions: the self-advertisement is coupled with an emphatic statement that in his eyes literary endeavour is paramount. The value that other people place on their birth and social standing he places on his work alone. There is no doubt that he means his published work in general.[87] The other interpretation, that the λόγοι are the historical traditions about Alexander,[88] does not hold water when examined in context. If Arrian were merely expressing devotion to the memory of Alexander and enthusiasm for his history, it would never justify the following sentence that it was on this score that he considered himself worthy of the first place in Greek letters, the literary peer of Alexander in arms.[89] Mere enthusiasm for the Alexander saga could not convey primacy in the field. Any illiterate could claim a lifelong enthusiasm with his history. The sequence of thought, as Bowie and Brunt have observed, is similar to that in Aelius Aristeides, who dreamed of himself and Alexander side by side, 'since we had both acquired supremacy as our lot, he in military prowess, I in oratory.'[90] Arrian is more involved, but his meaning is clear. The relationship between him and Alexander will be comparable to that between Homer and Achilles. This claim is based on his established literary renown. His works have made him a household name and mean everything to him. On that

[87] For the use of the singular λόγος to denote an entire work, see *Ind.* 32. 1 (ἐν τῷ ἄλλῳ λόγῳ); 43. 14.

[88] See, most recently and fully, Moles 167. According to this interpretation οἶδε οἱ λόγοι takes up τήνδε τὴν ξυγγραφήν and refers exclusively to the Alexander history. I would accept the reference back but not its exclusive connotation. The work on Alexander is included as one work in a general corpus—'these λόγοι of mine'.

[89] καὶ ἐπὶ τῷδε οὐκ ἀπαξιῶ ἐμαυτὸν τῶν πρώτων ἐν τῇ φωνῇ τῇ Ἑλλάδι, εἴπερ οὖν καὶ Ἀλέξανδρον τῶν ἐν τοῖς ὅπλοις. Schepens, *Ancient Society* 2 (1971) 260–2, has argued that the conditional clause (εἴπερ οὖν ... ὅπλοις) is not a simple comparison. He cites vii. 20. 1, claiming that there is a causal nuance. Arrian invokes the case of Alexander to substantiate his own pretensions. For his celebrity Alexander is dependent on Arrian, and conversely Arrian's renown rests on the importance of his subject. Schepens, like earlier commentators (notably Krüger) interpreted the λόγοι exclusively as the tales about Alexander and came to the conclusion that Arrian considered that his reputation depended on his choice of subject. This is unnecessarily elaborate. A more apposite parallel is vii. 2. 3, where the Indian sage Dandamis declares ὡς Διὸς υἱὸς καὶ οὗτος εἴη, εἴπερ οὖν καὶ Ἀλέξανδρος. This is indeed comparison, with a tinge of irony: the Indian was himself a son of Zeus just as much as Alexander. Our passage is similar in construction. Arrian counts himself supreme in Greek letters just as he considers Alexander supreme in war.

[90] Arist. 50 (*Sacred Tales* iii). 49: ὡς ἄρα ἀμφότεροι τὸ ἄκρον λάχοιμεν ὁ μὲν τῆς ἐν τοῖς ὅπλοις δυνάμεως ἐγὼ δὲ τῆς ἐπὶ τοῖς λόγοις. Cf. Brunt, *Arrian* ii. 540.

score he considers himself the literary counterpart of Alexander, competent to do for him what nobody has done before. The statement is an uncompromising claim to literary pre-eminence, made in a remarkably stylized and mannered form. Arrian was a writer with a well-established reputation. That reputation need not have come from history, for he is talking of literary excellence, the rhetorical and literary skills which would do justice to Alexander's career. The wording is compatible with Photius' statement that the works on Alexander came relatively early in the sequence of specifically historical writings, but it implies any number of successes in other genres. When he wrote the passage, Arrian was at the head of the literary profession. Can we go further? I think we can. The language of the *recusatio*, as we have seen, is very carefully chosen. Arrian implicitly criticizes the common practice of including biographical information (which he was to follow in the *Bithyniaca*[91]) and places himself above it. His reference to office, however, is specifically confined to local office (ἐν τῇ ἐμαυτοῦ). In a context which is closely coherent and varied in expression there is no viable alternative (ἡ ἐμαυτοῦ is a variation of πατρίς).[92] His offices are qualified as local offices. Arrian mentions only the positions he held in his native Bithynia, implicitly excluding office at Rome or in the imperial service.

---

[91] Phot. *Bibl.* cod. 93. 1 = *Bithyn.* Fl. 1 (Roos).

[92] I cannot see how πατρίς can refer to anything other than Nicomedia, which Arrian explicitly acknowledged as such (twice in Photius' excerpt of the preface of the *Bithyniaca*; see further Moles 165 f.). Rome, the 'common fatherland' of all senators (Brunt ii. 538), has been suggested as an alternative, but the qualification 'in my own land' is too precise to refer to the Roman cursus (Vidal-Naquet [above, n. 69] 320, who considers it self-evident that the offices were held 'dans le cadre de l'empire', is constrained to quote Arrian in expurgated form, omitting the qualification). One would expect either a reference to magistracies in general or a specific mention of Rome (as in Appian, *Prooem.* 15. 62: ἐς τὰ πρῶτα ἥκων ἐν τῇ πατρίδι καὶ δίκαις ἐν Ῥώμῃ συναγορεύσας). It is true that after his retirement Arrian might have referred to Athens as 'his' city (*Cyneget.* 1. 4; Wirth, *Studien* 29), but, in such close proximity to πατρίς (which occurs both before and after) ἡ ἐμαυτοῦ cannot be anything other than conscious variation. For Arrian his πατρίς was clearly his birthplace, as it was for that other consular historian from Bithynia, Cassius Dio (cf. Dio lxxv. 15. 3; lxxx. 5. 3). Dio of Prusa, who had honorary citizenship of Apameia, refers to Apameia as a *kind* of πατρίς but makes it plain that Prusa was his primary homeland (Dio Chrys, 41. 2, 3, 5: *contra* Moles 165). For the legal status of provincial senators, who were allowed to retain all the advantages of municipal citizenship without its financial burdens (Hermogenianus, *Dig.* 1. 1. 23 pr.: *Municeps esse desinit senatoriam adeptus dignitatem, quantum ad munera: quantum vero ad honorem, retinere creditur originem*), see Eck, *Chiron* 7 (1977) 371 ff.

There seems no reason for the limitation unless his experience of public office was indeed local. It cannot be claimed that he is writing in an exclusively Greek cultural context, for Arrian sees Alexander as an ecumenical phenomenon, of interest to mankind at large. In any case his thesis is that his literary work, particularly his work on Alexander, outweighs any office he has held. If his experience of public service extended outside Bithynia, the qualification is otiose and weakens the point. Nor can it be said that the magistracies of Nicomedia and Bithynia were too insignificant to be listed as personal distinctions.[93] The major provincial priesthoods in particular brought recognition in Roman circles as well as local celebrity. Compare the case of the Lycian rhetorician Heracleides. He was Lyciarch (provincial high priest), and Philostratus comments that the position, despite the insignificance of the Lycians, was highly regarded by the Romans.[94] What he says of Heracleides in fact echoes Arrian's own statement: he was notable for his birth and his local priesthood, but still more notable as a sophist. Arrian's claim that his name is far from unknown fits his literary pretensions rather than his social standing. His work is what he primarily emphasizes, and he is clearly addressing himself to an established readership.

The language of the *recusatio* implies an entrenched reputation and local distinction. It best fits the period before Arrian held office at Rome. If he had achieved senatorial rank, it is unlikely in the extreme that he would have omitted the fact and unlikely that he would have set his writings above it. Access to the senate was still rare for men from the Greek east and was proudly commemorated. A dignitary from Miletus, for instance, proclaimed himself 'the fifth from Asia in the whole of time to enter the senate, from Miletus and the rest of Ionia the one and only'.[95] Now Arrian was among the first of the Bithynian senators (only one person is known to have been elevated before him, a man of Italian stock from the *colonia* of Apameia).[96] He is not likely to have underrated the distinction or

---

[93] For a catalogue of the local distinctions of Greek senators see Halfmann 33 ff.
[94] Philostr. *VS* ii. 26 (pp. 612–13).
[95] *Didyma* ii. 199, no. 296; cf. Habicht, *ZPE* 13 (1974) 1–6; Halfmann 108–9, no. 12.
[96] Catilius (?) Longus. Cf. Eck, *ZPE* 42 (1981) 242–4 (improved reading of *CIL* iii. 335); Halfmann 115, no. 18.

to have placed it below his literary reputation. If he had done so, his language would have been more explicit and even more emphatic. The evidence has taken us to a tentative conclusion. The history of Alexander was written after Arrian had proved himself as a major literary figure but before he entered the senate. If he received senatorial rank by adlection early in Hadrian's reign, we can date the work some time towards the end of Trajan's reign, when Arrian was in his early thirties,[97] already a mature and successful writer.

---

[97] Arrian's statement (i. 12. 5) that he had been engaged in literary studies from his youth (ἀπὸ νέου) is no argument to the contrary (*pace* Moles 168). The sources which give an upper limit to the concept of youth are hardly typical (Xen. *Mem.* i. 2. 35 is a piece of special pleading by Charicles). On the other hand ἐκ νέου can be used to mean 'from one's early days' (cf. Arist, *NE* 1103$^b$24, 1179$^b$31). That is surely the sense in Arrian, and the expression is not incongruous in the mouth of a man in his thirties. One knows that in Latin *adulescentulus* can be used to describe a man well advanced in his thirties (Sall. *BC* 49. 2). Yet the Younger Pliny, writing at the age of 36 or 37 can still refer to his early twenties as a time when he was *adulescentulus* (*Ep.* i. 10. 2).

# 3

# THE HANDLING OF SOURCES

THE character of Arrian's work on Alexander stands out in
sharp relief. It could not be clearer that it is intended as a literary monument to the Macedonian conqueror. Arrian, as we
have seen, considers himself a worthy peer of Alexander in the
field of literature. He has no doubt about the success and
enduring popularity of his work and is supremely confident
that he can stop the transmission of falsehood.[1] Thanks to his
work the details of Alexander's career will become common
knowledge, as much so as the march of the Ten Thousand, and
for future generations his version of events will be definitive. He
was quite right, of course, and his outstanding success was not
merely due to the vicissitudes of manuscript transmission,
which preserved his work and discarded his competitors. The
literary qualities of his work were admired in antiquity, and he
became a model of historiography.[2]

Style was fundamental. The manner of presentation had
little to do with the techniques of historical research. Arrian's
readership was far less concerned with the actual facts of Alexander's reign than with their literary dressing. That is the main
thrust of Lucian's little treatise on historiography, which glosses
over the collection of material in a few perfunctory sentences
but dilates on the arrangement and stylistic embellishment of
the collected facts.[3] Now for the history of Alexander the factual material presented no problem. As far as sources went,
there was an *embarras de choix*, a strong contrast with the history
of Bithynia, which was much less clearly defined and required
more primary investigation. Arrian cut down the range of

---

[1] vi. 11. 2. See below ch. 4.

[2] Note in particular the comments of Photius *Bibl.* cod. 92. 46: ἐστὶ μὲν οὖν ὁ ἀνὴρ
οὐδενὸς τῶν ἄριστα συνταξαμένων ἱστορίας δεύτερος. For Arrian's posthumous fame see
*HCArr.* i. 36–8.

[3] Lucian *Hist. conscr.* 47–8. See further, G. Avenarius, *Lukians Schrift zur
Geschichtsschreibung* (Meisenheim/Glan, 1956) 85–104; F. Millar, *Cassius Dio* 32–3.

selection by confining himself to two primary authorities, Ptolemy and Aristobulus, whom he used as basic repositories of fact (for the *Indike* he used three: Nearchus, Megasthenes, and Eratosthenes).[4] He did not accept what they said without criticism, but he was for the most part confident that they provided an honest, unbiased view of events. Stories from other sources could be added if they were intrinsically interesting and remotely plausible,[5] but as a general rule he confined himself to two sources.

How did Arrian handle his material? For us that is one of the most important problems, and it is also one of the most intractable. Arrian seldom names his sources. He does so more than most historians of antiquity, but there are long tracts of narrative where he gives no indication. Book i is particularly bad, with only two explicit citations (both of Ptolemy) in its entire length.[6] Even when we can identify the source for a passage, it is usually impossible to detect how Arrian has adapted it. No part of the original texts is extant, and there is no scope for direct comparison of source and adaptation such as commends itself with Livy and Polybius.[7] Even the primary identification of source is often problematic. Arrian has recourse to a whole barrage of literary devices when he comments on his material.[8] When the detail is striking or suspicious, he may name his source explicity, but he is more likely to use an indirect formula (λέγεται or λόγος κατέχει) simply to break up the narrative flow and permit an excursion into *oratio obliqua*. We need look no further than the opening chapters of the work. Arrian begins with indirect speech and continues with the narrative of the Danubian expedition, all in accusative and infinitive construction. At i. 1. 6 he refers obliquely to his sources (λέγουσιν ὅτι), and the change of construction allows him to continue in direct speech. The narrative then proceeds without interruption as far

---

[4] For fuller detail see *HCArr.* i. 16–34.

[5] See below, ch. 4, for general discussion.

[6] i. 2. 7 = *FGrH* 138 F 1; i. 8. 1 = *FGrH* 138 F 3.

[7] Stadter, *GRBS* 17 (1976) 159–67, examines the use of Xenophon in Arrian's *Cynegeticus*. The results are interesting, showing how Arrian could vary his original even when referring closely and directly, but the sample is necessarily limited. Arrian did not there use Xenophon as a narrative source but referred to him peripherally as an anchor for his discussion of modern methods of hunting

[8] Discussed fully below, pp. 62 ff.

as i. 2. 7, where Arrian gives a figure for Macedonian casualties and appends his source (Ptolemy). It is evident that the whole narrative is based upon a single source, interspersed by editorial comments,[9] and there are other passages, notably those dealing with Ptolemy's exploits,[10] where one can assume adaptation of a single exemplar. In other cases he explicitly constructs a narrative from both Ptolemy and Aristobulus and refers to the composite account as a collective entity.[11] Without control sources one cannot hope to detect how he transfers from one source to another, still less how he modifies and embroiders his original material. What is a priori likely is that there is variation. Given his high estimate of his own work, Arrian would not have acted as the slavish copier of any source, no matter how highly he regarded it.

ARRIAN AND STRABO

If there is no original to set against Arrian's adaptation, the next best thing is to compare his narrative with another secondary source dependent upon the same material. Fortunately that is possible on a number of occasions, thanks to Strabo, who drew extensively upon Aristobulus and Megasthenes for his descriptions of India, Persia, and Mesopotamia. The two authors, historian and geographer, often excerpt the same material in considerable detail, and their narrative can be compared and contrasted. It is a complex exercise, for we cannot assume in advance that either author is meticulously accurate in reproducing his original. Both may be assumed to have made excisions and stylistic alterations and to have varied the presentation according to their wider literary ends. It is only when a third source covers the same material that we have a fairly reliable tool for comparison, and that is only available on

[9] The dependence continues. Arrian's account of the reception of the Celtic embassy (i. 4. 6–8) runs parallel to a passage in Strabo, explicitly based on Ptolemy (Strabo vii. 3. 8 [301 f.] = *FGrH* 138 F 2). Cf. *HCArr.* i. 64; Stadter, *Illinois Classical Studies* 6 (1981) 167–9.
    [10] e.g. iv. 24–5 (*FGrH* 138 F 18); v. 20. 8–24. 3 (F 22, 35).
    [11] e.g. ii. 12. 5; iii. 26. 1–27. 1. For a more controversial case (vii. 26. 3) see below, ch. 7.

one occasion. Diodorus Siculus has a brief survey of India, which is patently based upon Megasthenes and overlaps material in Strabo and in Arrian's *Indike*.[12] The comparison is not as helpful as it might be, for Diodorus' summary is typically perfunctory: the original is drastically abbreviated, stripped of much of its most colourful detail, and certainly distorted by negligence and error in excerpting.[13] As a result little more than the outline of Megasthenes' account survives in Diodorus.

One can see that Arrian has used the same material in approximately the same order in the opening chapters of the *Indike*, except that he uses Eratosthenes as his primary source for the basic geography of India. Otherwise his material overlaps and supplements that of Diodorus, particularly in the account of the seven Indian castes.[14] Strabo is more capricious. He uses more sources than Arrian and draws upon Megasthenes episodically as one among many authorities. Even when he adheres to Megasthenes for an extensive stretch of narrative he still varies the order of the original. That is clear from his account of the caste system. He begins with an account of the first three castes which runs parallel to Arrian and Diodorus.[15] Having mentioned that no private person is permitted to keep a horse or elephant (xv. 1. 41 [704]) he diverges on a lengthy account of Indian techniques of capturing and domesticating elephants, a passage which in Megasthenes' original followed the description of the caste system.[16] Strabo then leaves Megasthenes altogether, drawing on Nearchus for further details about the elephant (xv. 1. 43) and appending a brief account of the rest of the exotic fauna of India. He finally closes his digression, declaring that he will revert to Megasthenes' account at the point where he left it and concludes with the remaining four castes. This is, to put it mildly, a very extra-

[12] Diod. ii. 35–42. The text is printed, with references to parallel accounts, in Jacoby, *FGrH* 715 F 4.

[13] For Diodorus' general methods of working see J. Hornblower, *Hieronymus of Cardia* 18–32, 263–79.

[14] Arr. *Ind.* 11–12 (*FGrH* 715 F 19); cf. Diod. ii. 40–1.

[15] Strabo xv. 1. 39–41 (703–4); cf. Arr. *Ind.* 11 (*FGrH* 715 F 19); Diod. ii. 40.

[16] Strabo xv. 1. 42–3 (704–6); cf. Arr. *Ind.* 13–14, Diod. ii. 42. 1–2. Diodorus, who later reproduces Agatharchides' account of elephant-hunting in Ethiopia (iii. 26–7), omits the details of the chase, but there is no doubt that he preserves the general order in Megasthenes.

ordinary procedure. The logical order of the original is violently and explicitly disrupted with no apparent motive other than sheer desire for narrative variety. This same tendency has been noted elsewhere in Strabo, particularly in his version of Poseidonius' famous description of the Spanish mines. His account can again be compared with that of Diodorus, and it is again demonstrable that he deliberately rearranges the order of the narrative to suit his own literary purposes.[17]

Something of the same trait is evident in Arrian. Like Strabo he explicitly introduces alien material into Megasthenes' account of the caste system, but the passage, describing the brahmin philosophers' predilection for the shade of the banyan tree, is at least relevant to the general context and its source, Nearchus, is named.[18] Similarly he can anticipate. Dionysus' occupation of Nysa and the stories of early invasions by Sesostris and Semiramis are explicitly taken out of their context in Megasthenes and presented in a digression (ἐκβολή ... τοῦ λόγου), which interrupts Megasthenes' catalogue of Indian rivers.[19] Again the digression has some point, to underline the fallibility of Megasthenes, but it is somewhat clumsily inserted. There is a similar dislocation when he describes Nearchus' celebrated encounter with the school of whales. That incident, he says, took place at dawn, when the fleet was sailing from Cyiza (*Ind.* 30. 2). Now the voyage from Cyiza was described in the previous chapter (*Ind.* 29. 1), where Arrian gave a bare outline of the voyage to the extremity of the land of the Ichthyophagi. He clearly separated the more picturesque details of that section of the voyage and worked them up separately so that one episode could cap the next: first the outlandish habits of the Ichthyophagi, then the episode of the whales and finally the mysterious island of Nosala.[20] The curiosities are not dispersed but are combined to convey a stronger aura of wonder.

It is more difficult to compare the techniques of the two

---

[17] Strabo iii. 2. 9 (147) = *FGrH* 87 F 47; Athen. vi. 233B–E (F 48b); Diod. v. 35–8 (F 117). The passages are printed synoptically and discussed by W. Aly, *GGA* 189 (1927) 272–8.

[18] Arr. *Ind.* 11. 7–8 = *FGrH* 133 F 6.

[19] *Ind.* 5. 5–6. 1; cf. Strabo xv. 1. 6–7 (*FGrH* 715 F 11).

[20] Cf. Stadter 127–8, calling attention to divergences in Strabo xv. 2. 11–13 (*FGrH* 133 F 1b and c).

writers in detailed narrative, for we have no direct evidence for
the style of Megasthenes and Aristobulus and there are no verbatim citations of sufficient length to be useful. Some conclusions, however, can be drawn from their parallel versions of the
same text. A particularly good example is Megasthenes' description of Indian techniques of capturing and domesticating
elephants. Both Arrian and Strabo digest the passage at some
length and substantially agree on the facts.[21] Arrian is more
interested in the preparation of the holding enclosure and the
techniques of luring in the wild males, and supplies more information, but Strabo provides an excellent précis, disagreeing
on no single point.[22] When it comes to the breaking of the captured animals, Strabo becomes fuller and gives a clearer, more
comprehensible account of the procedure. When the animals
are subdued by hunger and demoralized by conflict with
domesticated elephants, the most skilled of the mahouts slip
down under the cover of the bellies of their mounts, surrep-
titiously hobble the feet of the wild elephants and order their
own beasts to batter them to the ground. They then secure a
raw-hide noose to each captive elephant, placing the rope in an
incision around its neck and attaching the free end to a tame
elephant. The captives can then be led off, the pain of the hide
rope in the open wound preventing their turning their heads to
dislodge the rider. All this appears clearly and succinctly in
Strabo. Arrian has most of the detail but it is less easy to make
sense of the passage and the key detail that the wild elephants
are harnessed to the tame beasts is only mentioned as a tailpiece
(*Ind.* 13. 13), whereas in Strabo it is properly placed at an
earlier stage.

The comparative lack of clarity is due to the more conscious
literary elaboration of Arrian. His style is artificially Ionic and
includes carefully chosen Herodotean idioms ($\mathring{\alpha}\tau\rho\epsilon\mu\alpha$ $\mathring{\epsilon}\chi\epsilon\iota\nu$ used
both transitively and intransitively: $\gamma\nu\omega\sigma\iota\mu\alpha\chi\epsilon\hat{\iota}\nu$ in the sense of
'concede victory': the variation of $\mathring{\alpha}\tau\acute{\alpha}\sigma\theta\alpha\lambda o\nu$ $\mathring{\epsilon}\rho\gamma\acute{\alpha}\zeta\epsilon\sigma\theta\alpha\iota$ and
$\mathring{\alpha}\tau\alpha\sigma\theta\alpha\lambda\acute{\iota}\eta$).[23] There is even a Homeric echo, again owing

---

[21] *FGrH* 715 F 20 (texts cited above, n. 16).

[22] Arr. *Ind.* 13. 2–8; cf. Strabo xv. 1. 42.

[23] $\mathring{\alpha}\tau\rho\epsilon\mu\alpha$ $\mathring{\epsilon}\chi\epsilon\iota\nu$: *Ind.* 13. 12–13; cf. Hdt. viii. 14. 1 (trans.), 16. 1 (intrans.);
$\gamma\nu\omega\sigma\iota\mu\alpha\chi\epsilon\hat{\iota}\nu$: *Ind.* 13. 13; cf. Hdt. vii. 130. 2; iii. 25. 5; $\mathring{\alpha}\tau\acute{\alpha}\sigma\theta\alpha\lambda o\nu$ $\mathring{\epsilon}\rho\gamma\acute{\alpha}\zeta\epsilon\sigma\theta\alpha\iota/\mathring{\alpha}\tau\alpha\sigma\theta\alpha\lambda\acute{\iota}\eta$:
*Ind.* 13. 12–13; cf. Hdt. iii. 80. 4, ii. 111. 2.

inspiration to Herodotus.[24] These stylistic devices are Arrian's own, paralleled in works other than the *Indike*, and they are superimposed upon the original text. The literary elaboration has been achieved here at some expense of clarity. The same is probably the case at the beginning of the extract (*Ind.* 13. 2). Strabo gives the dimensions of the holding enclosure quite simply as four to five stades in circumference and there is no reason to doubt that he has taken Megasthenes' figures. Arrian, however, gives no exact circumference but describes the open enclosure more picturesquely, 'large enough to accommodate the encampment of a great army'.[25] The imagery is surely his own, imposed upon Megasthenes' more prosaic original. Elsewhere the literary elaboration is more misleading. Arrian (14. 4) describes the elephants' devotion to their mahouts and claims that when their riders are killed they bear them off for burial or bestride their bodies. Strabo makes it clear that the beasts protect their riders when insensible (ἐξαίμους) or rescue them from the field, and his version is supported by Aelian (*NA* iii. 46), who clearly excerpted the same passage of Megasthenes. Arrian has read the passage a little carelessly, perhaps with his experiences of performing elephants (*Ind.* 14. 5–6) at the forefront of his mind, and constructed a pathetic picture of a Homeric *aristeia* with elephants as heroes. Similar carelessness is seen in minor omissions—Arrian slides over the phenomenon of musth in the male elephant, concentrating on the behaviour of the female alone,[26] and in the list of remedies for elephantine ailments he omits the use of melted butter in the treatment of wounds (which is duly included by Strabo and Aelian).[27]

Arrian is not of course unique in his propensity to minor error. There are comparable slips in Strabo. He suggests that the captured elephants are conditioned to obey orders by the soothing music of songs or drums, whereas it is clear from Arrian (supported by Aelian) that the music is designed to raise

[24] *Ind.* 13. 10: μάχη ἵσταται κρατερή: cf. Hom, *Il.* xiii. 333, xviii. 172; Od. xvi. 292. Herodotus uses the expression μάχη ... καρτερὴ γίγνεται (ii. 63. 3; cf. i. 76. 4, iii. 11. 3), which is in turn repeatedly echoed by Arrian (iv. 17. 2, 25. 1, 27. 8; *Parth./Succ.* F 5 [Roos] ).

[25] ὅσον μεγάλῳ στρατοπέδῳ ἐπαυλίσασθαι; cf. Strabo xv. 1. 42: ὅσον τεττάρων ἢ πέντε σταδίων.

[26] *Ind.* 14. 7; cf. Strabo xv. 1. 43.

[27] *Ind.* 14. 9; cf. Strabo xv. 1. 43; Ael. *NA* xiii. 7.

the animals' spirits and encourage them to feed.[28] It may be a preliminary to training but it has nothing directly to do with the actual process of instruction. Similarly, when describing the breaking of the wild animals, he suggests that the fighting with tame elephants took place at the same time as the starving of the captives. Again it is clear from Arrian's fuller text that the fighting only began when the wild animals were demoralized by hunger.[29] In both these instances Strabo is misleading, but the confusion has come in through contraction: Arrian's text is fuller on both occasions and supplies the missing details. By reducing his account to a précis Strabo has omitted meaningful material and garbled the general sense of the passage. His errors tend to be different in kind from those of Arrian, who is more prone to change the shape of the passage for literary or rhetorical ends.

More important than the errors is the general concordance of the two authors. Both narratives cover the same ground, present the same material in the same order, and supplement each other's descriptions. The divergences that we have noted are rare and trivial. This concordance is particularly useful when citations of source are involved. There is an important principle. When adapting material from an author, ancient writers may repeat everything, including citations of sources. Authorities may be quoted at second hand, not by reference to the original text but through a citation in their immediate exemplar. This is a common phenomenon, found in both Arrian and Strabo. Both authors, for instance, transcribe Eratosthenes' comparison of the river-creatures of India with those of Ethiopia and Egypt. They mention that the hippopotamus alone is not found in India and both cite a variant from Onesicritus, alleging the existence of the hippopotamus there.[30] The citation clearly occurred in Eratosthenes and was repeated by both secondary writers. More striking still is the reproduction of Eratosthenes' geographical survey of India. Both Arrian and Strabo repeat, in the same order, the estimates

---

[28] Strabo xv. 1. 42; cf. *Ind.* 14.3; Ael. *NA* xii. 44.

[29] Strabo xv. 1. 42: διαμάχονται . . . ἅμα καὶ λιμῷ καταπονοῦντες; cf. *Ind.* 13. 9.

[30] *Ind.* 6. 8; Strabo xv. 1. 13 (691) = *FGrH* 134 F 7. The chapter of Strabo contains an explicit citation of Eratosthenes. Cf. Berger, *Die geogr. Fragmente des Eratosthenes* 232–4.

of the area of India given by Ctesias, Onesicritus, Nearchus, and Megasthenes and quote them in the same context, as an appendix to Eratosthenes' figures.[31] It could not be more evident that the estimates of the earlier authors were collected and criticized by Eratosthenes and that his list was reproduced without comment by both Arrian and Strabo. Fortunately the problem does not occur frequently in Arrian. The vast majority of citations in his work on Alexander come from authors he claims to use directly, namely Ptolemy, Aristobulus, Nearchus, Megasthenes, and Eratosthenes, and, when he cites a particular name, the citation is usually direct. But these instances of indirect citation which are demonstrable should put us on our guard when we have to deal with quotations from authorities outside Arrian's standard repertoire. However explicit the citation may seem, it need not be taken from the original text.

So far the material examined has not been of great historical significance. It has, however, brought out some of the characteristics of the two authors. Strabo is stylistically sober, with few detectable mannerisms. He gives the gist of his original reasonably accurately but he is inclined to contract his subject-matter so drastically that unclarity can result. He can also take great liberties with the arrangement of the material, varying the order of presentation for no apparent reason. Arrian is far more sophisticated as a stylist, writing in a mannered and artificial prose. He retains the substance of his original but consciously rewrites it, and the stylistic transformation inevitably produces changes in meaning. The concentration on style also causes lapses in factual accuracy—the original may be misread or details capriciously excised. Both authors are reasonably faithful to the substance of the text they follow, but they are both prone to error, as we should expect. These results, obtained from material that is uncontroversial, may be extended to passages of more fundamental importance.

### ARISTOBULUS AND CYRUS' TOMB

Strabo and Arrian both give an account of Cyrus' tomb at

---

[31] *Ind.* 3. 6–8; Strabo xv. 1. 12 (689–90). There is complete agreement of fact and close verbal similarity. Strabo adds Daimachus to the list (*FGrH* 716 F 2), whom Eratosthenes elsewhere listed alongside Megasthenes, Onesicritus, and Nearchus as a source of fiction (Strabo ii. 1. 9. [70] = *FGrH* 721 F 2, Berger 77).

Pasargadae, and both refer explicitly to Aristobulus as their source. Arrian's is by far the fuller excerpt. He twice cites his source by name (vi. 29. 4, 10), and, apart from two brief excursions into *oratio recta*, he presents his material entirely in indirect speech. Strabo is equally explicit, again with two named citations of Aristobulus,[32] but his report is much compressed, only half the length of Arrian's. The two versions have much in common. The description of the tomb itself is exactly parallel. It was set in a garden, surrounded by a dense growth of trees, constructed with a rectangular base of squared stone, which supported a small stone chamber with a roof and an extremely narrow entry passage (according to Arrian a hard squeeze even for a man of moderate size).[33] This is a fairly accurate account of the actual Cyrus' tomb, the so-called 'Tomb of the Mother of Solomon' (see Fig. 1). It is a small, gabled tomb chamber set on a stone plinth built in six receding tiers. The doorway is particularly narrow, 1.39 m high and 78 cm wide, requiring the visitor 'to bend and scuttle awkwardly into the immured chamber'.[34] The only feature which is not brought out in the common description is the step construction of the base, and that may be an omission by Arrian, who emphasizes the other two features of the supporting plinth, its rectangular shape and its finely shaped stone blocks (vi. 29. 5). Strabo's description is far more general—a small tower, solid at the base but with a roof and sepulchre above. Nothing contradicts Arrian's fuller picture, but taken by itself it would be seriously misleading. We should envisage an edifice rising in a straight line from foundation to roof—and Strabo was clearly the inspiration for the erroneous identification of the cube-like Zendan-i Sulaiman (see Fig. 2) as Cyrus' tomb, a square tower solid at the base, its single chamber approached by a monumental staircase (and equipped with a relatively roomy entrance).[35] The true identification of Cyrus' tomb is no longer in question, but the very

[32] Strabo xv. 3. 7 (730) = *FGrH* 139 F 51b.
[33] Arr. vi. 29. 5: ὡς μόλις ἂν ⟨εἶναι⟩ ἐνὶ ἀνδρὶ οὐ μεγάλῳ πολλὰ κακοπαθοῦντι παρελθεῖν. Strabo: στενὴν τελέως ἔχοντα τὴν εἴσοδον.
[34] Full description in D. Stronach, *Pasargadae* (Oxford, 1978) 24–43; cf. *CH Iran* ii. 838–41.
[35] For discussion and bibliography see Stronach, *Pasargadae* 117–37; *CH Iran* ii. 848–52.

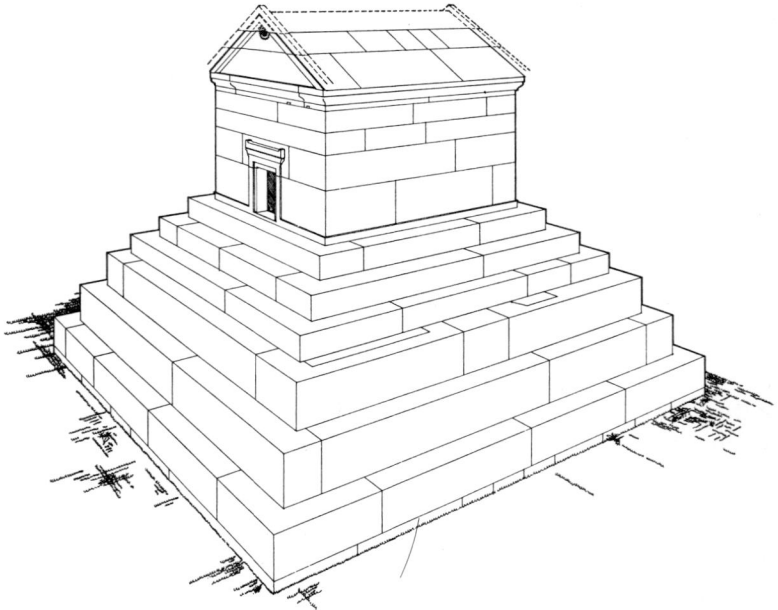

FIG. 1. A reconstruction of the 'Tomb of the Mother of Solomon'
*From D. Stronach,* PASARGADAE *(Oxford University Press, 1978),*
*by kind permission of the publishers*

brevity of Strabo's report has created problems, which the fuller version of Arrian largely resolves.

It is best to continue with Arrian's account. He goes on to describe the interior of the burial chamber as it was before 324. A gold coffin contained the remains of the great king and there was a couch beside it with a coverlet above and a carpet below, laid out with royal garments and precious ornaments. There was also a table. The passage is slightly corrupt thanks to a lacuna,[36] but the details are clear enough. The major items of furniture were the coffin, couch, and table and there was a plethora of minor offerings, clothes, and ornaments. From the interior Arrian moves to the surrounding enclosure with its house for the Magi who had guarded the tomb since the days of Cambyses, son succeeding father, and received daily rations of

---

[36] See below, p. 54.

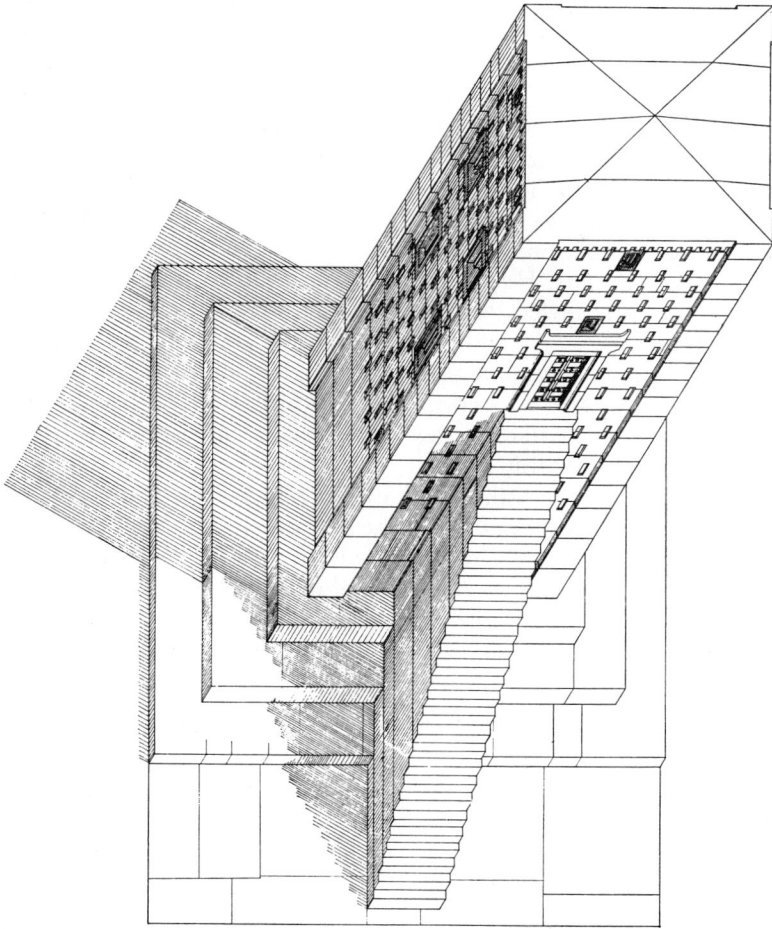

FIG. 2. A reconstruction of the Zendan-i Sulaiman

*From D. Stronach,* PASARGADAE (*Oxford University Press, 1978*),
*by kind permission of the publishers*

meat, corn, and wine and a horse each month for a sacrifice to
Cyrus (vi. 29. 7). He concludes with a rendering of the epitaph,
translating the original Persian into Greek. From description
Arrian turns to narrative. When Alexander reached Pasargadae in the early months of 324 he found the tomb robbed. The

coffin lid was removed, the remains ejected, and the coffin itself was mutilated in an attempt to remove it. Of the furniture and decorations only the coffin and couch remained. Aristobulus claimed that he was deputed to restore the tomb, which he did, replacing the lost offerings as far as possible and sealing the door with stone and clay. The Magi were interrogated under torture but proved ignorant of the whole affair (vi. 29. 9–11).

Strabo has much the same information, but it is rearranged, the details of the tomb robbery interwoven with the description of the monument. He claims that Aristobulus passed through the tomb and viewed its contents when he was first at Pasargadae (winter 331/0), and he briefly reviews them, giving the same details as Arrian: a golden couch, a table (with goblets), a golden coffin, and a good deal of clothing and precious ornaments. He then adds that the tomb was robbed subsequently, the couch and coffin broken, and the rest of the ornaments removed. That the tomb was not entirely stripped proved that it was the act of robbers not of the satrap. All this happened despite the presence of the guard of Magi and was one of the many acts of lawlessness that took place while Alexander was in the east. Strabo ends the extract with the epitaph, which he quotes verbatim, varying only slightly from the text in Arrian.[37]

It is an open question which of the versions comes closer to the original. Arrian's presentation is simpler and more logical,

---

[37] The epitaph raises problems. Plut. *Al.* 69. 4 has the same substance as Aristobulus but inflates the language. Onesicritus (*FGrH* 134 F 34) reported a dual inscription, one in Persian, the other in Greek but engraved in Persian letters, both with the simple message: 'here I lie, Cyrus, king of kings'. The later writer, Aristus of Salamis (*FGrH* 143 F 1), largely agreed with Onesicritus. The variation in content is not surprising. Hellenic speakers in Alexander's entourage would not understand the cuneiform script and would be as dependent on local interpreters as they were for the monument of 'Sardanapalus' at Anchiale (cf. *HCArr.* i. 193–5). There is no doubt that Alexander's men *did* see an inscription on the tomb—and it is worth noting that Onesicritus' rendering of Darius' sepulchral inscription at Naqs-i Rustan does cohere with parts of the extant text (*FGrH* 134 F 35; cf. R. G. Kent, *Old Persian: Grammar, Texts, Lexicon* 138, DNb, 11. 5–11, 40–5). Cyrus' tomb in its present state has no trace of any inscription, Achaemenid or Hellenistic, and it has been argued that the inscription was read not on the tomb but in the adjacent palace (Stronach, *Pasargadae* 26). It is more likely that the inscription has been lost. The doorway of Cyrus' tomb is much mutilated (Stronach 31 f. with plate 28a). There is no trace of the masonry with which Aristobulus sealed the entrance in 324 (Arr. vi. 29. 10), and much else will have disappeared. Perhaps the inscription was obliterated when the building was transformed into a mosque and adorned with Islamic inscriptions (Stronach 37 with n. 32).

but, as we have seen, he is quite capable of imposing his own canons of narrative construction upon his source material, and he may have varied Aristobulus' order of presentation. We can in fact explain the omission of one particular detail by reference to the wider construction of his work. Strabo claims that the survival of the coffin and couch proved that the satrap was not involved in the crime, whereas Arrian merely stresses that all that was movable was removed.[38] The omission may be fortuitous, but there is some reason for thinking that it is deliberate. It is clear from all sources that the supposed desecration of Cyrus' tomb had wide-ranging effects. According to Plutarch (*Al.* 69. 3), a Macedonian from Pella (perhaps the commander of the garrison at Persepolis)[39] was ultimately convicted of the offence, and Curtius makes it clear that accusations were made against the satrap. The context is murky, and we shall have to return to it, but Curtius is categorical that, when allegations were made that the tomb had been plundered, Orxines, the incumbent satrap of Persis, was accused of complicity in the crime (x. 1. 30–6). The attack was followed by further accusations, allegedly orchestrated by the royal favourite Bagoas, and Orxines was executed.[40] Now Arrian is interested in the career and fate of Orxines. He mentions his usurpation of the satrapy while Alexander was in India (vi. 29. 2) and records the accusations made when Alexander returned from Pasargadae to Persepolis (vi. 30. 2). These were the desecration of sanctuaries and royal tombs and the arbitrary execution of subjects,[41] and they correspond to the accusations made by the prosecutors suborned by Bagoas. Arrian dealt with Orxines in two sections, bracketing Aristobulus' account of Cyrus' tomb, and it looks as though he derived the material from Ptolemy.[42] At least the story is presented sequentially with no hint that Orxines was

[38] Strabo xv. 3. 7: δι' οὗ δῆλον γενέσθαι διότι προνομευτῶν ἔργον ἦν, οὐχὶ τοῦ σατράπου; cf. Arr. vi. 29. 9.

[39] For the possibility of a garrison at Persepolis see Berve i. 263.

[40] Curt. x. 1. 35–8. On Bagoas, see Badian *CQ* 8 (1958) 147–50. Recent attempts to discredit Curtius' evidence (e.g. L. C. Gunderson, in *Philip II, Alexander the Great and the Macedonian Heritage* 190–5) are not convincing.

[41] Similar accusations were made against the commanders in Media (Arr. vi. 27. 4; Curt. x. 1. 3) with similar political undertones (cf. Badian, *JHS* 81 [1961] 17–25).

[42] Assumed by Jacoby, *FGrH* ii.D 520, 522; Strasburger, *Studien* 132; Kornemann 88–9.

under threat until the accusations in Persepolis, whereas it is clear that Aristobulus regarded Peucestas as satrap designate of Persis while the army was still in Carmania.[43] Aristobulus seems to have been interested in Orxines, noting that his position was in jeopardy before Alexander entered his satrapy, and took some trouble to underline the frailty of one of the charges made against him. Arrian, however, took the more straightforward account of Ptolemy, in which Orxines was accused of multiple transgressions and summarily executed. The possibility of his involvement in the desecration of Cyrus' tomb anticipated the topic and introduced narrative complications. It was best excised altogether.

Even so, the greater distortion of the original seems to be in Strabo. He throws forward Aristobulus' commission to repair the violated inner chamber and to a slight degree echoes Arrian's wording. But he adds that Aristobulus actually saw the chamber before its desecration and saw it during his first visit to Pasargadae (ἰδεῖν δὲ κλίνην ... κατὰ μὲν οὖν τὴν πρώτην ἐπιδημίαν ταῦτ ἰδεῖν). Now there is nothing in Arrian about an earlier viewing of the tomb.[44] Aristobulus saw the inside of the chamber only when he was instructed to remove the traces of the violation and restore the decoration to its original state. The contents of the tomb are described a few sentences earlier in purely factual terms, but with no suggestion that it is an account based on personal observation. That might be a fortuitous omission, but there is no reason to think so. Arrian stresses the fact that Aristobulus mentioned his commission of restoration,[45] and one would expect him to have laid similar emphasis on the viewing of the unviolated tomb, if Aristobulus made such a claim. On the other hand Strabo could well have made a faulty inference from the wording of the original. Aristobulus stated that his commission was to restore the tomb to its pristine

---

[43] Arr. vi. 28. 3 = *FGrH* 139 F 50.

[44] The various emendations for ὁπότε ἕλοι at vi. 29. 9. (ἔλθοι ⟨ἐς⟩; ἴδοι) are superfluous and do not necessarily produce the iterative sense required to produce an earlier visit to Pasargadae. Cf. Brunt *Arrian* ii. 195 with n. 5. I see the optative as wholly indefinite, indicating a long-established desire on Alexander's part ('for his intention was to visit Cyrus' tomb at such time as he conquered [came to (?), saw (?)] the Persian capital'). Strabo's statement, it must be conceded, is always taken at its face value. Cf. Berve ii. 64, no. 121.

[45] vi. 29. 10 λέγει 'Αριστόβουλος αὐτὸς ταχθῆναι ...

state. Arrian represented this simply: κοσμῆσαι ἐξ ὑπαρχῆς.[46] There is no telling what was Aristobulus' original wording, but there is every possibility that he used some slightly ambiguous phraseology, suggesting the he decorated the tomb *again*, as it was before. That might have suggested that Aristobulus had an earlier commission and entered the tomb twice. Combined with the extremely vivid description of the contents, it could have given a very strong insinuation that Aristobulus had seen the unviolated tomb. Indeed, if we had only Strabo's version, we should be forced to conclude that Aristobulus entered the tomb at Alexander's bidding once only, when he was first at Pasargadae, and merely noted the later violation, whereas Arrian makes it clear that the first, and the only, commission was given in 324, after the violation.

A single visit to the tomb, as reported by Arrian, makes better sense of the rest of the tradition. In Curtius there is no suggestion of an earlier entry.[47] When he reached Pasargadae, in the winter of 325/4, Alexander had the tomb opened, so that he could pay his respects to the dead conqueror. Apart from a few crumbling artefacts there was nothing but the coffin in the tomb, and the expectations of legendary wealth were disappointed. That gave rise to allegations of tomb robbery. Now if the tomb had been visited six years before and an inventory made of its contents, there would have been no scope for allegations. The robbery would have been palpable and blatant. Is Curtius' story pure fabrication, as some have argued,[48] or is the first visit of Aristobulus a product of misreading by Strabo? Various factors tell in favour of the latter. In particular the enumeration of contents seems surprisingly lavish for the actual tomb. The inner chamber measures no more than 3.17 m by 2.11,[49] and in that narrow space was arranged, sardine-like, a sarcophagus, a couch, and an ornamental table, not to mention

---

[46] For the phraseology compare *Tact.* 44. 2.

[47] *Pace* Jacoby, *FGrH* ii.D 522 (followed by Gunderson 192), the order to open Cyrus' tomb (Curt. x. 1. 30) was patently given in 324. at the time of the discovery of the 'robbery'. Apart from Strabo only the Alexander Romance (Ps.-Call. ii. 18. 1) suggests that Cyrus' tomb was visited in 330, and even there it is not stated that Alexander forced an entry.

[48] e.g. Tarn ii. 321; Gunderson 190–5; Hammond, *Three Historians* 157. *Contra* Badian, *CQ* 8 (1958) 147–50. See also Berve ii. no. 195, who characterizes Curtius' narrative as 'rhetorisch stark entstellt'.

[49] These and other dimensions in Stronach, *Pasargadae* 27.

the plethora of clothing and ornaments. As early as 1884 Marcel Dieulafoy drew attention to the inconsistency and argued erroneously that the tomb of Cyrus should be located elsewhere.[50] The identification is no longer in doubt, but the veracity of Aristobulus automatically comes into question. Attempts to salvage the credit of his account have rested heavily on a single corrupt sentence of Arrian which suggests that the sarcophagus lay 'in the middle of the couch'.[51] Elsewhere the text is categorical that the couch and sarcophagus were placed side by side (καὶ κλίνην παρὰ τῇ πυέλῳ) and Strabo also suggests that they were not superimposed but stood separately. In that case the artefacts in the tomb would have been so compressed that there was no room for an observer to enter. It seems much more likely that Aristobulus' description rests upon the contemporary expectations of what was inside the tomb and reflects wishful thinking rather than personal autopsy.

We may perhaps go further and question whether the tomb had in fact been robbed. If there was robbery, it was not recent robbery. The Magi who guarded the tomb were found wholly innocent of any complicity, despite the most stringent investigation; and, despite the allegations against him, the satrap Orxines was cleared of the charges of desecration[52] (though other accusations of misgovernment were upheld). It is possible that the robbery took place generations before, so that no contemporary could be reasonably incriminated. But Curtius' account suggests that the robbery was not immediately obvious.[53] Perhaps the original grave furnishings had degenerated with age. If the coffin was not made of solid gold, the fittings could have rotted over the centuries, leading to a disintegration in which the corpse was dislodged. Once the allegations of robbery were made, the ravages of time could be

---

[50] M. A. Dieulafoy, *L'Art antique de la Perse* i (Paris, 1884) 25.

[51] vi. 29. 6: ἐν μέσῳ δὲ τῆς κλίνης ἡ πύελος ἔκειτο. Apart from the contradiction with the earlier description, the picture of a coffin 'in the middle of' a funerary couch is absurd. Polak's emendation ἐν μέσῳ δὲ ⟨τῆς τραπέζης καὶ⟩ τῆς κλίνης is accepted by Brunt, provides the sense required, and conforms with Arrian's usage (for the double genitive compare iii. 28. 8, v. 5. 5, 12. 1, 24. 1, *Tact.* 6. 6).

[52] See above, p. 51.

[53] Cf. Curt. x. 1. 32–3: Alexander has no suspicions of foul play before it is insinuated by Bagoas.

reinterpreted as the work of pillagers. The modest decayed relics of the tomb were seen as the sole survivors of the original furnishings, left behind because they were too bulky to remove. When Aristobulus received his task of restoration the robbery was an established fact, a crime under investigation, and he had no motive to question the official story. He described the rumours of the content of the tomb as fact and represented the state of the burial chamber as it was discovered in 324 as the result of grave robbery. He restored the furnishings to what was considered the original state and saw no reason to undermine the official story that the tomb had been violated during the wave of lawlessness that had prevailed while Alexander was in India. But he was honest enough to add that the first suspects were proved innocent and that the affair remained a mystery.

The fuller version of Aristobulus, that of Arrian, is by far the clearer and more credible. He may have trimmed away the allegations against the satrap, but otherwise he seems to have preserved the general narrative order of his original. Strabo by contrast is drastically abbreviated and he has thrown forward the account of the alleged robbery. It is easy to see why he does so. He is comparing Aristobulus' description of the tomb with those of Onesicritus and Aristus, both of which concentrated on the external aspect of the monument, the architecture and the funerary inscription. Accordingly he ends his extract with Aristobulus' citation of the inscription, which permitted an immediate comparison with Onesicritus. The details of the violation were unique to Aristobulus and Strabo presents them parenthetically as a historical note. The dislocation of the narrative order caused a severe distortion of sense: Strabo on his own account threw back the autopsy to the first stay at Pasargadae and inferred that Aristobulus saw the inner chamber in its pristine state. Arrian on the other hand was reporting the episode as a whole, an incident of intrinsic interest from his secondary source, and there was no reason to vary the narrative order. His fuller version can and should be used as a corrective to Strabo.

## THE PALLACOTTA CANAL

A more elaborate adaption of Aristobulus is to be found in the latter part of Book vii (19. 3–21. 7).[54] This passage begins with an explicit citation (19. 3), describing the arrival of ships from the Levantine coast to join Alexander's fleet on the Euphrates. Arrian moves to the object of the preparations, the expedition to Arabia. The new chapter begins with a vague reference to authority (λόγος κατέχει—20. 1), but presently (20. 5) there is another explicit citation of Aristobulus for the origins of the name of the island Icarus (Falaika). He now proceeds to the voyages of reconnaissance which Alexander commissioned in the Persian Gulf (20. 7–9), recapitulates a fragment of Nearchus describing the Straits of Hormuz (20. 8–10), and moves to the voyages of exploration on the Euphrates. The next reference to Aristobulus comes some time later, at vii. 22. 5, where he is cited as a variant, not the principal authority.

If there were no control source, it would be impossible to trace most of this material to any specific author. Fortunately there is a parallel report in Strabo (xvi. 1. 9–11) which establishes that Aristobulus is the direct source for everything except the reference to Nearchus. Not only does he repeat the details about the Euphrates fleet, but he adds that it was a preparation for the Arabian campaign, noting that Alexander was insatiable of conquest (a comment which Arrian repeats as his own).[55] He also mentions Alexander's desire to be honoured as the third god of the Arabs, a theme which Arrian (20. 1) presents as an unidentified λόγος. In Strabo the material is clearly attributed to Aristobulus, and it comes in a different context, explaining Alexander's engineering work on the Euphrates. Indeed Strabo's presentation is in general different from that in Arrian. He starts with Alexander's demolition of the weirs on the Tigris. Arrian also records the transaction, but in its correct chronological place, at Opis in summer 324, whereas Strabo associates it with the work on the Euphrates.[56] He goes on (xvi. 1. 9–10) to a general discussion of the Euphrates in flood and at low water. Then, with an explicit

---

[54] Printed as a single extract by Jacoby, *FGrH* 139 F 55. Cf. Pearson, *LHA* 183–5. The passage is summarized by Appian, *BC* ii. 153. 644, who is using Arrian rather than Aristobulus (see below, n. 65).

[55] τὸ δ' ἀληθὲς ὀρεγόμενον πάντων εἶναι κύριον: Strabo xvi. 1. 11 (741); cf. Arr. vii. 19. 6 (ὥς γέ μοι δοκεῖ).

[56] Arr. vii. 7. 6–7; cf. Strabo xvi. 1. 9 (740).

reference to Aristobulus,[57] he describes Alexander's work to clear the canal-system and enlarges on the new mouth created for the main Pallacotta canal. After that comes the motive for the work, the Arabian expedition. Arrian's narrative is differently arranged. The engineering operations are detached from the preparations against the Arabs and they are limited to the Pallacotta canal.[58] They are a diversion while the fleet is being prepared, and there is no suggestion of any military connection.

Despite the differences, both authors worked from the same source material. Strabo's general description of the Euphrates coheres with Arrian's specific description of the operations on the Pallacotta. Both mention the spring floods at the time of the melting of the Armenian snows.[59] The fields would be inundated were it not for a series of cuts which diverted the surplus water.[60] Strabo goes on to describe the need for constant maintenance. Otherwise the canals would silt up. The overflow created vast marshes and reed beds near the sea. The alluvial soil and its easy subsidence explain the relative ease of clearing the canal mouths and the enormous difficulty of damming them after the flood season. Most of this is in Arrian, but the details occur as a digression on the difficulties of clearing the Pallacotta and Arrian implies that the conditions were peculiar to it (21. 4–5). In particular he suggests that it is the Pallacotta alone which would divert the waters of the Euphrates if it were not dammed at low season, whereas Strabo is explicit that the problem was common to the entire canal network. Both authors, however, agree about the new cut made thirty stades from the old mouth of the Pallacotta, where the subsoil was strong enough to support a stable channel (Strabo xvi. 1. 11; Arr. 21. 6). There is a large amount of agreement on the facts but their arrangement is totally different. Strabo gives a general account of the problems of the Babylonian irrigation system and relates them to Alexander's planning against the

---

[57] xvi. 1. 11 (741) = *FGrH* 139 F 56.

[58] The only motive given is to aid the local agriculture (vii. 21. 6).

[59] Arr. vii. 21. 2–3; Strabo xvi. 1. 9 (740).

[60] τὸ ἐκπῖπτον τοῦ ῥοῦ καὶ ἐπιπολάζον ὕδωρ: Strabo. Cf. Arr. 21. 3: ὅτι δὲ ἐπιπολῆς ἐστιν αὐτῷ καὶ ὑψηλὸς ὁ ῥοῦς. The adverb ἐπιπολῆς is unique in Arrian and was clearly suggested by the common source.

Arabs, whereas Arrian deals with the Pallacotta as a phenomenon in its own right, unrelated to any wider plans.

Arrian is probably correct in his context for the construction of the new fleet. He states that Alexander found his main fleet (Nearchus' contingent) newly arrived in Babylon after voyaging from the Persian Gulf and notes that additional warships had been transported from the Phoenician coast.[61] Aristobulus is named as the source, and there can be little doubt that he reported the naval build-up in Babylon at its appropriate point in the campaign narrative. In Strabo's version the information comes retrospectively, to explain Alexander's invasion plans.[62] It is transferred from its chronological setting and adduced as background to the canal-clearing project. That is a dislocation of the narrative order, of a type with Strabo's procedure elsewhere. He has taken liberties in the arrangement of the subject-matter, but he has not seriously misrepresented it. Indeed he brings out one important theme. Aristobulus clearly related the canal work to the forthcoming Arabian expedition, emphasizing Alexander's military need to make the estuarine marshes accessible. There is no trace of this motif in Arrian,[63] nor of the pertinent detail that navigation was only possible if the canal system operated efficiently. Aristobulus stressed the military aspect of Alexander's work and Arrian omitted it.

There is also little doubt that the work on the Pallacotta was only part of Alexander's activity on the Euphrates. Strabo cites Aristobulus by name for the detail that Alexander steered his own ship and inspected the canals, damming some and clearing others.[64] It is a precise piece of information, and there is no reason for Strabo to have it garbled. Aristobulus dealt with a series of operations and, when he described the changing water-level of the Euphrates, he probably did so in a general passage of description relating to the entire canal system refur-

---

[61] For the historical context of these preparations see below, ch. 8.

[62] xvi. 1. 11 (741).

[63] The marshes are mentioned (vii. 21. 7, 22. 2), but the military context is excluded. Arrian places the mouth of the Pallacotta 800 stades south of Babylon (vii. 21. 1), which seems to dispose of Meissner's location north of the capital. Cf. B. Meissner, *Mitt. der Vorderasiatischen Gesellschaft* 1 (1896) 177–89, esp. 183; R. D. Barnett, *JHS* 83 (1963) 12.

[64] xvi. 1. 11 (741). Arrian includes the detail that the king steered his own ship, but presents it as a λόγος at a later stage (vii. 22. 2).

bished by Alexander. In that case Strabo comes closer to the original. The hypothesis is corroborated by a point of detail. When Strabo talks in general terms of the difficulty of damming he merely says that the work requires a multitude of hands (πολυχειρίας δεῖται). Arrian is more specific: the satrap of Babylonia ensures the damming of the Pallacotta with a work-force over ten thousand strong, and the exercise keeps them occupied for more than two months (21. 5). However large and important the Pallacotta, I do not think that it can have monopolized the efforts of such a colossal corvée. Aristobulus described the entire work-force attached to the Euphrates irrigation system and Arrian used the information in the specific context of the Pallacotta, the only canal he chose to describe.[65] Instead of following Aristobulus' general discourse on the Euphrates, he selected the most important of Alexander's operations, the creation of the new mouth, and reorganized the material to supply a commentary on it. The episode becomes more self-contained, narrated as a curiosity in itself. There is no thematic connection with the surrounding narrative. Alexander behaves as though the damming of the Pallacotta were an end in itself, and there is no suggestion that he was improving the navigability of the river for his war fleet.

The explanation, I think, is that Arrian wished to include all the material on the Arabian plans in a single digression. Accordingly he records the arrival of naval units from the Levantine coast, explains that Alexander was meditating an expedition against the Arabs, and expounds the reasons: the desire to be worshipped in Arabia and the proverbial abundance of the country, with its ample scope for city foundations (20. 2). The general description leads to the particular instance

---

[65] This virtually guarantees that the derivative version of Appian (*BC* ii. 153. 644) is taken from Arrian and not from Aristobulus. Appian also associates the flood control methods with the Pallacotta alone and garbles the sense, turning the possibility of the canal diverting the waters of the Euphrates (properly expressed by Arrian as an indefinite future condition) into an established fact (cf. *CQ* 22 [1972] 177, *contra* Wirth, *Studien* 22–5). Appian's adaptation of Arrian is not unlike Arrian's of Aristobulus. He uses the narrative to enlarge on the portents of Alexander's death and selectively extracts (and adapts) the material that is most germane to his purpose (639–40 = Arr. vii. 18. 2–4; 642–3 = Arr. vi. 16. 5–7, 17. 6; 644 = vii. 21. 1–5, 22. 1). By contrast a source other than Arrian was used for the wound at the Malli town (637), for Arrian has nothing about the adverse omen before the engagement, which is what most interests Appian.

of the islands of Icarus (Falaika) and Tylus (Bahrain), and
then to the voyages of discovery which provided the crucial information. So far he used material from Aristobulus. When describing the reconnaissance of the Straits of Hormuz by Hieron
of Soli, he reverts to Nearchus and paraphrases the report of the
sighting of Cape Maceta which he also used in the *Indike*.[66]
Hieron's reconnaissance of the Arabian desert vindicated Nearchus's determination to keep to the coast of Carmania. Here
Arrian's sources dovetailed and formed a satisfactory conclusion to the discussion of Arabia. His material was carefully
arranged to move from point to point and climax with the
altercation between Nearchus and Onesicritus. In all probability he combined reports which Aristobulus had scattered
over his campaign narrative (the commissions of Archias,
Androsthenes, and Hieron were hardly, as in Arrian, covered
in a single retrospective notice) and dealt with the Arabian
plans in a single excursus. There was no need to refer to them
subsequently, and the operations on the Euphrates could be
separated and described as a self-contained episode. We have
noted a similar phenomenon in Arrian's refusal to anticipate
the fate of Orxines, but here the compartmentalization of the
narrative is more drastic.

This analysis indicates that Arrian could operate on his
sources with considerable freedom, more so than is apparent in
the simpler narrative of the *Indike*. He selected material at will
and combined it to present an artistically satisfying whole. As
far as the actual sense goes, he does not seem to have altered the
data of his sources, but the original order and emphasis are
altered. The *tesserae* of the mosaic may be the same, but they are
worked into a different pattern. Given Arrian's avowed literary
pretensions, that is exactly what we should expect. He may be
dependent on his sources for material, but he rises above them
and creates a literary work that is wholly his own. Even when
we are confident of the ascription of the material, as in the
Pallacotta chapter, we have no guarantee that he preserved the
narrative sequence or the historical judgement of his exemplar.
The presentation is his own and it must be treated as such.

---

[66] vii. 20. 9–10; *Ind.* 32. 6–13 (cf. 43. 9). The substance of the two passages overlaps
exactly, but Arrian takes care to vary his terminology. For the comparison see Stadter
129–30.

# 4

# THE SECONDARY TRADITION

PTOLEMY and Aristobulus demonstrably provided Arrian with the bulk of his historical material. The rest of the rich and multifarious tradition he used selectively and he considered this material of secondary importance. In the preface he declares that where he has drawn upon authors other than his principal sources he has qualified what he writes as hearsay only (ὡς λεγόμενα μόνον). He adds that he has selected only such material as was memorable in itself (ἀξιαφήγητα) and has some measure of credibility.[1] The language and the thought, as so often, are Herodotean.[2] The historian conventionally expressed the obligation to provide his readers with all reports, even when their credentials were not impeccable, and Herodotus in a famous passage claims that it is his duty to report the traditions he received whether or not he believed them.[3] Arrian comes close to this position when (for the sake of completeness) he reports the rumours that Alexander was poisoned (ὡς μὴ ἀγνοεῖν δόξαιμι). He disbelieves the reports but feels that they are too widely attested to be simply omitted.[4] In the same way he repeats the tradition of the Bacchic revels in Carmania but appends a Herodotean disclaimer expressing his scepticism.[5] The criterion of narrative importance clearly outweighs that of credibility. Arrian uses his secondary material as a counterpoint. It enlarges upon or contrasts with the material

---

[1] Pr. 3: ἔστι δὲ ἃ καὶ πρὸς ἄλλων ξυγγεγραμμένα, ὅτι καὶ αὐτὰ ἀξιαφήγητά τέ μοι ἔδοξε καὶ οὐ πάντῃ ἄπιστα, ὡς λεγόμενα μόνον ὑπὲρ ᾿Αλεξάνδρου ἀνέγραψα. Cf. ii. 12. 8. See further HCArr. i. 20.

[2] For the use of ἀξιαφήγητος, unique to Ionic prose before it was taken up by writers of the Empire, see Hdt. i. 16. 2, 177. 1, v. 57. 2. (cf. Jos. AJ. xv. 412; App. BC iv. 16; Dio Cass. xlviii. 50. 4). Compare also Hdt. vii. 209. 5: ἄπιστα ἐφαίνετο τὰ λεγόμενα (cf. iii. 80. i).

[3] Hdt. vii. 152. 3. Cf. iii. 9. 2; v. 45. 2 with Jacoby, RE suppl. ii. 472 ff; Pearson, TAPA 92 (1941) 335–8; H. Erbse, Antike und Abendland 10 (1961) 19–34, esp. 24–5.

[4] Arr. vii. 27. 3.

[5] Arr. vi. 28. 1. See below, pp. 67 ff.

from his primary sources and provides a vehicle for literary comment.

Arrian's statement of method is clear enough, but it is frustratingly difficult to evaluate his practice. The subsidiary tradition is not often labelled as such, and Arrian does not confine his statements of qualification to material outside his major narrative sources. That is a principle of cardinal importance, and it is often overlooked—with fatal results.[6] Arrian has a wide range of expressions to denote scepticism or to avoid commitment. He may refer to the author by name, but more often he reports a tradition anonymously ('some have recorded', 'a story is told'). That may apply to material from Ptolemy and Aristobulus as well as the secondary tradition. Arrian states that it is only when his main authorities agree that he records the consensus as absolute truth. In other cases he selects what he regards as the more credible and memorable version. This is exactly the criterion he uses for his selection of material from subsidiary sources, and in both cases he clearly felt qualms about the historicity of some of the episodes recounted.

A good instance is the famous story of the sailor who retrieved the royal diadem from the Euphrates, to be rewarded for his service but punished for his presumption.[7] Arrian introduces it explicitly as a hearsay report ($\lambda \acute{o} \gamma o s$ δὲ $\lambda \acute{e} \gamma \epsilon \tau a \iota$ $\tau o \iota \acute{o} \sigma \delta \epsilon$), and he continues in *oratio obliqua*. But when he comes to the fate of the sailor, he reports a variant: Aristobulus' statement that the man was beaten is contrasted with the majority tradition that he was decapitated (vii. 27. 4). Arrian then appends another variant, that the person involved was the future king Seleucus. That manifestly comes from the subsidiary tradition and is a relatively late accretion, designed to supply a presage of Seleucus' subsequent majesty.[8] It differs both from Aristobulus and from the majority tradition, which insisted that the

---

[6] See, for instance, Tarn, *Alexander* ii. 45: 'Arrian (v. 1–2. 7) tells the story of Nysa at length as a λόγος—that is, Ptolemy did not give it.' The underlying assumption is that, when a statement is qualified, it is not taken from Arrian's primary source. The fallacy was clearly exposed by Schwartz (*RE* ii. 1241 ff.; see further Kornemann 21–30), but it still occurs with surprising frequency.

[7] Arr. vii. 22. 2–5 = *FGrH* 139 F55. The story is reported by Diodorus (xvii. 116. 6) in a slightly different context and (apparently) with a different outcome.

[8] vii. 22. 5. The passage was used and adapted by Appian (*Syr.* 56. 288–91: see above ch. 3, n. 65).

man who rescued the diadem was executed for his pains, and is added purely for interest's sake.[9] The authors who comprised the majority tradition are not named, but it is fair to assume that they included Arrian's primary sources, probably Nearchus and possibly Ptolemy.[10] The divergences in the reports of the story led Arrian to interpose a note of caution and to qualify the story as something less than undoubted truth.[11] There was probably a literary model. As Arrian surely knew, Herodotus recorded a very similar story about Xerxes, who purportedly rewarded and decapitated his own helmsman on his return from Greece (Hdt. viii. 118. 4). Herodotus is contemptuous of' the story, which he stigmatizes as incredible, and he twice refers to it as a current *logos*,[12] reporting it in *oratio obliqua*. Arrian was no doubt influenced by the precedent and gave his narrative a distinctively Herodotean flavour, casting doubt on the authenticity of an episode which was somewhat distasteful but multiply recorded.[13] In this case, then, the bulk of the material comes from Arrian's primary sources: the subsidiary tradition is used for the picturesque variant concerning Seleucus.

These considerations complicate any assessment of Arrian's use of sources. One simply cannot apply mechanical criteria, and in many cases a clear identification is impossible. The central portion of Book iv is a particularly nasty minefield, for there Arrian is dealing with episodes inimical to his general picture of Alexander. These are the stock *exempla* of the king's immoderation, his murder of Cleitus and the abortive introduction of *proskynesis*. They are episodes which Arrian cannot

[9] It allows Arrian to give a rhetorical appreciation of Seleucus, phrased in superlatives which echo his final encomium on Alexander (see below, ch. 6). Compare particularly the language of vii. 30. 1.

[10] Cf. Schwartz, *RE* ii. 1241 (*contra* Hammond, *Three Historians* 76: 'a λόγος, i.e. not verified by Ptolemy and Aristobulus'). The prelude to the rescue of the crown contains some elements of Aristobulus, corroborated by Strabo (xvi. 1. 11 [741]: see above, pp. 56 ff.): Alexander steers his own ship and visits the royal tombs of the marshes. Arrian may have combined his sources into a composite narrative before listing the variants separately.

[11] Compare the story of Alexander's desire to be worshipped as a third god of the Arabs (vii. 20. 1). Arrian presents this explicitly as a *logos*, but Strabo (xvi. 1. 11) again makes it clear that Aristobulus is the direct source.

[12] viii. 118. 1: ἔστι δὲ καὶ ἄλλος ὅδε λόγος λεγόμενος; 119. 1.

[13] Compare the use of λέγεται at i. 1. 1, where Arrian adopts a common introductory formula, perhaps inherited from Xenophon (*Cyrop.* i. 2. 1; cf. Dion, Hal. *AR* i. 9. 1). The narrative that follows is certainly based on his primary sources.

avoid, but he chooses to deal with them out of context, in a long
timeless digression. Not surprisingly, he is sensitive about the
subject-matter, which (he cannot deny) reflects adversely upon
his hero (iv. 9. 1, 12. 6), and he uses language that creates a certain detachment. He reports what is said, rather than narrating
fact on his own authority. Indirect speech tends to predomi-
nate, and there are consistent references to anonymous
reporters.[14] It is clear, however, that Arrian is still using his
principal sources. Aristobulus is cited by name for a variant tradition of the death of Cleitus, characteristically imputing full
responsibility to the murdered man.[15] Later he again appears
as the named source for the miraculous intervention of the
Syrian prophetess, and both he and Ptolemy are cited as
sources for the fate of Callisthenes and his involvement in the
Pages' Conspiracy.[16] In the case of Callisthenes' complicity
their consensus is contrasted with the prevailing agreement
that he was not directly incriminated in the conspiracy. Arrian,
then, used his full range of sources,[17] and we cannot infer from
the absence of citation that Ptolemy was not used throughout.[18]
No episode in the digression is said to have been omitted
from any source, and the material was controversial enough for
arguments from silence to be of some validity. The qualifications and the manifest reserve of Arrian's exposition are best
explained by the uncomfortable nature of the themes discussed.
He used a wide spectrum of sources and they can only be identified with any confidence when he himself labels them by
name. A similar technique is used in his commentary on the
various reports of Alexander's grief after the death of Hephaestion (vii. 14. 2–10). Arrian notes the separate traditions of

[14] iv. 8. 2 (λέγουσι); 9. 2–3, 7, 9 (λόγος κατέχει); 10. 3, 5; 12. 3.

[15] iv. 8. 9 = FGrH 139 F 29.

[16] iv. 13. 5 = FGrH 139 F 30; iv. 14. 1, 3 (FGrH 138 F 16–17, 139 F 31, 33).

[17] iv. 14. 4 comments on the diversity of the tradition and hints that Arrian had read
more than he chose to use. One version of the *proskynesis* affair is based, directly or indirectly, upon Chares of Mytilene (iv. 12. 4–5 = FGrH 125 F 146; see below, p. 113), a
source which cannot be traced elsewhere in Arrian. The range of material deployed in
these chapters is evidently wide.

[18] It is common doctrine that Ptolemy was used only from the beginning of iv. 13
(Schwartz, RE ii. 1240; Jacoby, FGrH ii.D 517; Strasburger, Studien i. 126) but the
grounds are curiously subjective ('Spuren seines Stils finden sich nicht'—Strasburger).
Kornemann 139 ff. was equally subjective to argue that a writer of Ptolemy's high
moral calibre could not have omitted Cleitus' murder, but he was on the right track.
Arrian *should* have drawn attention to silence on Ptolemy's part.

excess, commenting on their intrinsic plausibility and contrasts them with what was generally agreed.[19] Once again he drew upon the full range of sources, isolating what was singly reported and indicating the common ground.

There are relatively few instances where the secondary tradition can be reliably identified. That is usually only possible where Arrian indicates that an episode is omitted by Ptolemy and Aristobulus or otherwise reported in their work. An unambiguous case is the story of the hundred female warriors, alleged to be Amazons, who were introduced to the king in Media by the satrap Atropates. Arrian notes that the episode was not to be found in Ptolemy or Aristobulus or, for that matter, in any source which one would consider a reliable authority.[20] Having expressed his reservations, in language which deliberately echoes Thucydides,[21] Arrian embarks on a Thucydidean digression, applying arguments of probability to the question of the survival of the Amazons. They were, he considers, extinct by the time of Alexander, for otherwise they must have occurred in Xenophon's description of Trapezus and its surroundings. On the other hand it is implausible that they never existed. The mythological tradition was too rich, attested in numerous passages of Herodotus and in the *epitaphia* of the Attic orators and visually resplendent in Micon's great painting in the *Stoa Poikile*. The Amazons, then, had existed but had disappeared by Alexander's day, and, if Atropates did parade female warriors, they were local tribeswomen masquerading in Amazon dress.

This subject-matter was probably selected to provide a peg for the digression, which was hardly Arrian's own conception. There was a general debate about the historicity of the Amazons, most trenchantly expressed by Strabo, who ridiculed the whole concept of a community exclusively composed of females. Amazons were an absurdity even in myth, let alone in the clear light of history.[22] A reflection of this scepticism is found in the *Panathenaicus* of Aelius Aristeides, who referred to

---

[19] vii. 14. 2 πάντες τοῦτο ἀνέγραψαν: vii. 14. 8 ἐκεῖνα δὲ πρὸς πάντων ξυμφωνούμενα.
[20] Arr. vii. 13. 2–3.
[21] ἱκανὸς ... τεκμηριῶσαι (vii. 13. 3) echoes Thuc. i. 9. 4. Compare Dion, Hal. *AR*. i. 89. 4: ἀποχρῶσι ... τεκμηριῶσαι.
[22] Strabo xi. 5. 3 (504–5).

the Amazon invasion of Attica as fact but claimed that the victory destroyed the Amazonian empire, to such a degree that it is now dubious whether they ever existed.[23] The scepticism about the Amazons is acknowledged but used as a rhetorical paradox—if the Amazons' existence can be queried it is proof of the completeness of the legendary victory of Theseus. A less sophisticated reaction to the rationalist criticism can be traced in Diodorus,[24] who believes in a decline. After the death of Penthesileia in the Trojan War the Amazons dwindled to the point of utter debilitation; as a result the ancient tales have been considered fiction in modern times. Both Diodorus and Aristeides share a common ground with Arrian. They uphold the veracity of the Amazonian legend while admitting the non-existence of Amazons in any period of recent history. Arrian's argument is detailed but superficial. His negative arguments goes no further than the omissions in Xenophon and the review of myth is frankly perfunctory.

What is prima facie surprising is that there is no attempt to connect the discussion of Atropates' female warriors with the rest of the tradition of interaction between Alexander and purported Amazons. In particular there is no reference to the campaign of 328 in Sogdiana, when Alexander and his men thought themselves relatively close to the Black Sea and had expectations of meeting Amazons. Arrian himself notes that the Chorasmian king, Pharasmanes, claimed to be a neighbour of the Amazons.[25] and the conversation was clearly reported by one of his principal sources. In addition, one of the stock themes of the vulgate tradition was the visit of the Amazon queen, Thalestris, to Alexander's headquarters in Hyrcania.[26] Arrian

---

[23] Aristid. 1. 83–4. The sentiment is taken directly from the Attic orators (to whom Arrian makes a passing reference at vii.13.6). Lysias (2 [*Epitaph*.]. 4–6) claimed that the Athenian victory destroyed the Amazons, eradicating them even from their homeland, and the passage was copied by Isocrates (4 [*Paneg*.]. 68–70) and Demosthenes (60 [*Epitaph*.]. 8).

[24] Diod. ii. 46. 6 (the source is uncertain). At iv. 28. 4 he repeats the version of the Attic orators, that Theseus' victory resulted in a migration of Amazons from the Thermodon region.

[25] Arr. iv. 15. 4 The source is usually said to be Aristobulus (cf. Strasburger, *Studien* i. 127, following Schwartz and Jacoby), but there is no reason for excluding Ptolemy.

[26] Diod. xvii. 77. 1–3; Curt. vi. 5. 24–32; Justin xii. 3. 5. See the famous list of authorities cited by Plutarch (*Al.* 46. 1–2; cf. Strabo xi. 5. 4 [505] ). For discussion see Hamilton, *Plut. Al.* 123–7 (with bibliography).

makes no attempt to challenge the historicity of Thalestris' visit, even though it was a literary *topos*, the divergence of the sources noted by both Plutarch and Strabo.[27] More seriously Pharasmanes' statement about the Amazons is left without comment. It comes from a primary source, and Arrian seems unwilling to undermine its credibility or speculate what might have been at the basis of the Chorasmian monarch's claim.[28] Instead he extracts an isolated anecdote from the subsidiary tradition and uses it as the peg for a conventional digression on the Amazons. The treatment of the subject is conventional and illustrated from standard models of literature—Xenophon, Herodotus, and the Attic orators. This is almost standard procedure for Arrian. When he digresses on the fate of Thebes and argues that it was unprecedented in its rapidity and totality, the parallels he draws are taken exclusively from Thucydides and Xenophon.[29] The more recent and pertinent example of the destruction of Olynthus is altogether overlooked. Arrian's comment is conventional and taken from conventional sources outside the Alexander tradition. When he comments directly on the history of Alexander, he either restricts himself to single points of detail or repeats material already in his sources, such as Eratosthenes' critique of mythological invention.

Another item from the subsidiary tradition, closely related in its presentation, is the description of the Bacchic revels in Carmania, late in 325. Arrian states that he does not find the episode credible, because it is not mentioned by Ptolemy, Aristobulus, or any other reliable source.[30] The details of the revel largely cohere with those in Plutarch and the vulgate tradition.[31] Arrian, however, goes further and suggests that the revel was an imitation of the legendary celebrations of Dionysus on his return from India. Indeed Arrian claims that the very origin of the triumph may be traced back to Dionysus and

[27] Plut. *Al.* 46. 1–2; Strabo xi. 5. 4 (505).

[28] Nor does he relate his two references to Amazons. He merely states that Atropates' female warriors did not appear in Ptolemy or Aristobulus, and omits any mention of the earlier episode.

[29] Arr. i. 9. 1–5. The inspiration for the digression is Thucydides, and the vocabulary is demonstrably borrowed from him (see further *HCArr.* i. 84–8).

[30] Arr. vi. 28. 2. The language deliberately mirrors that in vii. 13. 3 (see above, n. 21).

[31] Plut. *Al.* 67. 1–6; Diod. xvii. 106. 1; Curt. ix. 10. 24–8. For discussion of the source tradition see, most recently, P. Goukowsky, *Essai sur les origines du mythe d'Alexandre* ii (Nancy, 1981) 47 ff.

his cult epithet Θρίαμβος.[32] This material is demonstrably late. The origins of the Roman triumph are shrouded in mystery, and there was considerable speculation in antiquity. Varro had notoriously associated the victory cry 'Io triumphe' with the cult title of Dionysus, and there is general agreement in modern times that there was some connection, but at best an indirect connection, the term reaching Rome through the medium of Etruria.[33] There is no evidence of Dionysiac military celebrations in the Greek world and no possibility that the Roman institution of the triumph could have been borrowed directly from a Dionysiac original. Arrian has repeated a false etymology, evolved after the full development of the legend of the triumphal Dionysus, at a time when the Roman triumph was a familiar institution in the Greek east. The tradition was established by the late first century BC, when Diodorus explained the epithet *Thriambos* by the fact that Dionysus was the first to have celebrated a triumph,[34] but it was clearly a comparatively late evolution. Dionysus' return from the east had been described in outline by Euripides, and Antimachus of Colophon may have made the starting point India itself.[35] The concept of the conquering Dionysus had its origins before Alexander, and the tradition may well have influenced the king's behaviour, inspiring a Bacchic revel. But a revel was not a triumph, and Dionysus'

---

[32] καὶ Θρίαμβόν τε αὐτὸν ἐπικληθῆναι . . . καὶ τὰς ἐπὶ ταῖς νίκαις . . . πομπὰς ἐπὶ τῷ αὐτῷ τούτῳ θριάμβους. There is a trace of this tradition in Curtius (ix. 10. 24), who cites variant explanations of Alexander's Dionysiac revel, one of them being that Dionysus instituted the triumph (*sive illud triumphus fuit ab eo primum institutus*). In that case his source, clearly late, may have been Timagenes (cf. ix. 5. 21).

[33] Varro *LL* vi. 68. For full (but not always convincing) discussion of the origins of the triumph see H. Versnel, *Triumphus* (Leiden, 1970), esp. 21 ff. (cf. 26: 'θρίαμβος never had the meaning "procession" in Hellas'). See also L. Bonfante Warren, *JRS* 60 (1970) 57; *Gnomon* 46 (1974) 575–6.

[34] Diod. iii. 65. 8 (πρῶτον τῶν ἁπάντων καταγαγεῖν θρίαμβον); iv. 3. 1. Both passages represent late material, apparently derived from a handbook of mythology (Schwartz, *RE* v. 673 f.).

[35] Eur. *Bacch.* 13–20; Diod. iii. 65. 7 (Antimachus). *Pace* Goukowsky (above, n. 31) 12–13, there is nothing to prove that Diodorus' entire narrative is based on Antimachus or that Antimachus explicitly mentioned India. On the other hand the common view that the tradition of Dionysus' return from India is a fabrication of the Alexander period (cf. A. D. Nock, *Essays on Religion and the Ancient World*, ed. Z. Stewart [Oxford 1972] i. 134–44) rests on no evidence. Euripides traced the influence of Dionysus as far east as Bactria, and by the time of Alexander the god may well have been associated with India. It would explain the attested manufacture of myth better if there were already a connection.

return from India was not celebrated with military overtones, even in Ptolemy Philadelphus' grand procession.[36] Arrian's source makes the military connection explicit and includes the false etymology of the triumph. That is hardly likely to have occurred before the great celebrations of Scipio Asiaticus and Manlius Vulso in the early second century BC. Whatever source Arrian used for the episode, it was obviously a late compilation, written against a background of Roman domination.

The report of the revel, comes as an appendix. It follows thematically from the arrival of Stasanor and Phrataphernes with a vast train of pack animals and provisions, an event recorded in other sources as the immediate prelude to the Carmanian bacchanale.[37] The revels were omitted by Ptolemy and Aristobulus, but Arrian noted the report in his subsidiary source and considered it sensational enough to be included as a story, even though he totally disbelieved it. There was also a thematic link with the previous narrative. At the beginning of Book v Arrian digresses to describe Alexander's experiences at the city of Nysa in the Cophen valley (modern Swat). The passage differs from the description of the Bacchic revels in that it is largely from the primary narrative tradition. It is presented in direct speech, with occasional excursions into *oratio obliqua*, and one detail (the conscription of Nysaean cavalry) is taken up in the subsequent campaign narrative.[38] The story was popular and multiply reported in the Alexander tradition (first occurring as early as Theophrastus).[39] Alexander was welcomed by the people of Nysa, whose populace claimed to be descended from followers of Dionysus, settled in a colony before the god's return to the west, and tangible traces of the god's

[36] Callixeinus, *FGrH* 627 F 2. 31–2 = Athen. v. 200D. In her excellent commentary E. E. Rice (*The Grand Procession of Ptolemy Philadelphus* [Oxford 1983] 29, 83) talks of a 'symbolic army' of Dionysus. The symbols are far from obvious. The 'troops' are little girls, mostly in civilian dress (200E). The only things suggesting an army are a few girl charioteers with light shields and thyrsos lances and a few female prisoners of war (200F–201A).

[37] Arr. vi. 27. 6. Cf. Plut. *Al.* 66. 7; Diod. xvii. 105. 8; Curt. ix. 10. 22 (cf. 17).

[38] Arr. v. 1. 1–2. 7. Indirect statement at v. 1. 1, 2. 3–4 and excursions from *oratio recta* into the accusative and infinitive at v. 1. 4 and v. 2. 4 (on this see *HCArr.* i. 21). Arr. vi. 2. 3 explicitly takes up v. 2. 4. It is generally (but not universally—see above, n. 6) accepted that the story of Nysa comes from Arrian's primary sources (Schwartz, *RE* ii. 1241; Strasburger, *Studien* i. 128–9).

[39] Theophr. *HP* iv. 4. 1. Cf. Curt. viii. 10. 7–18; *Metz Epit.* 36–7; Justin xii. 7. 6–8; Diod. xvii *arg.* λγ; Plut. *Al.* 58. 6–9.

presence (in the form of ivy[40]) were still visible on the slopes of the neighbouring mountain, which was named Mt. Meros after the legend of Dionysus' birth from the thigh (*meros*) of Zeus.

The historical substrata of the story do not concern us here.[41] It seems fact that Alexander and his entourage believed that Nysa was originally founded by Dionysus, and the visit was reported in similar detail by all the principal sources for Alexander. There is no hint of scepticism in Arrian's report of the king's actions, and he underlines Alexander's compulsion to accept that the city was a Dionysiac foundation (v. 2. 1). Where he declares himself ambiguous is in his attitude to the Dionysus myth. Eratosthenes had stigmatized the entire legend of Nysa's foundation as a Macedonian invention for the greater glory of Alexander. Strabo summarized his criticisms,[42] and Arrian was manifestly affected by them (v. 3. 1–4). He expresses some of Eratosthenes' doubts, notably the objection that there was no tradition of a Dionysiac conquest in any eastern country but India,[43] but he leaves the doubts unresolved, in a statement of Laodicean neutrality—what seems incredible on purely rational calculations of probability gains some credence when one takes the divine into one's calculations. As a statement of principle this is totally conventional, following Lucian's maxim that a myth should be narrated without any guarantee that one believes it, so that the reader may make up his own mind on the subject,[44] and, like so much in Arrian, the genesis of the thought can be found in Herodotus.[45] But Arrian totally avoids discussion. He expounds Eratosthenes' rationalizing criticisms but blandly circumvents them, using the vacuous and unanswerable argument that the ways of the divine are beyond human reason.

Arrian is not seriously indulging in criticism when he recounts the events at Nysa. His aims are primarily artistic. He had ended Book iv with the arrival at the Indus and the cross-

---

[40] That was the basis of Theophrastus' comment. Cleitarchus (*FGrH* 137 F 17) noted that the plant locally known as σκινδαψός resembled the ivy of Greece.

[41] See, most recently, Goukowsky (above, n. 31) ii. 21–33; Brunt, *Arrian* ii. 438–42.

[42] Strabo xv. 1. 7–9 (687–8). Cf. Berger, *Die geogr. Fragmente des Eratosthenes* 77 f.; Jacoby, *FGrH* 721 T 3.

[43] v. 1. 2; cf. Strabo xv. 1. 9.

[44] Luc. *hist. conscr.* 60. See, more explicitly, Arr. v. 3. 1 and *Ind.* 1. 7.

[45] Hdt. ii. 123. 1.

ing of the boundary with India proper. The Nysa episode was omitted from the campaign narrative,[46] to be expounded out of its chronological context and make an impressive beginning to the new book. The motif of emulation of the divine was emphatically restated, and the section on India could start with a satisfyingly exotic episode, bringing together myth and historical actuality. It is probably no coincidence that Nysa also bulks large in the first chapter of the *Indike*, where the non-Indian origins of the populace are emphasized (with implicit reference to the exposition in the Alexander history proper).[47] The episode made a proper starting-point for both expositions and helped link together the two works. As we have seen, the narrative is firmly based on Arrian's major sources, and he accepts as fact its key elements, the conversation with Acuphis and the visit to Mt. Meros.

There is only one qualification, where Arrian reports a tradition that many of the prominent Macedonians crowned themselves with ivy and worked themselves into a state of Bacchic exaltation. Arrian suggests that the story is fiction (εἰ δή τῳ πιστὰ καὶ ταῦτα) and introduces it as a variant report.[48] The earlier report of the happenings on Mt. Meros runs roughly parallel to Curtius' account, agreeing on the flora of the mountain and that the Macedonians invoked the god by his various titles.[49] Either the events were standardly reported in the tradition or a common source is used. The variant, however, takes the theme one stage further, implying that senior members of the Macedonian staff were out of control, in an actual frenzy.[50] Arrian is unwilling to accept the story as authentic but it is too picturesque to be dropped without comment. The same applies to the later celebration in Carmania. It was a colourful episode, illustrating the theme of Dionysiac emulation, but it was also unattested in the primary sources and portrayed Alexander in

[46] The appropriate place for the visit would be in the vicinity of the lacuna at iv. 24. 1. See the synoptic table in Goukowsky (above, n. 31) ii. 22.

[47] Arr. *Ind.* 1. 4–7. Compare *Ind.* 1. 4 with v. 1. 5.

[48] v. 2. 7: οἱ δὲ καὶ τοῦτο ἀνέγραψαν.

[49] v. 2. 5: Mt. Meros abounds in ivy, bay trees, and woodlands of every type (Curt. viii. 10. 13–14). v. 2. 6: invocation of the god by his several cult titles (Curt. viii. 10. 16).

[50] Curtius mentions behaviour *like* that of bacchantes (viii. 10. 15) but his source did not necessarily speak of divine possession, only of invocation, sacrifice, and feasting, all of which is mentioned in Arrian's main story (v. 2. 6). The comparison with the Carmanian revel is added by Curtius himself (viii. 10. 18).

an unacceptably dissolute state. Arrian accordingly includes it in his narrative but indicates his scepticism, exactly as he includes the stories of poisoning for the sake of completeness, even though he disapproves of and disbelieves them (vii. 27. 1–3). The secondary tradition in these cases is drawn upon for supplementary exotica, not in any sense as a control source for the main narrative.

Arrian's description of the stay at Nysa reveals his artistic techniques, the withholding of material for presentation later in the narrative, when the dramatic effect is greater. A more elaborate example comes at the opening of Book vii, where Arrian begins with his fullest characterization of Alexander's imperial ambitions and moves on to the celebrated spectacle of the self-immolation of the Indian sage, Calanus. The two themes are connected by a bridge passage in which Arrian explains Alexander's sympathy for philosophy, which led him to solicit the services of Calanus, and observes that his drive to achieve worldly success prevented his being seriously affected by the ethics of the Indian philosophers. The sentiment is illustrated by three separate episodes: an exchange with unnamed ascetics , who reminded the king of his mortality (vii. 1. 5–2. 1), the meeting with Diogenes in Corinth (2. 1), and finally Alexander's failure to recruit the sage Dandamis (2. 2–4). The last episode is presented in direct speech and is evidently excerpted from Megasthenes, Arrian's primary source in the *Indike*. Strabo excerpted the same material and his account of the interview with Dandamis agrees with and supplements that of Arrian.[51] But Strabo records the episode as one of the variant traditions on Calanus, whereas Arrian uses it as an additional example of Alexander's sympathy with philosophy and an introduction to his account of Calanus' death. In the latter he is not altogether successful, for Megasthenes' strictures on Calanus as a slave to worldly pleasure are followed by an account of the sage's death which stresses his superhuman fortitude (vii. 3. 6). Arrian leaves the contradiction unresolved, for the reader to make his own decision.

---

[51] Strabo xv. 1. 68 (718) = *FGrH* 715 F 34. The sage's name is given as Mandanis (so at xv. 1. 64, with a textual variant). That seems an error of Strabo or of his transcribers. Arrian's Dandamis is the otherwise universally attested spelling (*contra* Brunt, *Arrian* ii. 492).

The first episode, the admonition of the ascetics, cannot be ascribed to any single source. The subject-matter is not attested in any other historical authority and there is no overlap with anything recorded in any extant fragment of the Alexander tradition.[52] There is, however, an interesting parallel from the period of Arrian. A papyrus of the early second century AD containing a collection of Cynic diatribes preserves extensive segments of a lengthy dialogue between Alexander and Dandamis.[53] The work is an eclectic compilation, portraying Dandamis as a classic Cynic sage, but there are clear traces of the main lines of thought in Arrian. Alexander is characterized as an eager listener with some affinity for higher things but corrupted by Greek ambition.[54] There are also reflections of Megasthenes, particularly Dandamis' insistence upon vegetarianism and the criticism of Calanus' desertion.[55] But there are also echoes of the advice of the sages in the first episode of Arrian. Alexander is warned that he possesses only the ground that he walks upon and is subject to common mortality,[56] and his conquests are disparaged as ruinous to himself and to mankind.[57]

These parallels cannot be pressed too hard, but it is undeniable that the episode of Alexander's encounter with the brahmin sages had become a stock *exemplum* in popular philosophy by the early Empire and that there was a conventional picture of the king as an aspirant to moral virtue but trapped in the toils of military success. That was a picture which Plutarch consciously reversed, representing Alexander as a philosopher in action not merely in aspiration. For him the meeting with Diogenes is used as an illustration that Alexander's calling was the practical implementation of philosophy,[58] and he refers to the Indian sages (echoing Megasthenes) not as moral censors

---

[52] There are obvious similarities with the tradition of Alexander's cross-questioning of the brahmins of Southern India (cf. Hamilton, *Plut. Al.* 178 f.).

[53] Full text published by V. Martin, 'Un recueil de diatribes cyniques, Pap. Genev. inv. 271', *MH* 16 (1959) 77 ff. (esp. 83–90). There is a good discussion by G. C. Hansen, 'Alexander und die Brahmanen', *Klio* 43–5 (1965) 351–80.

[54] Col. ii. 45–9: ἐνῆν τι καὶ ἐν αὐτῶι [θεῖον πνεῦ]μα, ἀλλά κτλ. Cf. Arr. vii. 2. 2.

[55] Col. i. 20–6 (vegetarianism: cf. Strabo xv. 1. 68; Arr. vii. 2. 4); col. iv. 19–25 (criticism of Calanus).

[56] Col. i. 1–8 (ἴσην σοι ἔχω γῆν καὶ πᾶς ἄνθρωπος); cf. Arr. vii. 1. 6.

[57] Col. ii. 3–12.

[58] Plut. *de Al. f.* i. 10 (331F–332A). For a more conventional interpretation of the story see *ad princ. inerud.* 5 (782A–B) with Hamilton, *Plut. Al.* xxxii.

but as worthy partners of Diogenes who would be introduced to Cynic teachings by his conquests.[59] But Plutarch is deliberately playing with paradox and turning the convention upside-down. A more straightforward example is Dio Chrysostom's fourth discourse on kingship, which represents a fictional conversation between Diogenes and the young Alexander. There again the king is depicted as basically sympathetic to higher things, but overmastered by his desire for fame ('the most ambitious of men and the greatest lover of glory')[60] and Diogenes' role is to shock him into a state of mental sobriety (4. 77).

Arrian's exposition fits into this conventional framework. Alexander listens with equanimity to the explicit criticisms of the Indians and of Diogenes, but he is not seriously moved by them. The examples used as illustration are clearly standard and the sources were probably familiar ones. Megasthenes' account of the meeting with Dandamis seems to have been regularly used, and the same may apply to the first episode, the meeting with the critical sages. Arrian will have used the material at first hand (his digest of Megasthenes is so close to Strabo's that we must accept that he was working from the original), but his choice of the illustrative examples was probably predetermined by the subject—and he will have chosen the sources most commonly used in the rhetorical debate. His originality here is minimal. He uses his comment deftly enough, to join together the first two major episodes of Book vii, but the thought is a rhetorical commonplace and the historical detail pre-selected. The sources (other than Megasthenes) cannot be isolated, but it is safe to assume that they were commonly used in the philosophical rhetoric of his day.

It is hard to separate the primary and secondary tradition. Arrian's use of sources outside the regular campaign narrative is complex, and where he is suspicious of his material he expresses his doubts and uses indirect statement irrespective of whether his source is a major narrative authority or a representative of the minor tradition. Generally the secondary material is used for minor additions, to add colour and a Herodotean

    [59] Plut. *de Al. f.* i. 10 (332B).
    [60] Dio Chrys. 4. 4, cf. 49–51; 60. For analysis see now J. L. Moles, 'The Date and Purpose of the Fourth Kingship Oration of Dio Chrysostom', *Classical Antiquity* 2 (1983) 251–78, esp. 272–4.

note of scepticism, but rarely, as with the detail of Atropates' Amazons, it provides a peg for a literary digression.[61] As yet, the sources have eluded identification but some of the material has been shown to be late and with strong affinities to the rhetorical tradition. On that basis we can now move to the most elaborate and controversial uses of the secondary sources.

## THE CRITIQUE OF HISTORICAL ERROR

The fullest discussion of material from the secondary tradition comes in the context of Alexander's wound at the Malli town. Here Arrian begins (vi. 11. 1) with a variant report of the extraction of the arrow from the wound (by Perdiccas or by the Coan doctor, Critodemus) and adds that there are many other details which have been uncritically accepted and need correction. This is explicitly a digression and Arrian notes the fact when he closes his exposition.[62] It is also a highly elaborate literary structure, combining various elements common in ancient historiography. The first is the insistence that previous work on the subject is riddled with error and requires emendation by the author. That is a theme that can be traced directly back to Hecataeus, who claimed to report the truth as he conceived it in contrast with the many ludicrous opinions then in vogue (οἱ γὰρ Ἑλλήνων λόγοι πολλοί τε καὶ γελοῖοι ... εἰσίν).[63] Subsequently it became almost conventional for the historian to parade himself as the champion of truth over traditional error. The most striking parallel is provided by Dionysius of Halicarnassus, who claims that there was general ignorance of the origins of Rome and that Greek readers were deluded by false opinion based on chance reports. The avowed aim of his own work is therefore to remove the errors and replace them

---

[61] A good parallel is the story of Alexander crowning the tomb of Achilles and envying the hero his chronicler (Arr. i. 12. 1). The λόγος is placed at a pivotal point in the narrative, to introduce Arrian's justification of his own history (cf. Stadter 75; *HCArr.* i. 104).

[62] vi. 11. 8: ἐν ἐκβολῇ τοῦ λόγου (cf. *Ind.* 6. 1, 17. 7).

[63] *FGrH* 1 F 1. The passage is echoed by Herodotus (ii. 2. 5). See Jacoby, *FGrH* i. 1 (Kommentar) 535 (with bibliography); K. von Fritz, *Die griechische Geschichtsschreibung* i. 71 f.; C. W. Fornara, *The Nature of History in Ancient Greece and Rome* (Berkeley 1983) 5–7.

with truth.[64] That is precisely the contrast that we find in
Arrian: falsehood has been compounded by repetition and
must be countered with the facts. But there is a more immediate model for the digression. Arrian is patently influenced by
Thucydides' famous critique of prevailing opinion (i. 20). The
setting is the same. Thucydides remarks that there is a tendency
for stories to be uncritically accepted, gives three examples of
the phenomenon, and concludes bitterly that most people have
no stomach for the labour involved in establishing the truth. In
Arrian the structure of the digression is repeated, as is the terminology. The rare word ἀταλαίπωρος is evidently a direct echo
of Thucydides, and the Thucydidean flavour is reinforced by
another obvious borrowing in the same sentence.[65] Arrian's
exposition, then, like his excursus on the fate of Thebes, was
direct imitation of a great historical model. Like Thucydides,
he claims to apply a corrective to popular error and both his
structure and his language owes a direct debt to his predecessor.

Arrian begins his critique with a note that the universal
story[66] is that Alexander received his wound in the territory of
the Oxydracae. This he refutes by turning to his historical
sources and retailing a detail that he had deliberately held in
reserve for the excursus: Alexander's attack affected the Malli
alone and it was over before the Oxydracae could give assistance (vi. 11. 3). The refutation is cogent, but it is difficult to see
which authors were responsible for the fiction Arrian attacks.
Other historical sources, notably those used by Plutarch and
Strabo,[67] claim that the engagement took place in Malli territory and do not mention the Oxydracae. On the other hand
Curtius states explicitly that the town in which Alexander was
wounded belonged to the *Sudracae*.[68] Unfortunately it is uncertain how faithfully he reproduced his source. A little earlier

---

[64] Dion. Hal. *AR* i. 4. 2, 5. 1. For a more polemical variation on the theme see Jos. *BJ* i. 1–2.

[65] ἀταλαίπωρος Thuc. i. 20. 3 (closing the digression), so Arr. vi. 11. 8. For ἐκβολὴ τοῦ λόγου in the sense of 'digression' (above, n. 62) see Thuc. i. 97. 4. The opening of Thucydides' critique (i. 20. 1) exactly parallels Arrian vi. 11. 2 in sense, if not in vocabulary.

[66] ὁ πᾶς λόγος (vi. 11. 3 and 4).

[67] Plut, *Al.* 63. 2; Strabo xv. 1. 33 (701).

[68] Curt. ix. 4. 26: *perventum deinde est ad oppidum Sudracarum.*

both he and Diodorus speak of a campaign against the Oxydracae *and* the Malli,[69] and it seems that the vulgate tradition
(unlike Arrian) conceived the two peoples forming a common
resistance.[70] Curtius is clearly abbreviating his source and may
have had the erroneous impression that the campaign concerned the *Sudracae* alone.[71] But it is indubitable that his source
knew of both the Malli and the Oxydracae and did not dis-
tinguish between them.

Whatever the source of the error, it was clearly pervasive in
the rhetorical schools of the Empire. Lucian, for instance, quite
casually describes Alexander's wound ἐν Ὀξυδράκαις.[72] The
same is true of Plutarch. In his *Life of Alexander* he transcribes a
unitary source, probably Aristobulus, which is quite categorical that the Malli inflicted the wound on Alexander.[73] He also
uses the same material in the two epideictic speeches *On the Fortune of Alexander*,[74] but here he was operating from memory and
patently contaminates the historical material with rhetorical
practice. He repeats with declamatory hyperbole the description of the celebrated leap into the Indian town but locates it ἐν
Ὀξυδράκαις.[75] The weight of rhetorical convention prevailed
over the historical tradition. How that situation had evolved
we can only guess, but it is a fact that the conventional belief in
Arrian's day was that the engagement took place among the
Oxydracae, and it is that convention, not a specific historical
account that Arrian is attacking.

The same is true of Arrian's second example. The substitution of the Oxydracae for the Malli leads him to the nomencla-
ture of Alexander's final battle against Darius. The universal
belief that it was fought near Arbela is confronted with the evidence of Ptolemy and Aristobulus, who located it at Guaga-
mela, five or six hundred stades from Arbela. Again it is
difficult to identify a source for the original confusion. To be

[69] Curt. ix. 4. 15; Diod. xvii. 98. 1. So *Metz Epit.* 75 and Justin xii. 9. 3.
[70] *Metz Epit.* 78 is explicit. The same is implied by Diodorus (98. 1–2). So Curt.
ix. 4. 24.
[71] His choice of words may be influenced by his earlier narrative, which stated that
the *Sudracae* provided the general for the allied forces (ix. 4. 24).
[72] Luc. *Dial. Mort.* 12. 5. So Paus. i. 6. 2.
[73] Plut. *Al.* 63. 2–16. Compare 63. 9 with Aristobulus, *FGrH* 139 F 46. Cf. Hamilton,
*Plut. Al.* 176–8.
[74] *de Al. f.* i. 2 (327B); ii. 9 (341C)—both references locate the episode ἐν Μαλλοῖς.
[75] *de Al. f.* ii. 13 (343D), an elaboration of the material at *Al.* 63. 3–4.

sure, Diodorus and Curtius do not give the name Gaugamela, but they give a detailed itinerary of the progress of Darius before the battle,[76] and it is clear that their common source mentioned the river Bumelus and was explicit that the engagement took place a considerable distance away from Arbela. On the other hand it became conventional shorthand for writers referring in passing to the battle to locate it by reference to Arbela, and the phenomenon was regularly noted. Plutarch underlines that the battle was located at Gaugamela, not, as was generally reported, at Arbela, while Strabo adds that the Macedonians themselves transferred the site from the less familiar village to the famous city, so influencing subsequent historians.[77] That is almost exactly the explanation Arrian gives, and it is possible that there is a common source for the criticism. More probably it was a literary commonplace, a regular example of the perversion of fact, which need not derive from any single source. What is certain, however, is that the substitution of Arbela for Gaugamela was a constant feature of rhetoric. Plutarch, despite his concern for accuracy in the *Life*, refers casually to the victory at Arbela in the first speech *On the Fortune of Alexander* (*Mor.* 326F), and Arrian himself is infected by the fashion when he separates himself from his sources and writes rhetoric of his own (iii. 22. 4). Once again Arrian would seem to be attacking an error simultaneously popular in rhetorical and literary practice and well known as such.

From questions of geography Arrian moves to questions of fact, noting that there was disagreement in the sources about the identities of the officers who defended Alexander at the Malli town and also about the number of wounds he received (vi. 11. 7). He contrasts one (unidentified) version with Ptolemy's statement that the king received a single wound in the chest. Ptolemy's version was the version he retailed in his narrative of events at the Malli town, and there is every reason to believe that his account of the episode, which is unitary, is derived in general from Ptolemy.[78] In that case he is singling

---

[76] Curt. iv. 9. 9–10; cf. Diod. xvii. 53. 4. Compare Curt. iv. 16. 8–10, v. 1. 3, 10; Diod. xvii. 64. 3.

[77] Plut. *Al.* 31. 6; Strabo xvi. 1. 3 (737); cf. Arr. vi. 11. 6.

[78] Arr. vi. 10. 1 = Ptolemy, *FGrH* 138 F 25. For the general ascription of vi. 6–10 to Ptolemy see Strasburger, *Studien* i. 131.

out variants within his primary source tradition. The precise sources that he is using are not identifiable. It is clear that there was general disagreement (maybe deriving from first-hand recollections of the event itself, which would inevitably have been confused) when it came to the identity of the officers close to Alexander. Where Ptolemy mentions Abreas other sources name Limnaeus,[79] and the source used by Plutarch in the *Life* did not apparently name Leonnatus.[80] Here the disagreement was patent and Arrian did not consider it worth his while to give details.

The discussion of wounds is a little more helpful. Aristobulus, according to Plutarch, noted that Alexander sustained a second wound in the neck, and Plutarch seems to embroider on that nucleus a few pages later when he claims that this neck wound was inflicted by a club.[81] That is the version we find in the *Life* (*Al.* 63. 9), and it seems inevitable that it goes back to Aristobulus. This is not quite the variant in Arrian, which records a wound inflicted by a club, but it is a blow to the helm and occurs *before* the fateful arrow shot. All these elements are combined in a full-blown rhetorical account in Plutarch's second speech *On the Fortune of Alexander*, which mentions a blow on the helmet by a cleaver and subsequently the club wound in the neck.[82] Given the confusion at the time there is nothing surprising in the sources reporting different wounds at different stages of the mêlée and there is no difficulty in ascribing the variant to one of Arrian's primary authorities. Aristobulus is excluded,[83] but it is possible that it derives from Nearchus, who presumably gave his own account of the episode.

Arrian has moved from correction of popular error to the exposition of variants, which he notes but does not criticize in detail. He is evidently unwilling to choose between them (although his explicit reference to Ptolemy makes his prefer-

---

[79] Plut. *Al.* 63. 8; Curt. ix. 5. 15–16 ('Timaeus'). Cf. Berve ii. no. 474. On the propaganda implications of the source tradition see Errington, *CQ* 19 (1969) 235–6: *contra* J. Roisman, *CQ* 34 (1984) 382.

[80] He is, however, mentioned (alongside Ptolemy and Limnaeus) at *de Al. f.* ii, 13 (344D).

[81] *de Al. f.* ii. 9 (341C) = *FGrH* 139 F 46. Cf. *de Al. f.* i. 2 (327B); ii. 13 (344D).

[82] *de Al. f.* ii. 13 (344C–D).

[83] I do not see why Strasburger (*Studien* i. 131) and Kornemann (84) ascribe the variant to Aristobulus. Aristobulus made the minor wound a neck, not a head wound (cf. Brunt, *Arrian* ii. 134 n. 4) and said that it was the second, not the first sustained.

ence clear). But he now returns to excoriation of falsehood, the greatest error in the entire Alexander tradition. Some (unnamed) writers have recorded that Ptolemy participated in the action, receiving the title of *Soter* for his defence of the fallen Alexander, whereas Ptolemy himself reported that he was absent from the siege and fought elsewhere on a separate mission (vi. 11. 8). At first sight this resembles the critique of the location among the Oxydracae: Arrian refutes the falsehood using an element of the narrative that he has reserved for this occasion. That is indeed his procedure, but it is not, it seems, an original piece of research. Curtius notes exactly the same disagreement: Cleitarchus and Timagenes reported that Ptolemy participated in the battle, whereas Ptolemy himself stated that he was away on an expedition.[84]

This is a famous and doubly interesting passage. In the first place it names sources for the aberrant tradition, notably Cleitarchus. Secondly it has been argued that Ptolemy was reacting against his own self-glorification, altruistically setting the record straight in the interest of truth.[85] This last view is hardly correct. Neither Arrian nor Curtius suggest anything polemical in Ptolemy's account of the matter. He merely noted that he was on an expedition (as so often) and had not returned at the time of the siege. That can indeed be inferred from Arrian's own narrative, which reports a commission to Ptolemy to lead the rearguard down the Acesines to the confluence with the Hydraotes.[86] Immediately afterwards Alexander made his push across the desert into Malli territory. It was easy enough to conclude that Ptolemy was not present at the celebrated siege. His silence in the matter was no doubt famous and used as an example of refutation by omission. An individual notorious for his self-praise passed over an episode which would have redounded to his credit—it therefore did not occur. Curtius' wording is interesting. His phrasing echoes a similar *topos* in Livy and prefigures one in Tacitus. Livy refutes exaggerated casualty figures in Valerius Antias by noting that Cato (*haud*

[84] Curt. ix. 5. 21: *Ptolemaeum, qui postea regnavit, huic pugnae adfuisse auctor est Clitarchus et Timagenes, sed ipse, gloriae suae non refragatus, afuisse se missum in expeditionem memoriae tradidit.*

[85] See, most recently, Schachermeyr, *Alexander in Babylon* 215–17 (following Jacoby, *RE* xi. 625). Tarn's counter-arguments (*Alexander* ii. 27–8) were not successful.

[86] Arr. vi. 5. 6–7; cf. 13. 1.

*sane detractator laudium suarum*) did not give exact numbers for the enemy he killed.[87] Secondly the story that Nero was guarded by snakes in his infancy is ridiculed by reference to statements by that notoriously monomaniac emperor that only *one* snake was ever seen in his chamber.[88] Curtius followed a literary model, and there is no reason to suspect that he used Ptolemy direct (any more than Livy necessarily went directly to Cato).[89] Ptolemy's silence may have been famous in its own right.

Curtius alleges that Cleitarchus related Ptolemy's presence at the siege, and it has often been suggested that Cleitarchus is the target of Arrian's attack. That cannot be. In the first place Curtius says nothing of Ptolemy defending Alexander's body alongside Peucestas. He merely states that Cleitarchus reported his presence (*adfuisse*) at the siege. There is no suggestion that he played a spectacular role. Secondly his narrative of events in the Malli town (which runs parallel to Diodorus') has no major role for Ptolemy: the defenders of the king are Peucestas, Limnaeus, Leonnatus, and Aristonous.[90] It is possible that the common source was an author other than Cleitarchus, but, given the general pattern, it is easier to conclude that Curtius' account is, here as elsewhere, based on Cleitarchus and that Ptolemy played a relatively minor part in Cleitarchus' story of the siege—so minor that it was passed over by Diodorus.[91] Now Arrian criticizes the story at a much later stage of its development.[92] The parallels that can be adduced for it are all

---

[87] Livy xxxiv. 15. 9 ( = Cato F 92 Peter).

[88] Tac. *Ann.* xi. 11. 3. The echo of Livy was noted by Syme, *Tacitus* 349.

[89] See the detailed discussion of H. Tränkle, *Cato in der vierten und fünften Dekade des Livius* (Ak. der Wiss, und der Lit.: Abh. 4. Mainz, 1971), concluding that Cato *was* Livy's immediate source (27). See also J. Briscoe, *Commentatary on Livy xxxiv–xxxvii* (Oxford, 1981) 63–5.

[90] Curt. ix. 5. 14–16. For the general description compare Diod. xvii. 98. 3–99. 4 with Curt. ix. 4. 26–5. 21; *Metz Epit.* 76–8 (note particularly Diod. 99. 1 with Curt, 5. 1; 99.2 with Curt. 5. 4–5; 99.3 with Curt. 5. 11). Diodorus, as so often, cuts his description short and deals with the defence of Alexander in a few words (99. 4), but there is nothing inconsistent with Curtius' account.

[91] That is better than the favoured explanation that he was omitted because Diodorus (and *Metz Epitome?*) was aware of the controversy surrounding the detail (Jacoby, *FGrH* ii.D 495; Goukowsky, *Diodore xvii* 257; Hammond, *Three Historians* 65). Hamilton, in *Greece & the E. Mediterranean* 143, is agnostic.

[92] Necessarily after the adoption of the title Soter by Ptolemy I, at a time when its historical origins were forgotten (so Brunt, *Arrian*, ii. 134 f., n. 6). Cf. Habicht, *Gottmenschentum*[2] 109 f., 257 ff.

late. The fullest version comes in Pausanias' brief epitome of Ptolemaic history, where the founder of the dynasty is said to have been the chief agent in saving the king's life at the siege (again set ἐν ᾿Οξυδράκαις), and the story is fully fledged in the Alexander Romance.[93] Once again, it was a stock element of rhetoric. We have seen how Plutarch lets the reference to the Oxydracae slip into his speech *On the Fortune of Alexander.* The same happens with Ptolemy. In the *Life* he is, quite properly, not mentioned at the Malli town. In the speeches, however, Plutarch is less careful, and Ptolemy's name intrudes twice, displacing Peucestas from his central role.[94] The popular tradition was evidently strong enough to override his recollection of the historical evidence.

How the tradition developed is a mystery. It is a reasonable enough assumption that Cleitarchus began the fiction by his erroneous statement that Ptolemy was present at the siege. At a later stage the false explanation of the name Soter was superimposed, and Ptolemy was promoted to centre stage alongside Peucestas. That development had taken place by the first century AD, and there is certainly a possibility that the Alexandrian historian, Timagenes, played a hand in it. He is named by Curtius alongside Cleitarchus and certainly dealt with Ptolemy's supposed actions at the Malli town. Unfortunately the content and character of his work remain enigmatic[95] (a fact which has encouraged rather than deterred modern speculation), and it is impossible even to guess at the extent to which he modified Cleitarchus' exposition. All that can be said is that Arrian's criticism seems directed against specific literary presentation (ἔστιν οἳ ἀνέγραψαν) rather than general rhetorical practice. That literary source was not Cleitarchus but an author (or authors) writing relatively late, after the tradition had been fully embroidered.

The criticism of historical error is an elaborate, carefully structured digression. Its inspiration was Thucydides and, like Thucydides, Arrian expounds and corrects various popular

---

[93] Paus. i. 6. 2 (on the source see Seibert, *Das Zeitalter der Diadochen* 50 f.); Ps.–Call. iii. 4. 14–15 (Ptolemy and Peucestas side by side).

[94] *de Al. f.* i. 2 (327B); ii. 13 (344D); cf. *Al.* 63. 8.

[95] Jacoby, *FGrH* 88, lists twelve 'authentic' fragments, only one of which (the reference in Curtius) deals with the period of Alexander.

errors. Those errors are errors familiar from rhetorical practice. It is only with the final example that he takes issue explicitly with a historical authority, and that authority is relatively late. There is no indication that Arrian drew on the first generation of Alexander historians for this subsidiary material. His sources on the contrary seem to fall into two distinct groups: the main narrative authorities (Ptolemy, Aristobulus and, in the last two books, Nearchus) and the secondary tradition, which embraces a whole spectrum of material, literary and non-literary. Arrian uses it not to provide evidence for ⟨the history of Alexander's reign but to illustrate a purely literary theme, the prevalence of mistaken belief. The material selected is understandably late, written after the full development of the fictions he stigmatizes.

### THE ROMAN EMBASSY

We may now turn to the most famous incident recorded in the secondary tradition, Alexander's reception of a Roman embassy.[96] Arrian presents the story as a subsidiary *logos* not mentioned by Ptolemy or Aristobulus, and for once he names his authorities. They are Aristus and Asclepiades.[97] This information is a little disappointing. Of Asclepiades we know nothing at all; he is cited only by Arrian and only in this single context.[98] Aristus is slightly less obscure. We know from Strabo that he wrote significantly later than Aristobulus and Onesicritus,[99] and there survives a sprinkling of fragments, the most important of which is his description of Cyrus' tomb. That, as

[96] The literature is substantial, the verdict largely against the historicity of the episode. For reviews of the problem see Seibert, *Alexander der Grosse* 172–3; O. Weippert, *Alexander-imitatio und römische Politik in republikanischer Zeit* (Augsburg, 1972) 1–10. Recent contributions have, on the whole, been more receptive to the idea that an embassy of some sort approached Alexander. See M. Sordi, 'Alessandro e i Romani', *Rend. dell. Ist. Lombardo* 99 (1965) 445–52; Schachermeyr, *Alexander in Babylon* 218–23, *Alexander der Grosse* 552–4; Brunt, *Arrian* ii. 497 f.

[97] Arr. vii. 15. 4–6 = *FGrH* 143 F 2 (Aristus); 144 F 1.

[98] Various identifications are noted and scouted by Jacoby, *FGrH* ii.D 531. It might be worth considering the Bithynian polygraph, Asclepiades of Myrlea (*FGrH* 697), a contemporary of Pompey whose *Bithyniaka* must have been known to and used by Arrian. We have no means of guessing the context in which he mentioned the Roman embassy.

[99] Strabo xv. 3. 8 (730) = *FGrH* 143 F 1. There is nothing except the name to suggest an identification with the favourite and minister of Antiochus II (Athen. X. 438D). Strabo (xiv. 6. 3 [682]) only seems to know of him as a writer, and gives no hint of high office.

far as we can tell from Strabo's brief summary, was derivative and inaccurate, and the prognosis is not good for his account of the Roman embassy. There has been a strong tendency to dismiss the whole episode as unhistorical, a romance which has the future mistress of the world pay homage to Alexander and have her future greatness acknowledged by the king in an inspired prophecy. The assumption that the episode is fictitious has important historiographical consequences. It is known from Pliny that Cleitarchus briefly reported a Roman embassy, and, if the report is invention, it can only have been devised when Rome was a power significant enough to be a household name. Only then would the invention redound to the greater glory of Alexander. If, then, the embassy is an invention, Cleitarchus, who knew and retailed the invention, must have known of Rome's rise to greatness, and it would be hardly credible that he wrote before the Pyrrhan wars.[100] That is the strongest single argument for the late dating of Cleitarchus and a critical point for the evaluation of the entire vulgate tradition.

Arrian's report of the Roman embassy is embedded in a larger description of embassies soliciting Alexander's favour in the spring of 323 (vii. 15. 4–6). All the delegations mentioned are non-Greek, from Africa and the far west. Now it is clear from Arrian and other sources that a plethora of embassies descended on Alexander's court in the months before his death, and they arrived at different times. Arrian notes casually that an embassy from Epidaurus crossed Alexander's path when he was on his way to Babylon (vii. 14. 6) and adds that on his arrival there were several Hellenic embassies awaiting him (vii. 19. 1).[101] Diodorus also notes the presence of Greek and Macedonian ambassadors at Babylon, but he associates them with missions from the African coast and the northern Balkans.[102] In Arrian's account there is a clear separation, which

[100] Fully argued by Tarn, *Alexander* ii. 21–6 and accepted with reservations by Pearson, *LHA* 232–3. Jacoby (*FGrH* ii.D 497), who believes in an early date for Cleitarchus and a fictitious Roman embassy, fails to give any cogent reason for the invention.

[101] A second group of ambassadors was received after Alexander's return from the Pallacotta (Arr. vii. 23. 2; cf. Brunt, *Arrian* ii. 495–7; Goukowsky [above, n. 31] i. 185–6).

[102] Diod. xvii. 113. 1–4; Justin xii. 13. 1–2. It is often argued that Diodorus lumped together all the embassies that arrived during the last months (cf. Brunt, *Arrian* ii. 495), but there is no cogent reason to think so. The Bruttians and Etruscans are notable absentees from his list and may have been mentioned elsewhere.

must be conscious. Greeks and non-Greeks appear in separate
contexts, and the reception of non-Greeks is built up into an
elaborate passage of discussion and comment. Arrian first mentions embassies (comprising Libyans, Bruttians, Lucanians,
and Etruscans) which encountered Alexander on his way to
Babylon, offering crowns in honour of his conquest of Asia.
Next he embarks on indirect speech: it is said (λέγεται) that the
Carthaginians and other western peoples sent embassies, soliciting Alexander's friendship and asking him to settle inter-
state disputes. That made Alexander truly appear lord of earth
and sea. Finally Aristus and Ascelepiades are explicitly cited for
the Roman embassy.

Arrian is openly sceptical about the Romans, mentioned (so
he claims) neither by Roman historians nor his preferred
sources, Ptolemy and Aristobulus. But his scepticism is confined
to that one episode. He has no doubts about the second batch of
embassies, from Carthage and the west, and it looks as though
the information comes from one at least of his major sources.[103]
Then why does Arrian qualify his report and present it in indirect speech? The best explanation I can find is that Arrian is
combining material that is generically related but chrono-
logically discrete. The embassies from the west were a memorable and self-contained theme, an illustration of Alexander's
universal reputation at the time of his death, and Arrian chose
to record them as a narrative entity. He began with the note of
the arrival of the first embassies while Alexander was still en

[103] It is usually taken as axiomatic that λέγεται marks a transition to the secondary
tradition (Jacoby, *FGrH* ii.D 496; Tarn, *Alexander* ii. 374 [dogmatic]; Brunt, *Arrian* ii.
498 f.). But there is nothing implausible about any of the delegations listed. Even the
Iberians were in contact with the great powers of the west and must have heard the
news of Alexander's conquests. Nor is it impossible that many of the tribal names (and
costumes) were completely new to the Greek world. The wider names were doubtless
familiar but not those of the obscurer tribes who chose to send embassies. Again, it is
not even unlikely that the more distant embassies excited wonder and inspired the comment that Alexander was lord of earth and sea. In the context of court flattery, which
placed the king above Heracles and the Dioscuri, that was hardly extreme. Ptolemy,
Aristobulus or even Nearchus may well have reported the comment. It is not (*pace* Tarn
ii. 376) the same as Justin's rhetorical flourish (xii. 13. 2) that all peoples of the world
did homage to Alexander as their destined king. Rather it is an illustration of the effect
*on Alexander's courtiers* of the flood of outlandish embassies, and the sentiments expressed
are natural enough under the circumstances. There is no cogent reason to suspect late
fabrication. If Ptolemy Philadelphus could be eulogized as lord of every land and sea
(Theocr. xvii. 91–2; cf. Momigliano, *Secundo Contributo alla storia degli studi classici*
[Rome, 1960] 433), so indeed could Alexander at the height of his glory.

route to Babylon. That came from a narrative source, either Ptolemy or Aristobulus. Arrian then looked ahead to the reception in Babylon and reported the other embassies from Africa and the west. He probably changed sources, for he seems reasonably well informed about the purpose of these second embassies,[104] whereas he is noticeably vague when he talks about the embassies which met him on the road and the later Greek embassies which were waiting in Babylon.[105] In that case the λέγεται formula at vii. 15. 4 marks a change of source and a slight chronological progression, but all the material before the introduction of the Roman embassy comes from Arrian's major authorities.

The Roman embassy itself concludes the theme of diplomatic overtures from the non-Hellenic world. Arrian elaborates on Alexander's universal monarchy, adding an anecdote which he is deeply suspicious of but which shows the ruler of the contemporary world honoured by the world power of the future and foretelling its greatness. The subject of universal empire could not be more aptly concluded. But the anecdote is taken out of context. We cannot infer that Aristus or Asclepiades placed the encounter in Babylon. Arrian has selected it for artistic reasons, to provide a narrative climax, and he did not necessarily find it in the same chronological context as the other embassies. It is chosen because it is the most impressive instance of Alexander's recognition by foreign powers and, in the version in which Arrian quotes it, it was clearly famous in his day. The chronological dislocation will be seen to have important repercussions for the historicity of the episode.

As it stands, the version transmitted by Aristus and Asclepiades is unhistorical. On the face of it there is nothing implausible in Alexander enquiring about and admiring the institutions of a free people (which had the good sense to offer him homage). The same is attested, for instance, of the Ariaspians of the lower Helmand and the Indians of Nysa.[106] Nor is it totally beyond the bounds of possibility that Alexander made some

---

[104] Requesting the king's friendship and his good offices in settling local disputes. The latter motive is also attested in Diodorus (xvii. 113. 2).

[105] ὑπὲρ ὅτων μὲν ἕκαστοι πρεσβευόμενοι οὐκ ἀναγέγραπται vii. 19. 1. Cf. vii. 14. 6.

[106] Arr. iii. 27. 5; v. 2. 2. Compare his questioning of the Celts, which Ptolemy reported (*FGrH* 138 F 2; Arr. i. 4. 6–8).

comment about the Romans' potentiality for empire. What, however, is most implausible is that such assertions and such signal honour paid to a foreign people were ignored by both Ptolemy and Aristobulus. Alexander's admiration for the Ariaspians was duly recorded and one would expect the same of the Romans. There was no reason to pass over so memorable a tribute. If the tradition is first found in the demonstrably late work of Aristus, it should be considered a romantic fiction, concocted after Rome became a major power in the eastern Mediterranean. It should be emphasized that this version is highly flattering to the Romans. There is no implicit gloating over the fact that the future masters of the world offered submission to Alexander or any hint of the hostile animus that later infuriated Livy. The Romans have their intrinsic worth recognized and Alexander 'makes some presage of their future power'. That need not even imply world empire, γῆς καὶ θαλάσσης σκῆπτρα καὶ μοναρχία, as it appears in a passage (possibly interpolated) of Lycophron's *Alexandra*.[107] The language is consistent with Rome's position after (or even during) the first Punic War, while the city was still an object of curiosity in the east but not yet an imperial power with numerous enemies in the Greek world.

Early or not, the story as it is elaborated by Arrian's sources is a fiction. The more substantial question is whether it is total invention or an embellishment of a historical nucleus. Was there a Roman embassy sent to Alexander in 323? It so, there would be an element of fact to inspire the imagination of later writers. The sole evidence of substance is a famous passage of the Elder Pliny discussing the history of the Latin town of Circeii. Once it was an offshore island, Circe's island in Homer, but now, he claims, it is part of the mainland.[108] He refers in particular to the testimony of Theophrastus, who gave the dimensions of the island as eighty stades in circumference.

---

[107] Lyc. 1226–31. On the problems of the passage see, most recently, Stephanie West, *JHS* 104 (1984) 127–51, arguing the case for interpolation. For a defence of a 3rd-cent. dating (combined with thorough disbelief in the Roman embassy), see Momigliano, *Secondo Contributo* 431–46 (cf. 442 n. 32). For the thesis that it was Timaeus who raised Rome to the status of a world power alongside Carthage see Momigliano, *Terzo Contributo alla storia degli studi classici e del mondo antico* (Rome, 1966) 44–7.

[108] Pliny, *NH* iii. 57–8 (*FGrH* 137 F 31). Cf. J. R. Hamilton, *Historia* 10 (1961) 452–5; Badian, *PACA* 8 (1965) 9–10.

Theophrastus, he maintains, was the first author to write with especial care about the Romans. Before him Theopompus merely mentioned the fact of the city's capture by the Gauls and Cleitarchus, the next to refer to the Romans, recorded only the embassy sent to Alexander. There can be no doubt about the basic sense of the passage. Pliny claims that Theophrastus was the first to give details about the Romans. They were mentioned in earlier literature by Theopompus and Cleitarchus, both of whom referred to Rome in a single specific context, in Cleitarchus' case the embassy to Alexander.

If Pliny is accurate, then a Roman embassy was mentioned by an author who wrote immediately after the king's death[109] and had no obvious reason for inventing it. But can we assume the accuracy of the passage? Certainly there is a degree of garbling. In the wider context Pliny implies that Circeii was an island in Theophrastus' time and had ceased to be so since.[110] But in the extant passage of the *Historia Plantarum* (v. 8. 3) Theophrastus is quite explicit that Circeii is a promontory of the mainland and that its island state was a thing of the past. At best Pliny's memory of the text is fallacious.[111] But it is the inference that is false. He is quite correct when he quotes Theophrastus for the dimensions of the island, eighty stades in circumference. The statement is taken out of context and forced into an inference that is contradicted by the text as a whole. There seems little reason a priori to doubt that Pliny is correct about the preceding facts: Theophrastus recorded the capture of Rome and Cleitarchus mentioned an embassy to Alexander. Both statements are parenthetical, justifying the statement that Theophrastus was the first alien writer to give details about the Romans, and they are presented by Pliny as well-known facts.

Cleitarchus mentioned a Roman embassy and did so not long after Alexander's death. It has been argued that he based his account upon autopsy, but that is supported only by Pliny's

---

[109] That is the overwhelming implication of Pliny's text: Cleitarchus' work appeared after Theopompus and before Theophrastus. Tarn's attempt to avoid the conclusion (*Alexander* ii. 22) was sheer sophistry and has been rightly rejected.

[110] *quicquid ergo terrarum est praeter X̄ p. ambitus adnexum insulae post eum annum* [sc. 314 BC] *accessit Italiae.* On the problems of Pliny's dating of the *Historia Plantarum* see Hamilton (above, n. 108) 452 f.

[111] He may simply have noted the sentence with the dimensions of Circeii (τῆς δὲ νήσου τὸ μέγεθος περὶ ὀγδοήκοντα σταδίους) and forgotten the context.

desperately vague qualification: *hic iam plus quam ex fama*. If the text as printed is sound, the phrase may refer backwards to Cleitarchus or forwards to Theophrastus.[112] Both have been argued. The logic, such as it is, of the passage is in favour of Theophrastus. Pliny refers to the older traditions of the island of Circeii based upon the *Odyssey* and passes to the more accurate information of Theophrastus. He could now give topographical measurements which were based upon fact, not mere hearsay. Unfortunately the resumptive pronoun *hic* refers most naturally to the proper noun immediately preceding.[113] It does not seem to me impossible that it refers back to the opening of the sentence and marks the close of the rather clumsy explanatory parenthesis, but, as has been observed, it is hard to find a satisfactory parallel. Even if the phase refers backwards it need not imply autopsy on Cleitarchus' part. It merely states that he reported the Roman embassy as more than a rumour. That would indicate that Theopompus modified what he said about the capture of Rome, suggesting that it was a tradition based on hearsay, whereas Cleitarchus reported the embasssy as an unqualified fact. He need not have witnessed the embassy personally to report it as more than *fama*.

We are left with Pliny's statement that Cleitarchus reported a Roman embassy. There is no internal evidence to controvert it. It is, however, mildly problematical that the statement recurs in none of the sources which have been considered derivative from Cleitarchus. In particular Diodorus and Justin have complementary accounts of the embassies which Alexander received at Babylon, and neither mentions the Romans. Diodorus refers to the delegations from Europe and Africa, but the European embassies are apparently confined to the Balkans.[114] Justin is slightly fuller, mentioning communities from the

[112] Editors of Pliny (notably Jan-Mayhoff and Rackham) tend to close the parenthesis at *missam* and refer back the following *hic* to the primary subject of the sentence. Jacoby extended the parenthesis to *fama* (after Detlefsen) and was in turn followed by Tarn. Cf. Pearson, *LHA* 233–4. In his later years Jacoby reverted to the traditional punctuation (*FGrH* 840 F 24a).

[113] Noted and stressed by Badian, *PACA* 8 (1965) 9. In the previous clause Pliny uses another demonstrative (*ab eo próximus Clitarchus*). Here *eo* clearly refers back to the immediate antecedent (Theopompus). Desire for variation may have induced Pliny to use *hic* to designate the remoter main subject.

[114] Diod. xvii. 113. 2 (Greeks, Macedonians, Illyrians, the inhabitants of the Adriatic coast, Thracians, and neighbouring Gauls).

northern Mediterranean from Sardinia to Spain, including some from Italy.[115] If either source was excerpting a list of embassies which included Rome, there was no reason for the city not to be named and given emphasis. But, as we have seen, there is nothing that compels us to date the Roman embassy to the first stay in Babylon. Delegations were coming and going all through that last year, and long before Chares attests the presence of foreign embassies at Susa in very considerable numbers.[116] The major agglomeration may have been at Babylon but there will have been additional hearings for delegations which were late in being sent or were delayed on their journey, as must have been frequently the case. If the Romans were late-comers, they will have been casually noted by Cleitarchus in some context immediately before the king's death.[117] That is a period very summarily covered by both Diodorus and Justin, who, if they used Cleitarchus, must have discarded the majority of his narrative. The record of minor embassies from the west would be passed over as lacking in interest. There is, then, no historiographical ground for rejecting Pliny's statement that Cleitarchus mentioned a Roman embassy. What, however, is certain is that he laid no emphasis upon it, merely noting the fact that it was received, perhaps in a list of minor embassies from the west. In that case we cannot assume a falsification. Cleitarchus had no reason for naming the Romans unless they actually came to Alexander's court. If he were concocting the tradition for the greater glory of Alexander, he must have made a more impressive feature of it. We can now explain the silence of Ptolemy and Aristobulus. The Roman embassy was one of a great multitude from the west and cannot have impressed them greatly. At the time the Romans would have been far less memorable than the Etruscans or even the Brut-

---

[115] Justin xii. 13. 1. Without other evidence it is impossible to infer what Trogus originally said about these embassies or what detail he chose to give (Hammond, *Three Historians* 186 n. 46). He may have dealt with relations with Rome in another context (according to the *Prologus* of Book xii he dealt extensively with events in the west in digressions not excerpted by Justin) or, as a Roman of the Augustan era, he may have ignored the entire tradition of the embassy to Alexander.

[116] Athen. xii. 538c, 539a = *FGrH* 125 F 4.

[117] Arr. vii. 23. 2 records a second wave of Hellenic embassies. There must have been many delegations not recorded in any source. Few, I hope, would endorse Tarn's axiom that every embassy that arrived at court was recorded in the *Journal* (see below, ch. 7) and reflected in Ptolemy (*Alexander* ii. 23, 374).

tians, and there was no reason for either author to name them unless they had an interest to record every delegation, major or minor, that approached Alexander. This is one of the occasions (and there are several others) where Cleitarchus' account can be shown to have contained more detail than either Ptolemy's or Aristobulus'.

The tradition could only be disproved from the Roman side, by showing that it was impossible for the Romans to approach Alexander. That Arrian attempts to do on a priori grounds. Against the argument from silence, the absence of record in Roman tradition and the principal Alexander historians, he sets an argument from probability.[118] The Roman state was then a free state and could not have made overtures to an alien king, particularly when it meant a journey so far from home and there was no fear to compel them or hope of gain to attract them. It is a technique used by Arrian elsewhere, notably in his discussion of the size of the force with Porus' son (v. 14. 5) and the location of the kingdom of Geryon (ii. 16. 6),[119] and, if the premisses were sound, the logic would be acceptable. That of course is not the case. The Romans had every reason of practical policy to approach Alexander. It had been known for more than a year that he had grandiose plans of conquest in the western Mediterranean and could be expected to impinge on the destiny of Rome in a very tangible way. In 323 the city was in the early stages of the second Samnite War, and it was a prudential move to gain the favour of a great and powerful ally, or at least deny the Samnites that advantage. The gains must have been obvious, as well as the losses if they let their case go by default.

There may indeed have been a particular dispute that required diplomatic attention. According to Strabo the Latin city of Antium had been involved in acts of piracy and Alexander complained to Rome, as later did Demetrius Poliorcetes.[120] The information is unique and cannot be checked, but it is not impossible. Etruscan inroads on Greek shipping were a constant irritation and led directly to the establishment of an

---

[118] οὐδὲ ... ἐπεοικὸς ἦν κτλ.: vii. 15. 6.

[119] And, of course, the excursus on the Amazons (vii. 13. 4–6: see above, pp. 65 f.) The inspiration comes ultimately from Herodotus (Hdt. vii. 239. 2).

[120] Strabo v. 3. 5 (232). Cf. Schachermeyr, *Alexander in Babylon* 219–20.

Athenian colony in the Adriatic to protect the city's interests (c.325/4)[121] The Athenians will not have been the sole power affected; and it is by no means unlikely that complaints were made to Alexander as soon as he returned from India and that he responded with remonstrances to the offending parties. The Romans may well have followed the lead of the Etruscans and sent an embassy to justify their position. As for the suggestion that it was unthinkable for the Romans of the early Republic to approach an alien king, it is immediately refuted by the undeniably historical embassy sent to Ptolemy Philadelphus in 273 BC.[122] The monarch approached then was not on the point of a western campaign and in no position to make a direct impact on Rome. It would have had far more importance in 323 to open contacts with Alexander.

All that remains is the silence of Roman historians, none of whom (Arrian claims) mentioned the embassy. That, if true, is not surprising. The diplomatic overture had no immediate or long-term effect. Once Alexander was dead and his western plans were shelved there was no need to pursue negotiations with his successors. Accordingly the memory of the event lapsed and it was not transmitted to Timaeus and the early Roman annalists. On the other hand the embassy was noted by Cleitarchus at least of the Alexander historians and set on record as an incident of casual interest. It was there for later generations to use and combine with Roman annalistic material, but few Romans would have relished the fact that their ancestors had offered homage, if not submission, to the world conqueror. It was more comforting, if mendacious, to ignore the episode and claim with Livy that the Romans lived in blissful ignorance of Alexander's name.[123]

Some basic facts are now certain. A Roman embassy did approach Alexander in 323 and its presence was recorded by Cleitarchus, writing in the first generation after the king's

---

[121] *IG* ii². 1629. 220 ( = Tod, *GHI* 200). Cf. W. Will, *Athen und Alexander* (Munich, 1983) 112, who believes that the Athenians were acting with the approval of Alexander.

[122] Val. Max. iv. 3. 9; Dion, Hal. *AR* xx. 14. 1–2: Livy, *Per.* 14; Dio F 41; Justin xviii. 2. 9. Cf. M. Holleaux, *Rome, la Grèce et les monarchies hellénistiques* (Paris, 1921) 60–83; E. Will, *Histoire politique du monde hellénistique* i. 172–3. In this case the diplomatic initiative seems to have come from Ptolemy.

[123] *Ne fama quidem illis notum*: Livy ix. 18. 6.

death. Cleitarchus saw nothing exceptional in the episode, but, as Rome's power increased, the dramatic possibilities of the meeting were realized. Aristus and Asclepiades retailed an elaboration highly flattering to both parties: Alexander recognized the intrinsic worth of the Romans and foretold their greatness. That was the version Arrian chose to excerpt and criticize, and he clearly chose it for its rhetorical potential and also for the opportunity it provided to eulogize Roman institutions. This does not exclude his knowing other versions of the story. He merely says that it was omitted by Roman authorities and by Ptolemy and Aristobulus. Other versions probably existed and were not mentioned. Arrian somewhat earlier (vii. 1. 4) gives a variant report of the plans of western conquest, which suggests that Alexander was attracted to Italy because of the growing reputation of Rome. The source here can hardly be Aristus, for whom Alexander apparently was first acquainted with Romans when he met the embassy. Another writer had clearly turned Rome into a significant factor in his calculations, anticipating her world-wide reputation. But that source was again late. There is no indication here or elsewhere that Arrian used Cleitarchus' work.

# 5

## THE PROBLEM OF THE SPEECHES

I T is a popular assumption that in Arrian's time the formal orations, which were a mandatory feature of historical writing, were free compositions, enabling the author to give a bravura display of rhetorical technique.[1] They dramatized the personalities and issues involved but had little to do with factual reporting. The Polybian insistence that speeches should be a documentary record,[2] if it ever had been observed, was now stone dead. That, at least, is the impression one might gain from the scanty attested comments on historical methodology. Lucian succinctly states three criteria for successful speeches: relevance to the subject-matter, consistency with the character of the speaker, and clarity of presentation.[3] He adds that in these matters the historian has more licence to use rhetoric and display skill with words. Factual accuracy is not prescribed or even mentioned. One gains the impression that the speeches are to be a rhetorical *cadenza*, an embroidery on the historical narrative designed for the maximum of dramatic effect.

Other evidence tells in the same direction, notably Dionysius' famous critique of Pericles' last speech in Thucydides, which concentrates solely on supposed rhetorical defects.[4] But other statements suggest a different philosophy. Diodorus has a celebrated denunciation of the excessive use of speeches, which

---

[1] See, in general, Avenarius, *Lukians Schrift zur Geschichtsschreibung* (Meisenheim/Glan, 1956) 149–57; F. W. Walbank, 'Speeches in Greek Historians', *The Third J. L. Myres Memorial Lecture* (Oxford, 1965) esp. 18–19; Fornara, *History in Ancient Greece and Rome* 142–68. See, however, Fornara 143: 'the fact does not seem to have been sufficiently appreciated that the ancients unfailingly endorsed the convention that speeches must be reported accurately'.

[2] Polyb. xxxvi. 1. 2–7; xii. 25a. 5; 25i. 8. Cf. P. Pédech, *La méthode historique de Polybe* (Paris, 1964) 254–302; Walbank, *HCP* iii. 651–3.

[3] Luc. *hist. conscr.* 58; cf. Avenarius (above, n. 1) 149–51. Compare Quint, x. 1. 101 (on Livy): *ita quae dicuntur omnia cum rebus tum personis accommodata sunt*; Dion. Hal. *Th.* 36.

[4] Dion. Hal. *Th.* 43–7. See the commentary of W. K. Pritchett, *Dionysius of Halicarnassus: On Thucydides* (Berkeley, 1975).

he may well have taken from Duris of Samos.[5] Speeches which are too long or too frequent bore the reader and debase history into a derivative of rhetoric. Many are inserted capriciously, so as to be irrelevant to the time and place at which they were supposed to have been delivered. He does not deny that speeches add variety to the narrative. They should be used when things have been said well and appositely, for one should not omit what deserves record and has utility for the reader. Here Diodorus apparently claims that the historian has the obligation to give a factual record of the substance of a speech, when it is morally edifying, and to make the best of its content. If his precept were followed, historians would report fact, embroidering the content for rhetorical emphasis but retaining the thread of what was supposed to have been said.

The same principle seems to underlie an interesting passage of Dio of Prusa.[6] There the orator addresses a powerful, unnamed friend and gives him a reading list of suitable authors. The great model for men of action, he claims, is Xenophon. In the *Anabasis* his speeches are superbly adapted to character and unsurpassably persuasive. The persuasiveness is ascribed to their factual content. Xenophon's speeches are not based on hearsay or literary imitation but on actual experience. They have their impact because they are what he did say. Once more there is an assumption that a speech in a narrative history should correspond to fact. That assumption was widespread. Even Dionysius seems genuine in his criticism of Thucydides. He simply does not believe that a trained orator like Pericles could have hectored the *demos* in the way described.[7] The speech may be good as rhetoric but it is inconsistent with the circumstances of delivery. But theory and practice do not always go hand in hand. From a reading of Dionysius' theoretical statements one would assume that his speeches *were* records of fact. One needs, he writes, reports not only of famous battles

---

[5] Diod. xx. 1. 1–2. 2. Cf. Fornara (above, n. 1), 147–51.

[6] Dio Chrys. 18. 14–17. Cf. 17: ἅτε γὰρ, οἶμαι, μιγνὺς ταῖς πράξεσι τοὺς λόγους, οὐκ ἐξ ἀκοῆς παραλαβὼν οὐδὲ μιμησάμενος, ἀλλ᾽ αὐτὸς πράξας ἅμα καὶ εἰπών, πιθανωτάτους ἐποίησεν.

[7] Dion. Hal. *Th.* 44. At 45 he claims that the procedure for a historian 'who wished to represent reality' was to make Pericles speak humbly and use words that would turn away wrath (cf. Ael. Arist. 28. 71–2).

but also of the speeches by which the result was achieved.[8] In the *Antiquitates*, however, it is unfortunately indisputable that the speeches are freely invented by Dionysius. There may or may not be an authentic record underlying a historian's speeches, and it is rare that they can be checked against documentation.

## A TEST CASE AND SOME GENERAL PRINCIPLES

An illuminating example is provided by the senatorial debate at Rome of 1–4 January 43 BC, when the question of war with Antony was debated. The outlines are established for us by Cicero, and we have his own *Fifth Philippic*, the published version of what he said on the first day of the debate. We also have two pairs of speeches devoted to that same occasion by the historians Appian and Cassius Dio. They differ markedly in tone and content. Dio is by far the more voluminous, and his version has attracted more attention.[9] He sets the scene at the beginning of the debate. Cicero opens proceedings with a long harangue, attacking Antony and urging immediate war (Dio xlv. 18–47). He is answered by a speech of comparable length from Q. Fufius Calenus, who defends Antony's actions and develops an invective of remarkable virulence against Cicero (xlvi. 1–28).

It must be said at once that the exchange in Dio is a travesty of historical fact from beginning to end. Calenus actually spoke first, proposing that negotiators be sent to Antony.[10] There was clearly no invective against Cicero, merely an attempt to forestall war. Cicero on the other hand began by attacking the compromise, claiming (as he had in the *Third Philippic*) that

---

[8] Dion. Hal. *AR*. vii. 66. 3. For an appreciation see Schwartz, *RE* v. 938: 'Dionys selbst die in endloser Menge und Breite sich abspinnenden Reden komponiert hat.' Cf. also S. Usher, *ANRW* 30 (1) (1982) 832–7.

[9] See particularly A. V. van Stekelenburg, *De redevoeringen bij Cassius Dio* (Delft, 1971) esp. 78 ff. More general discussion in F. Millar, *Cassius Dio* (Oxford, 1964) 52–6.

[10] Cic. *Phil.* v. 1–5. On the role of Calenus see H. Frisch, *Cicero's Fight for the Republic* (Copenhagen, 1946) 169–71. It is clear from the *Tenth Philippic* (2–6) that Calenus constantly opposed Cicero during the early months of 43. Their *perpetua dissensio* was presumably well known and made it natural for Dio to cast him in the role of critic of Cicero.

Antony's actions were those of a declared enemy of the state. Some of this material appears in Dio, but very little. The divine intervention of the young Octavian, which Cicero alleges prevented Antony bringing his troops to sack Rome, is described in terms reminiscent of the *Fifth Philippic*.[11] But the similarity ends there. Dio ransacks the corpus of Philippic orations for subject-matter, which he rearranges in a new invective, supplemented by non-Ciceronian material extracted from his earlier historical narrative.[12] But that is only part of the story. Cicero's speech is carefully contrived to be answered and over-topped by Calenus.[13] The polemic is turned against Cicero, and there are generous borrowings from the tradition of the Sallustian invectives.[14] Cicero is tarred with the brush he used to blacken Antony's reputation and at the same time his accusations are countered in a novel and sophisticated manner. In particular Antony's actions at the Lupercalia are interpreted as an attempt to *deter* Caesar from assuming the monarchy.[15] Dio is consciously writing for an oratorically sophisticated audience, steeped in the invective literature of the Ciceronian period and appreciative of his manipulation of the diverse material. What he is *not* doing is reproducing the content and flavour of the debate.

Appian is very different.[16] His flat style contrasts absolutely with Dio's malicious and sparkling invective, and the two speeches are far shorter. They are also more unbalanced. Cicero is set up as a man of straw, with a few feeble arguments

[11] Dio xlv. 38. 2–4; cf. Cic. *Phil*. v. 21; iv. 3.

[12] The denunciation of Antony's actions as *magister equitum* (xlv. 27. 5–28. 4) combines the unhistorical detail that the office was illegally held for a year, a detail taken from his earlier exposition (xlii. 21. 1–2), with the famous tirade in the *Second Philippic* directed against Antony's drunkenness and dissipation (Cic. *Phil*. ii. 62–9). Compare also xlv. 29. 2 with xlii. 27. 2.

[13] Dio xlvi. 8. 2 = xlv. 30. 2; 11. 1–2 = 27. 1–2; 14. 1. 3, 4 = 28. 3, 4. See further van Stekelenburg (above, n. 9).

[14] Cf. G. Jachmann, 'Die Invektive gegen Cicero', *Miscellanea Academica Berolinensia* (Berlin, 1950) ii. 1. 235 ff.; E. Gabba, *RSI* 69 (1957) 317 ff. Parallel texts are printed by A. Kurfess in the Teubner *Appendix Sallustiana* (fasc. 2: *invectivae*) 22–4.

[15] xlvi. 17. 5–8, 19. This development is apparently original.

[16] The speeches have been little discussed. Schwartz (*Hermes* 33 [1898] 219) dismissed Appian's historical tradition as romance. There is a more reasoned (but brief) appreciation by E. Gabba, *Appiano e la storia dei guerre civili* (Florence, 1956) 167 n. 1 and a longer exposition in *RSI* 69 (1957) 328–36. See now the commentary by D. Magnino, *Appiani Bellorum Civilium Liber Tertius* (Florence, 1984) 166–71.

for his interlocutor to demolish.[17] The exchange is set at a different time, the last day of the debate instead of the first.[18] Cicero responds to a diversionary move by the tribune Salvius who had postponed the vote on war with Antony. His interlocutor is L. Calpurnius Piso. Piso is not otherwise attested participating in the debate,[19] but his intervention is embedded in Appian's historical narrative and there is no reason to dispute that he did make a speech in favour of conciliation. But does what he said correspond to what we read in Appian? The last day of the debate is poorly served by the historical record. Cicero confirms the general tenor of Appian's narrative, that the feeling of the meeting was strongly in favour of war until the final day.[20] But it is hard to conceive that Cicero argued as lamely as Appian suggests or that Piso's response was so systematically arranged. What is more, Appian avoids invective. Cicero's accusation of Antony and Piso's defence are firmly centred on the issues of the debate and deal with the events following Caesar's death.

Some of Appian's material corresponds vaguely to passages in the *Philippics*. The claim that the honours voted for Antony's enemies are an implicit admission that he is a public enemy echoes what Cicero says in the exordium of the *Fifth Philippic*,[21] and the indictment of Antony's behaviour at Brundisium resembles one of the more famous passages of that oration.[22] But the similarities are few and vague. Appian's material more often seems a rewriting of aspects of his earlier narrative. The description of the unrest at Brundisium owes far more to his own presentation of the episode than it does to Cicero,[23] and Piso's reflections on Octavian's occupation of Rome are clearly

[17] App. *BC* iii. 52–3. 213–220 (Cicero); 54–60. 222–48 (Piso).

[18] *BC* iii. 50. 205 ff. On the chronology see Frisch (above, n. 10) 178–83. Appian notes only three days of debate, not four (Cic. *Phil.* vi. 3), but his account of the opening of the debate is very perfunctory and he may have conflated the first two days.

[19] At iii. 50. 205 he is said to be Antony's chief representative in Rome. That is not unlike what Cicero later alleges (*Phil.* xii. 1, 3). He may have been critical of Antony's behaviour in August 44 (*Phil.* i. 10), but that is not inconsistent with a defence of Antony early in 43 to prevent an unnecessary war. Nic. Dam. (*FGrH* 90 F 130 §111) also alleges (dishonest) neutrality in mid 44. That presumably changed by the end of the year, when Antony was directly under threat.

[20] Cic. *Phil.* vi. 1–3. Cf. Frisch 181 f.

[21] App. *BC* iii. 52. 213; cf. Cic. *Phil.* v. 3–5.

[22] *BC* iii. 53. 218; cf. *Phil.* v. 22; iii. 10–11.

[23] Cf. *BC* iii. 43. 175–8.

influenced by the earlier description of the event.[24] On the other hand there are statements that stand unique, unrelated to anything in the rest of Appian. Most notable is the claim that Antony proposed an official enquiry into the state of the treasuries at the time of Caesar's death, offering informers ten per cent of any moneys recovered.[25] There is no trace of that in Appian's narrative (or indeed anywhere else), nor is there of the equally remarkable statement that Antony's law on the exchange of provinces included a provision that he should go to war with Decimus Brutus if he failed to surrender the Cisalpina to him.[26] It is most unlikely that these details were freely invented by Appian. More probably they come from a source which purported to give the substance of Piso's speech. Appian adapted the material and added colour from his earlier narrative, but the nucleus of the speeches was already present in his sources. Whether that nucleus corresponded at all to what was said on the fourth day of the debate is another question, unanswerable without further detailed evidence.

These two pairs of speeches could not be more different. Whereas Dio gives an elaborate invective, demonstrably of his own invention, Appian seems to keep within the confines of his source material and attempts to do justice, however haltingly, to what was reported as said. Authors' techniques and abilities did vary widely, and there can be very few reliable criteria of assessment when no original survives for comparison. That problem becomes acute when we turn to Arrian. In his history of Alexander there are relatively few extended speeches and no comments about intention or method.[27] Virtually every speech has been acclaimed as a genuine report or damned as rhetorical fabrication according to the prejudices of the individual

[24] *BC* iii. 58. 240 ff.; cf. iii. 42. 173 (3,000 men with Octavian); 45. 184 (Antony enters Rome with a single cohort); 46. 187–8 (the reception at Tibur). The examples of Antony's moderation (iii. 57. 234 ff.) are again based on the earlier narrative, notably the recall of Sextus Pompeius (iii. 4. cf. M. Hadas, *Sextus Pompey* [New York, 1930] 63 ff.).

[25] *BC* iii. 54. 224. There may be a reference to this tradition in Dio xlv. 24. 1, though it is turned against Antony.

[26] iii. 55. 226. There is nothing corresponding in the historical narrative (iii. 27–30). On the background see W. Sternkopf, *Hermes* 47 (1912) 357–81.

[27] The speeches are conveniently listed and discussed by Tarn, *Alexander* ii. 286–96 (cf. Brunt, *Arrian* ii. 528–34). For the earlier speeches (ii. 7. 3–9, 17) see *HCArr.* i. 204–6, 238–9.

scholar; and the problem has been complicated by the view, long prevalent, that Arrian was a wholly derivative writer with no literary qualities of his own. An extreme example is the analysis of the Opis Speech by Fritz Wüst,[28] which quite properly isolates a strong rhetorical element and then tries to identify the source of the rhetoric, canvassing, it would seem, every possibility but Arrian himself.

Arrian certainly had the technique to compose effective speeches. Equally he could elaborate on reported speeches in his sources. The *Indike* proves him a master of lively dialogue, and the Alexander history has any number of passages where he slips into *oratio recta* to add vividness to the narrative.[29] He could extend the technique to longer orations, and there were several alternatives open to him. At the simplest level, he could turn a reported speech into a rhetorical creation of his own, using the material but reshaping it. Alternatively, he could expand an attested nucleus with free additions of his own. Lastly, he might even introduce a composition of his own, totally unrelated to anything reported in his sources. It is impossible to give proof positive of authenticity or fabrication, but I think that certain questions can be systematically applied and can sharpen the focus of discussion:

   (i) Is it attested elsewhere that a speech was delivered on this occasion?

  (ii) How far does the subject-matter cohere with what is reported by other authorities?

 (iii) How much of the speech consists of rhetorical *topoi*?

 (iv) What thematic links can be traced with the rest of the author's work?

  (v) Is there any statement which could not have been made by the purported speaker?

 (vi) Is there any statement which could not have been invented by the historian?

Using this framework I shall examine some of Arrian's most substantial passages of direct speech. The results will be seen to be different and, I hope, instructive.

---

[28] F. R. Wüst, 'Die Rede Alexanders de Grossen in Opis', *Historia* 2 (1953–4) 177–88, esp. 186–8.

[29] Cf. i. 13. 3–7; iv. 8. 7, 12. 5; v. 1. 3, 11. 4, 19. 2–3; vii. 1. 6.

## THE SPEECH AT OPIS

The most elaborate single speech in Arrian is Alexander's address to his mutinous troops at Opis (vii. 9. 1–10. 7). It is vivid and highly rhetorical; and its content has been assigned confidently to Ptolemy, rather less confidently to Cleitarchus, and, with some diffidence, to Arrian himself.[30] In this welter of confusion one thing at least is certain. Alexander *did* make a speech at Opis—or rather several speeches. Plutarch records the disturbances briefly, noting that the king roundly abused his men.[31] There is a similar picture in the vulgate tradition. Justin describes the Macedonian troops contumaciously clamouring for discharge and urging Alexander to campaign in future with his father Ammon.[32] The king responded with reproof and milder remonstrances, but finally he leaped from the tribunal, arrested thirteen of the ringleaders, and had them led off to execution. This same complex of events recurs more briefly in Diodorus, who records a speech by Alexander at exactly the same point.[33] Curtius, as usual, is more consistently rhetorical, but he follows the same outline: first contumacious demands for discharge (x. 2. 12–14), then an address by the king (x. 2. 15–29), and finally his reprisals against the thirteen ringleaders (x. 2. 30).

Arrian's narrative is much the same. He agrees with Justin about the gibe against Ammon, and he has the figure of thirteen for the mutineers arrested.[34] There is no hint that he was

---

[30] Kornemann 158–64 (Ptolemy); Tarn *Alexander* ii. 290–6 (Ptolemy, with late interpolations); Schachermeyr, *Alexander der Grosse* 493–4 n. 595 (fundamentally Ptolemy); Wüst (above, n. 28) 187 'dann kommt für deren Verfasser wohl nur Kleitarch in Frage'; Brunt, *Arrian* ii. 533 'this is an epideictic display by A(rrian)'. Strasburger, *Studien* i. 133, followed Droysen in denying Ptolemaic authorship.

[31] Plut. *Al.* 71. 1–4, esp. 4: καὶ πολλὰ μὲν ἐλοιδόρησεν αὐτοὺς πρὸς ὀργήν.

[32] Just. xii. 11. 5–8.

[33] Diod. xvii. 109. 2–3. Pace Hammond, *Three Historians* 107, I see no reason to assume that Diodorus used a different source from that of Justin/Trogus. Both give the same events in the same order (including the detail that Alexander arrested the mutineers with his own hand) and in both accounts the mutiny immediately follows the discharge of the army's debts. The gibe against Ammon is indeed recorded in an earlier context by Diodorus (108. 3), but it occurs in a general statement that the army repeatedly (πολλάκις) criticized Alexander's pretensions to divine sonship. That is no doubt correct (*Greece & the E. Mediterranean* 64), and, if so, there is no reason to exclude Diodorus' source having mentioned the gibe on the later occasion. Diodorus omitted it along with the rest of the details of the troops' contumacy, noting only that objections were voiced.

[34] Arr. vii. 8. 3; cf. Curt. x. 2. 30 (the arrest comes after the speech).

using the subsidiary tradition at this point and it would seem that there was relative agreement about the happenings at Opis. The main difference in Arrian comes with the placing of the speech. In the vulgate tradition it occurs before the arrest of the ringleaders while in Arrian it is subsequent. That may stem from a genuine disagreement in the sources, but alternatively the arrangement may be Arrian's own, designed to give a dramatic unity to the scene. There is no attempt to persuade. The king harshly punishes the obvious mutineers and berates the rest. The passion and outrage then passes from the stage-setting to the speech itself. But clearly a speech was made, and the fact was recorded in all traditions.

Other than Arrian, Curtius is the only writer to report the content of the speech. At first sight his version is very different, its material disjointed and with abrupt changes of mood. The opening with its questioning of the troops has no counterpart in Arrian, nor does the weak and pathetic sequel that Alexander is in a unique predicament, deserted by his entire army.[35] But there is some common ground. The contrast between past and present is important. In Arrian it is a primitive past, mitigated by Philip and transformed by Alexander (vii. 9. 2), whereas Curtius simply contrasts the frugality of life under Philip with the present luxury (x. 2. 23). More significantly, both writers underscore the scantiness of Alexander's resources at his accession, compared with the immensity of his later achievement. The same figures are given. At the beginning of the reign the treasury contained no more than sixty talents, and there were 500 talents of debt inherited from Philip.[36] This contrast was a favourite one, recurring three times in Plutarch alone.[37] But elsewhere the figures are differently reported: Aristobulus spoke of resources of 70 talents, Onesicritus of debts of 200 talents.[38] The primary tradition obviously contained variant reports of Alexander's early finances, and the agreement of Arrian and Curtius is all the more striking. The material does

---

[35] Curt. x. 2. 20. The theme recurs in the speech at the Hyphasis (ix. 2. 32–3).

[36] Arr. vii. 9. 6 (adding that Alexander contracted more than 800 talents of debt in his own right); Curt. x. 2. 24. The common ground was emphasized by Kornemann 159–60 and discounted by Tarn, *Alexander* ii. 296.

[37] Plut. *Al.* 15. 2 ( = Aristobulus, *FGrH* 139 F 4; Duris, *FGrH* 76 F 40; Onesicritus, *FGrH* 134 F 2); *de Al. f.* i. 3 (327D–E); *de Al. f.* ii. 11 (342D).

[38] Cited in n. 37, above.

not occur elsewhere in the extant narrative of either author, and it presumably derives ultimately from a common report of Alexander's speech.

There is a similar common reference to the recent discharge of the army's debts,[39] but this time the context is very different. In Arrian the episode is cited as one of the king's benefactions, whereas Curtius uses it as fuel for invective, proof of the worthlessness of the army. What is more, both authors recounted the incident in the immediate prelude to the mutiny,[40] and it was a natural theme for either to use. Finally they both emphasize the ingratitude of the army and the king's determination to turn to the barbarians (Arrian by implication only).[41] Some agreement, then, exists, but it is relatively limited and can be reduced to a simple nucleus. 'Your demand for discharge is unreasonable and ungrateful. I have brought you from poverty to world empire, and that from very few resources other than my personal qualities. It is my achievement, not yours, and you have profited from it. If you deny me now, I shall not stop you. Go home and be proud of your desertion, if you can; I shall now turn to the subject peoples.'

So much for the framework. What of the details of Arrian's speech? First and foremost, it is highly rhetorical. That is patent from the first to the last syllable. The final emphatic ἄπιτε, so much admired by Tarn and claimed to be impossible in the mouth of a Greek,[42] is on the contrary a nice piece of rhetorical *bravura*. Aristotle notes that the most appropriate style in which to end a speech is that which has no conjunctions, and he cites as his example the three tremendous imperatives which conclude Lysias' speech against Eratosthenes.[43] The rest of the peroration is elaborate and artificial. Beginning with a sarcastic and chiastic introductory phrase (ἐπειδὴ πάντες ἀπιέναι βούλεσθε, ἄπιτε πάντες),[44] Arrian builds up a sustained catalogue of the king's achievements, continues with a savagely

---

[39] Arr. vii. 10. 3; Curt. x. 2. 25.

[40] Arr. vii. 5. 1–3; Curt. x. 2. 9–11.

[41] Curt. x. 2. 27–8; Arr. vii. 10. 7 (παραδόντες φυλάσσειν τοῖς νενικημένοις βαρβάροις).

[42] Tarn, *Alexander* ii. 295–6 (qualifications are expressed in an *addendum* [452], but the position is unchanged); cf. Brunt, *Arrian* ii. 236 f. n. 8.

[43] Arist. *Rhet.* iii. 1420ᵃ 6–8, citing Lys. 12. 100.

[44] Plut. *Apophth. Lac.* 219E; Ael. *VH* ii. 19: ἐπειδὴ 'Αλέξανδρος βούλεται θεὸς εἶναι, ἔστω θεός.

ironical comment on the deserters' future reputation in the eyes of god and man, and concludes with a single abrupt imperative. The whole is an elaborately worked rhetorical entity.

The opening of the speech with its compressed indictment of Macedonian ingratitude also owes much to rhetorical models. The most pertinent comparison, I think, is with the peroration of the last great speech of Xenophon's *Anabasis*. There Xenophon reviews his labours in the interest of the Ten Thousand, beginning with a turn of phrase highly reminiscent of Arrian: ἀναμνήσθητε γὰρ ἐν ποίοις τισὶ πράγμασιν ὄντες ἐτυγχάνετε, ἐξ ὧν ὑμᾶς ἐγὼ ἀνήγαγον.[45] Arrian makes the contrast more elaborate, with a double comparison between Alexander and his subjects,[46] but the sequence of thought is the same, as is its literary expression. The same kind of elaboration occurs a little later in the speech, where Arrian apparently works on Xenophon's protest that, if they kill him, his men will have killed their benefactor who has shared their hardships and perils and kept vigil for them.[47] The general sentiment recurs in Arrian, developed as a catalogue of Alexander's wounds in the service of his men. But the reference to sleep is unmistakable. Alexander claims that he shares the same food as his men and takes the same sleep: but his food is, if anything, inferior to theirs and he has often kept awake so that they could sleep.[48] The phrasing directly recalls Xenophon, but the context is changed and the antithesis more forced. There is a similar elaboration a few sentences earlier. Arrian makes Alexander turn on his men and allege that they are the real beneficiaries of conquest: 'You are the satraps, you the generals, you the taxiarchs' (vii. 9. 8). Once more the wording is borrowed from Xenophon, but in the *Anabasis* the context is an appeal to an actual audience of generals and taxiarchs.[49] Arrian uses the same emphatic formulation, which gains rhetorical force when addressed to an

---

[45] Xen. *Anab.* vii. 6. 24. Xenophon contrasts the sorry situation of the Ten Thousand before he enlisted the aid of Seuthes with their present comfort (24–33).

[46] Arr. vii. 9. 1: ὡς γνῶναι ὑμᾶς πρὸς ὁποίους τινὰς ἡμᾶς ὄντας ὁποῖοί τινες αὐτοὶ γενόμενοι ἀπαλλάσσεσθε.

[47] Xen. *Anab.* vii. 6. 36: πολλὰ μὲν δὴ ἀγρυπνήσαντα, πολλὰ δὲ σὺν ὑμῖν πονήσαντα καὶ κινδυνεύσαντα καὶ ἐν τῷ μέρει καὶ παρὰ τὸ μέρος. The striking final phrase ('in and beyond the call of duty') is exactly echoed by Arrian in another context (iii. 26. 4).

[48] Arr. vii. 9. 9: προαγρυπνῶν δὲ ὑμῶν οἶδα, ὡς καθεύδειν ἔχοιτε ὑμεῖς.

[49] Xen. *Anab.* iii. 1. 37: ὑμεῖς γάρ ἐστε στρατηγοί, ὑμεῖς ταξίαρχοι καὶ λοχαγοί.

audience of common soldiers.[50] He deliberately echoes and modifies his classic model, much as Cassius Dio consciously improves on the material from the *Philippics*.

Arrian's main source of inspiration appears to be himself. The speech has numerous references to the earlier exposition, and the closest correlations are with his version of Alexander's speech at the Hyphasis. That harangue ends with a passionate claim that the king had shared his troops' sufferings and that they had an equal share in the rewards of conquest (v. 26. 7–8). There are unmistakable verbal echoes in the Opis speech,[51] and the same simple material is cleverly manipulated. Alexander's promises to his men that he will make them the envy of those who depart are echoed in the peroration at Opis, in which the veterans discharged are to be the envy of those at home; and the terminology also recurs in the historical narrative.[52] Once again the inspiration comes directly from Xenophon's *Anabasis*, where Cyrus promises his troops fortune and prosperity.[53] Arrian uses the *topos* on three separate occasions but varies the formulation according to the immediate context.

The creation of variety is one of Arrian's chief aims. That emerges very clearly from the catalogues of conquest which are prominent in these speeches. The first, at the Hyphasis (v. 25. 4–5), begins as a simple enumeration of conquered peoples in roughly chronological order and develops into a list of rivers, culminating with the Hyphasis itself. The second, in the middle of the Opis speech (vii. 9. 7–8), is a list of possessions gained for the Macedonians by Alexander's victories, and the phraseology is adapted to suit the theme.[54] The last and most elaborate is the catalogue in the peroration at Opis (vii. 10. 5–7). This has two objects, to highlight the achievement of the king and to denigrate the troops who deserted him. It begins with the victory at

[50] Tarn, *Alexander* ii. 291, argues that Alexander here 'turned to a knot of officers as he spoke'; Wüst (above, n. 28) 182 correctly speaks of a 'rhetorische Verallgemeinerung'.

[51] Cf. v. 26. 7–8 νῦν δὲ κοινοὶ μὲν ἡμῖν οἱ πόνοι ... ἥ τε χώρα ὑμετέρα ἐστι καὶ ὑμεῖς σατραπεύετε: vii. 9. 8–9 ... καὶ ἡ ἔξω θάλασσα ὑμέτερα ὑμεῖς σατράπαι κτλ. (this also echoes Xenophon—above, n. 49): vii. 10. 1 καὶ τίς ὑμῶν ἢ πονήσας οἶδεν ἐμοῦ μᾶλλον.

[52] Arr. v. 26. 8; vii. 10. 5; vii. 8. 1. The close correlation of the latter passages tells against attempts to salvage the preserved text μένουσι at vii. 8. 1 (Wüst, *Historia* 2 [1953/4] 418 n. 2; Hammond, *CQ* 30 [1980] 469–71).

[53] Xen. *Anab.* i. 7. 4.

[54] The emphasis is on the acquisition of territory and wealth, contrasting *Alexander's* victories with the empire of his people—the effort is his, the profit is theirs.

Gaugamela over the Persians, the Medes, and Bessus' contingent of Bactrians and Sacae,[55] then briefly refers to the conquest of central Iran, associating the Uxii of the Zagros with the Drangians and Arachosians around the Helmand lakes far to the east. The catalogue next moves north to the Caspian. Rather strangely the Hyrcanians and Parthians to the south and south-east of the sea are linked with the Chroasmians of the lower Iaxartes, which Arrian conceived as a tributary of the Caspian. Arrian may have in mind his earlier geographical excursus, where (following Eratosthenes) he places the Chorasmians and Parthians in close proximity, apparently on opposite sides of the Taurus range.[56] But the context in the speech is very different, and Arrian may simply be juxtaposing names of peoples whom he considered to live in the same area, dimly remembered from the earlier narrative. That is patently the case with the Uxii and the Arachosians.

Next the catalogue flicks impressionistically eastwards, over the Caspian Gates to the Hindu Kush and then to the great rivers of the north-east, the Oxus and the Iaxartes/Tanais. It proceeds by water, by the Indus and the rivers of the Punjab (which allows a hit at the Macedonian troops),[57] to the Ocean, which Arrian recalls Alexander having approached by both mouths of the Indus.[58] Next comes the Gedrosian desert, with a recollection of Nearchus' statement that it had never been previously traversed by an army (which Arrian had explicitly cited in his earlier narrative).[59] Finally there are rapid references to the passage of Carmania and Oreitis and Nearchus' voyage in the Indian Ocean, arranged without apparent regard for the geographical or chronological sequence. Perhaps there is an echo of the earlier description of the decorations at Susa, where Leonnatus' triumphs in Oreitis are placed before

[55] Σάκας at vii. 10. 5 refers back to the army list at iii. 8. 3, where Arrian gives the native name (with an explanatory gloss). Elsewhere he refers to the nomads of the north-east as Scythians (cf. *HCArr*. i. 289).

[56] Arr. v. 5. 2; cf. Berger, *Die geogr. Fragmente des Eratosthenes* 172. There is a similar combination of peoples (Chorasmians, Hyrcanians, Parthians, and others) in a problematic passage of Herodotus (iii. 117. 1: see, most recently, Diakonoff in *CHIran* ii [1985] 131 f.).

[57] vii. 10. 7 εἰ μὴ ὑμεῖς ἀπωκνήσατε.

[58] Cf. vi. 18. 2, 20. 2.

[59] Arr. vi. 24. 2 (also in Strabo xv. 1. 5 [686] = *FGrH* 133 F 3). The passage is also echoed at *Ind*. 26. 1 and 32. 1.

the account of Nearchus' *periplus*.[60] That may help explain
why Susa and not Opis is made the terminus of the campaign.
It was the more memorable city and meant more to Arrian's
readers, but it was also explicitly mentioned in the context of
Nearchus' return (vii. 5. 6) and has obtruded into the speech in
place of Opis. This final catalogue is then a recapitulation and
variation of themes already expounded, emphasizing the immensity and uniqueness of Alexander's conquests and paving
the way for the excoriation of the Macedonians which follows.
The irony of the final sentence is paralleled in Curtius (x. 2. 28)
and may have been present in the common source. It also
faintly echoes the peroration of Xenophon's speech to the Ten
Thousand.[61] But the contrast with the carefully contrived list
of conquests is Alexander's own and lends force to the irony.

What precedes is again dependent on Arrian's earlier narrative. The list of wounds (vii. 10. 2), as we know from Plutarch,[62]
was a standard item in the rhetorical repertoire, but Arrian has
given it a twist of his own, claiming that the king bore the traces
of every weapon devised. There is a brief recapitulation of the
sword wound at Issus (ii. 12. 1), the catapult wound at Gaza
(ii. 27. 2), and the arrow wound near Maracanda (iii. 30. 11);
and the passage as a whole may be influenced by the excursus
on Alexander's most serious wound of all, at the Malli town.
After this blatant rhetoric there is a quick fire of recollections:
the marriages at Susa (vii. 4. 8), the cancellation of debts (vii.
5. 1–3), and finally rewards for valour and for death in the
field. In this last reference Arrian patently echoes his description of the honours paid to the fallen at the Granicus. The terminology is borrowed from the earlier passage,[63] and Arrian
has generalized the awards, suggesting that every soldier who
fell in battle received what was given to the heroes of the Granicus. As a universal statement it is perhaps not without founda-

[60] Arr. vii. 5. 5–6.

[61] Xen. *Anab.* vii. 6. 38 οὐδὲ τούτοις δοκεῖτε βελτίονες εἶναι τοιοῦτοι ὄντες περὶ ἐμέ.

[62] Plut. *de. Al. f.* i. 2 (327A–B); ii. 9–10 (341A–D); cf. *Al.* 58. 1. For a comic inversion
of the theme see Luc. *Dial. Mort.* 12. 5.

[63] i. 16. 4–5: χαλκαῖ εἰκόνες ἐν Δίῳ ἑστᾶσι ... γονεῦσι ... ἀτέλειαν ἔδωκε καὶ ὅσαι ἄλλαι
... λειτουργίαι ἢ ... εἰσφοραί. vii. 10. 4: χαλκαῖ δὲ αἱ εἰκόνες τῶν πλείστων οἴκοι ἑστᾶσιν, οἱ
γονεῖς δ' ἔντιμοί εἰσι λειτουργίας τε ξυμπάσης καὶ εἰσφορᾶς ἀπηλλαγμένοι. The moulding
of the passage, as has been noted (Wüst [above, n. 28] 188), echoes Simonides'
encomium for the dead at Thermopylae (Diod. xi. 11. 6 = Simonides F 362 [Page]).

tion. Plutarch claims that orphaned children of Macedonian soldiers were given state pensions,[64] and in his later years Alexander could certainly afford to be lavish in rewarding the families of the dead. But the inference is Arrian's own. He has generalized from a single instance in his earlier narrative and produced an effect similar to that at vii. 9. 8, where he implies that the whole army collectively could be seen as royal satraps and generals.[65]

The most interesting instance of self-borrowing comes at the beginning of the speech, in the picture of Macedon before Philip:

When Philip inherited you, you were indigent wanderers, clad in skins for the most part, pasturing a handful of sheep on the mountains and being worsted in their defence by Illyrians, Triballians, and the neighbouring Thracians. He gave you cloaks to wear in place of your skins; he brought you down from the mountains to the plains, making you a match for the barbarians on your border, so that you gained your salvation by your inborn courage, no longer by reliance on the strength of your surroundings. He made you city dwellers and adorned you with good laws and customs.    (Arr. vii. 9. 2)

This passage is often quoted as basic evidence for the early history of the kingdom, but, as it stands, it is an absurdity.[66] The idea that Philip turned the Macedonian people from nomads to agriculturalists, bringing them from the mountains to the plains, would have invited ridicule from an audience well aware that they and their forebears had been domiciled in the great plain between the Axios and Haliacmon for uncounted

---

[64] Plut. *Al.* 71. 9. In the same context he notes that the Opis veterans were to receive crowns and προεδρία at festivals in Macedon. That perhaps is some warrant for Alexander's claim (vii. 10. 3) that the majority of his men had received gold crowns. I would, however, endorse Tarn's view (*Alexander* ii. 293) that the passage is a generalization based on the report of the gold crowns for valour which were conferred upon senior officers at Susa (vii. 5. 4).

[65] For the general principle compare Lysias' speech against Ergocles (28. 3–4), where it is implied that the Athenian assembly as a whole was affluent enough to be liable for levies on capital. Cf. M. M. Markle, in *Crux* (History of Political Thought 6 [1/2]; 1985) 281–3.

[66] There have been some recent attempts to give the passage a particular historical context, referring it to *specific* urban projects in Upper Macedonia and the plain of Philippi (J. R. Ellis, *Philip II and Macedonian Imperialism* 58 f.; N. G. L. Hammond, *History of Macedonia* ii. 659–60). That, I fear, makes nonsense of the context, which must refer to the generality of Macedonians.

generations. The general picture of Macedonian poverty is inconsistent with the archaeological evidence of luxury and sophistication long before Philip's time, most notably illustrated in the staggering funerary finds at Sindos.[67] At a more trivial level, there is no evidence that the Triballians had any contact with Macedon before Philip's reign; their one attested incursion to the south was the great attack on Abdera in 376,[68] and that was well outside Macedonian territory. The natural enemies of the Triballians were their neighbours in Paeonia and the Odrysian kingdom of Thrace.[69]

This sketch of Macedonian history is wildly inaccurate, and one is inclined to ask for its origin. There is a simple answer. It is based on a passage of the *Indike*, where Arrian transcribes Megasthenes' story of the civilizing influence of Dionysus.[70] Before the god's arrival the Indians were nomads, without cities or laws. Their clothing was skins and their food tree-bark and raw meat. It was Dionysus who gave them cities and laws and taught them the art of agriculture. The resemblance is undeniable, and there may be another source of inspiration in Nearchus' report of Alexander's actions against the Cossaei (he founded cities to transform them from nomads into tillers of the earth).[71] It looks as though Arrian created his own foundation myth, setting Philip in the role into which Megasthenes had cast Dionysus, the establishment of civic life and an agricultural economy.[72] Certainly Arrian was impressed by the contrast between nomad and farmer, whom he saw as the respective types of barbarism and civilization; and in the *Bithyniaka* he has a reverse fable of the Scythians consciously exchanging a life of agriculture and city dwelling for their classically nomadic

---

[67] See the outline description in *Archaeological Reports* 1981/2, 35–6; 1982/3, 37; 1983/4, 44.

[68] Diod. xv. 36. 1–4; Aen. Tact. 15. 8–9. Cf. F. Papazoglou, *The Central Balkan Tribes in Pre-Roman Times* (Amsterdam, 1977) 15–17, arguing that Triballian raids were only feasible after the Macedonians had annexed Paeonia and Dardania.

[69] Thuc. iv. 101. 5.

[70] Arr. *Ind.* 7. 2–7. The material is also digested by Diodorus (ii. 38. 5; cf. *FGrH* 715 F 4, 12).

[71] Arr. *Ind.* 40. 8. On this passage see P. Briant, *État et pasteurs au Moyen-Orient ancien* (Cambridge, 1982) 100–12, esp. 105.

[72] It is possible that Anaximenes of Lampsacus constructed a similar fiction, casting Alexander the Philhellene in the role of founding father (P. A. Brunt, *JHS* 96 [1976] 151–3; see, however, Griffith, *History of Macedonia* ii. 705–9; R. Develin, *Historia* 34 [1985] 493–6).

mode of existence.[73] If, then, Arrian was inventing his own picture of Philip the civilizer, the transformation from nomadic to
urban culture would have been an obvious framework.

Within that framework comes the problematic conjunction
of Illyrians, Triballians, and Thracians as traditional enemies
of Macedon. The collocation recurs in Alexander's speech at
the Hyphasis (v. 26. 6) in a somewhat different context. There
Alexander is made to contrast the rewards of conquest in the
east with the profitless task of repelling the neighbouring
Thracians, the Illyrians, and the Triballians. That is a clear
reference to the early campaigns of the reign; Arrian lumps
together the first three peoples to be mentioned in his narrative
history.[74] In the Hyphasis speech they are rightly adversaries
of the present, but in the Opis speech Arrian goes a step further
and converts them into timeless enemies of the state. He may
not have been unique in this. Dio of Prusa also couples together
Illyrians and Triballians as past overlords of Macedon,[75] but
there is no hint (despite his Bithynian origins) that he has influenced Arrian. The thematic links in his work are sufficient to
explain the conflation. Once again a theme from the historical
narrative is recapitulated simply in the Hyphasis speech and
rhetorically elaborated in the more complex oration at Opis.

Is there anything in the speech which is not a manipulation
of motifs already expounded? Very little. The most obvious instance is the review of Philip's historical achievements (vii. 9.
3–5). That is largely accurate, if one makes some allowance for
the rhetorical elaboration. Most (but not all) of Thrace *was*
annexed, the strategic coastal cities of Methone, Pydna, and
Amphipolis *were* acquired, the mines of Pangaeus *were* exploited
without interference by the neighbouring Thracians.[76] The
worries sometimes evinced about the statement that tribute was
paid to Athens are unwarranted.[77] The remark comes in an

[73] Arr. *Bithyn.* F 54 (Roos p. 218; Stadter 160). Arrian cites the Scythians as a phenomenon parallel to the Indians in their state of nature before the advent of Dionysus
(*Ind.* 7. 2).

[74] Arr. i. 1. 4 ἐλαύνειν ἐπὶ Θρᾴκης, ἐς Τριβαλλοὺς καὶ Ἰλλυριούς ... καὶ ἅμα ὁμόρους
ὄντας οὐκ ἐδόκει ὑπολείπεσθαι.

[75] Dio Chrys. 2. 9.

[76] Diod. xvi. 8. 6–7; Steph. Byz. *s.v.* Φίλιπποι. Cf. Griffith, *History of Macedonia* ii.
249–50.

[77] e.g. F. Hampl, *Der König der Makedonen* (Leipzig, 1934) 81; see, however, Kornemann 161.

elaborate contrast, juxtaposing the state of Thebes and Athens
before and after Philip's reign. It is not too much of an exaggeration. Strepsa at least paid tribute from 453, if not before,[78]
and the Attic orators made much of what they supposed to
have been Macedon's subjection in the past.[79] Either Arrian
or, for that matter, Alexander could take an item of Athenian
propaganda and contrast the humiliating past with the glori-
ous present.

The final statement about the Corinthian League is more
problematic. Factually it is correct and, I would argue, the title
ἡγεμὼν αὐτοκράτωρ is authentic.[80] But the body which elected
Philip is termed 'all the rest of Greece', and, as the text stands,
the contrast is with the Peloponnese, explicitly named in the
previous clause. That cannot be. Philip was appointed leader of
the Hellenic expedition by all Greeks inside and outside the
Peloponnese, and there is either inaccuracy or misstatement.
One explanation might be that Arrian followed a source which
recorded the invasion of Laconia and the abstention of the
Spartans from the League charter and contracted what he
read,[81] inferring that all the Peloponnese held aloof. More
probably (as Kornemann thought) 'the rest of Greece' is used
as a technical term, meaning southern Greece *apart from
Macedon*. The expression is used unambiguously elsewhere in
Arrian and recurs in a number of Hellenistic contexts.[82]
Originally this phraseology must have been framed in Macedon or at Macedonian instigation, to counter the propaganda
that Macedonians were non-Hellenic barbarians and to suggest
that the country was an integral part of Greece. Such an ideology was alien to Arrian, who elsewhere makes an automatic

---

[78] For the evidence see Hammond, *History of Macedonia* i. 116–19.

[79] Dem 3. 24, 7. 12, 11. 16. Didymus allegedly proved that the Macedonians paid
tribute in his (lost) commentary on Demosthenes *On the Crown* (Didym. *in Dem.* col. 12.
35–7).

[80] For discussion see *HCArr.* i. 48 f.; Griffith, *History of Macedonia* ii. 630.

[81] Arrian was well aware of the Spartan refusal (i. 1. 2, 16. 7) and should not have
garbled the sense through ignorance (but note his confusion over the site of
Gaugamela—p. 78, above).

[82] Arr. ii. 14. 4 εἰς Μακεδονίαν καὶ εἰς τὴν ἄλλην Ἑλλάδα; cf. Polyb. vii. 9. 3–7, *SIG*³
680 (both Macedonian contexts). The parallels tell against the theory that ἄλλην at ii.
14. 4 is simply pleonastic (as μὴ ὅτι τὸ Μακεδονικὸν ἀλλὰ καὶ τῶν ἄλλων ξένων at
iii. 26. 4). Cf. Schachermeyr, *Alexander der Grosse* 667–71, *contra* Instinsky, *HZ* 174
(1952) 560; Badian, *Studies in the History of Art* 10 (Washington, 1982) 51 n. 72.

contrast between Greeks and Macedonians,[83] as he does in the previous sentence, where the conquest of Phocis is said to have made a highway out of the road to Hellas (vii. 9. 4). If he used the expression 'the rest of Greece' to denote the lands south of Macedon, then he must have borrowed it from some inter-mediate source.[84] The same applies if there is an implicit refer-ence to Spartan recalcitrance: unless there is a lacuna in the text, Arrian has perpetrated an incompetent abridgement of a longer account. It looks as though the review of Philip's career was not his unaided composition but taken from some report in his sources.

The impression is strengthened when we note that the next item in the speech is Alexander's review of his own achieve-ments, which begins with material common to Curtius, the figures for his resources and indebtedness at the start of his reign.[85] I would conclude that Arrian had a vestigial report of the Opis speech which began with a brief review of Philip's suc-cesses and contrasted them with Alexander's even greater tri-umphs. This synopsis was elaborated by transforming Philip into the creator of Macedonian society and developing Alex-ander's catalogue of triumphs into a complex thesis that all his efforts were for the profit of his subjects. The whole speech, as we have amply seen, is a display piece, echoing the simpler model of Xenophon and reworking themes already expounded in the historical narrative. The original nucleus cannot be traced to any specific source. Either Ptolemy or Aristobulus could have given some suggestion of the content of Alexander's harangue; and the similarity with Curtius' narrative (which is clearly based on the vulgate tradition) indicates a measure of agreement in the original sources—the king arraigned his troops for rank ingratitude and dismissed them in contempt. That we may well believe. But the greater part of the speech in

[83] Most explicitly and strikingly at ii. 10. 7 and iv. 11. 7. Other instances are noted by Brunt, *Arrian* i. xxxvii, n. 33.

[84] There is a reference in the sentence to the κοινόν of Macedonians. Possibly Arrian's source referred simply to Philip's appointment as *hegemon* of Macedon and the rest of Greece (as ii. 14. 4). Arrian then superimposed the theme of the election being in the interests of all Macedonians at large (echoing, as Brunt notes, the words of Cyrus in Xenophon [*Cyrop.* i. 5. 8] ). That modified the sense, but the reference to 'the rest of Greece' was left in isolation without the immediate contrast with Macedon.

[85] See above, p. 102.

Arrian can be shown to be rhetorical elaboration. Neither in its shape nor in its detailed content can it bear any relation to what was actually said by Alexander.

## CALLISTHENES ON *PROSKYNESIS*

A complete contrast to the Opis harangue is Callisthenes' speech opposing the introduction of *proskynesis* (iv. 11. 1–9). This is part of a debate staged at a symposium at Bactra in the spring of 327. Arrian's story begins with an address by the sophist Anaxarchus, which he reports in *oratio obliqua*. Alexander's achievements are extolled as surpassing those of Dionysus and Heracles, and it is claimed that the king deserves divine honours at the hands of the Macedonians even more than his great forebears. Callisthenes' reply, reported directly, closed the debate and forced the king to drop the whole issue of *proskynesis*. The same story recurs in Curtius (viii. 5. 5–22), who agrees that Callisthenes led the opposition but names Agis of Argos and Cleon of Sicily as the sponsors of the proposal.

The entire tradition of the debate has regularly been denounced as apocryphal,[86] for two reasons. In the first place the debate is part of a wider controversy over the deification of Alexander. It is a popular view that the introduction of *proskynesis* had wholly secular motives, to impose Persian ceremonial on all subjects, Greeks and orientals alike. On this interpretation the act of *proskynesis* did not imply that the man honoured was conceived as divine, and nobody offering *proskynesis* to Alexander would think that he was performing a cult act. Secondly there is an anecdotal report, deriving from Alexander's chamberlain, Chares of Mytilene.[87] Here the ceremony takes place at a small symposium, and there are no speeches. Each guest at the party offered *proskynesis* in turn and received a kiss from the king. Callisthenes avoided the act, was detected and denied his kiss. This is a circumstantial story,

---

[86] e.g. T. S. Brown, *AJP* 70 (1949) 240–4; J. P. V. D. Balsdon, *Historia* 1 (1950) 372–9; Hamilton, *Plut. Al.* 150; Brunt, *Arrian* i. 536–8. More recently the tradition has been accepted as fundamentally correct: L. Edmunds, *GRBS* 12 (1971) 386–90; E. Badian, in *Ancient Macedonian Studies in Honor of Charles F. Edson* (ed. Dell and Borza: Thessaloniki, 1981) 28–32, 48–54; P. Goukowsky, *Essai sur les origines du mythe d'Alexandre* i. 47–9.

[87] Plut. *Al.* 54. 4–6; Arr. iv. 12. 3–5 ( = *FGrH* 125 F 18).

derived from a contemporary source, and it has been held to be inconsistent with the tradition of the debate.

Neither argument is satisfactory. Both the traditions recur in Plutarch; first the public occasion at which Callisthenes expressed the objections of the elder Macedonians, deterring the king from introducing *proskynesis*, and then the extract from Chares. There is no suggestion that the stories are mutually exclusive, and they are certainly not so.[88] The ceremony described by Chares was small in scale, confined to people who had supposedly expressed a prior desire to do *proskynesis*,[89] and it was largely successful. Only Callisthenes baulked, and his refusal was unobtrusive. This experiment may have encouraged the king to choreograph a more public display at a formal banquet. Then it was Callisthenes' opposition, forthright and uncompromising, which won the approval of the Macedonian traditionalists and put a stop to the entire project. Secondly there can be little doubt that most Greeks of Alexander's day *were* scandalized by the act of *proskynesis*. It had many connotations, all offensive, and one of them was religious. Whether performed in standing or kneeling position, it was an act associated in Greek contexts with worship.[90] Whatever the political intentions behind the innovation, a Greek would inevitably associate the act of *proskynesis* with formal acts of worship.[91]

We may accept that Alexander's divinity was repeatedly discussed at court during the years of the Sogdian campaigns. It is

[88] Plut. *Al.* 54. 3–6 (the tradition of the debate is recorded very briefly). I cannot accept Badian's argument (n. 86 above, 50–1) that Chares' story is tainted, presented with a bias against Callisthenes, to trivialize his opposition. No doubt Chares had no love for Callisthenes and did not wish to cast him in a heroic role, and he *may* have omitted the story of the debate. But nothing excludes his account of the symposium being factual, the details basically correct. Other sources concentrated on the more important and public debate. Goukowsky's view (i. 47) that two different scenes in the same drama are at issue seems to me the right one, but I would argue that the symposium of Chares comes first. It is agreed that Callisthenes' public opposition resulted in the abandonment of any attempt to impose *proskynesis* (Arr. iv. 12. 1; Plut. *Al.* 54. 3; Justin xii. 7. 3). After that the ceremony described by Chares would have been a gross charade.

[89] Arr. iv. 12. 3 πρὸς οὕστινας ξυνέκειτο αὐτῷ τὰ τῆς προσκυνήσεως. This may indeed be an implicit hit at Callisthenes.

[90] On the act of *proskynesis* at the Persian court see E. Bickerman, *PdP* 18 (1963) 241–55; R. N. Frye, *Iranica Antiqua* 9 (1972) 102–7. On Greek modes of worship see particularly F. T. von Straten, 'Did the Greeks Kneel before their Gods?', *Bulletin Antieke Beschaving* 49 (1974) 159–89.

[91] See the pointed and pertinent remarks of Badian (above, n. 86) 53.

a thematic strand in both Arrian and Curtius. According to
Arrian the quarrel with Cleitus began with an adverse comparison between Alexander's achievement and those of the
Dioscuri and Heracles, and it was insinuated that only the
malignity of contemporaries prevented adequate recognition of
the services of living men.[92] This first stage of the quarrel is not
recounted in detail elsewhere; but Plutarch (*Al.* 50. 1) confirms
that its occasion was a sacrifice to the Dioscuri and, given Alexander's known emulation of the heroes of the past,[93] some
comparison of their respective merits was not out of place. The
topic reappears in the staging of the *proskynesis* debate. The
arguments of the flatterers at Cleitus' banquet are exactly
reproduced in the introductory speech of Cleon, as presented
by Curtius, and there is the same emphasis on the envy of contemporaries for the success of the living.[94] Similarly in Arrian
(iv. 10. 6–7) Anaxarchus repeats the adverse comparison and
stresses the necessity to recompense present benefits with
present honours.

This thematic link certainly comes from the original sources,
but it is an unresolved question what specific source (or
sources) provided Arrian's narrative base for these chapters.
Aristobulus can probably be excluded, for he said nothing
about the origins of the quarrel with Cleitus,[95] and so cannot
have retailed the flatterers' comments about the Dioscuri. It is
not intrinsically impossible that Ptolemy himself is at the base
of the story. Arrian does not cite him for variants, but on the
other hand he does not suggest that he said nothing about the
Cleitus affair or about *proskynesis*; and Arrian does note his
silence on occasion.[96] He certainly did state as fact Callis-

---

[92] Arr. iv. 8. 1–3. Cf. *Greece & the E. Mediterranean* 62–4.

[93] On this trait, already celebrated in Callisthenes' account of the visit to Siwah
(*FGrH* 124 F 14a), see Brunt, *Greece & Rome* 12 (1965) 209; *Arrian* i. 464–6; Edmunds
(above, n. 86) 369–81.

[94] Curt. viii. 5. 8 and 11: *ne Herculem quidem et Patrem Liberum prius dicatos deos quam
vicissent secum viventium invidiam.*

[95] Arr. iv. 8. 9 = Aristobulus, *FGrH* 139 F 29.

[96] e.g. vi. 28.2, vii. 14. 3, on which see ch. 4. It is usually assumed that Ptolemy found
both the Cleitus affair and the introduction of *proskynesis* too embarrassing to mention
(e.g. Schwartz, *RE* ii. 1240; Strasburger, *Studien* 126) but that is totally subjective. One
might equally argue (with Kornemann 139 and Pearson, *LHA* 191 n. 20) that the episodes were too celebrated to be ignored in any chronicle of the reign. Unfortunately
Kornemann's attempts to trace Ptolemy's hand under Arrian's terminology can be
plausible only to the converted.

thenes' complicity in the Pages' conspiracy,[97] and might be expected to have explained the background and the reasons for his enmity against Alexander. On the other hand it is hard to envisage that the man who institutionalized the cult of the king in Egypt also retailed an account which depicted resistance to the very idea of ruler-worship. It is perhaps best to attribute the tradition of the debate to Arrian's secondary sources, which did explain the rift between Alexander and his historian (iv. 14. 1) and may well have given an account unflattering to the king, stressing the effects of adulation and identifying a circle at court which consistently assimilated him to the gods. At all events this account resembles the vulgate tradition in Curtius and cannot be lightly dismissed.

There is, as we have seen, considerable agreement between Arrian and Curtius as regards the setting of the debate. In form there is also some similarity between the two accounts. A brief summary of the case for deification is given in *oratio obliqua*, and it is then refuted in a direct speech by Callisthenes. Arrian's version concentrates more explicitly on the contrast between Alexander and the recognized gods. Anaxarchus is made to say that the king deserved worship because of his achievements and because (unlike Dionysus and Heracles) he was Macedonian-born. He should therefore receive divine honours now, rather than wait until his translation to the heavens. Callisthenes' reply is an uncompromising statement of the absolute gulf between human and divine honours. He goes on to attack the very institution of *proskynesis* as a creation of barbarian arrogance, inappropriate for Greeks or Macedonians—or for a Hellenic king. Curtius' version is more concentrated. His Callisthenes admits that Alexander will eventually be deified but insists that such honour is premature in his lifetime. Even Heracles and Dionysus (*sic*) had to shuffle off their mortal coil before their admission to heaven. There is a warning that a human assembly can no more make a god than it can a king, and the speech concludes with a secular objection to *proskynesis*: the victors should not learn court etiquette from the vanquished.

Some of this corresponds to material in Arrian. Both authors point the analogy between creating kings and creating gods, and both express repugnance at the barbarian nature of *prosky-nesis*. But there is one fundamental difference. Arrian's Callisthenes will have no truck with any divine honours offered to a mortal (iv. 11. 2–14), whereas in Curtius he is not only prepared to accept such honours after Alexander's death but confidently expects them. That is anachronistic, a retrojection of the intellectual attitudes of the early principate. Then the conventions of apotheosis did insist that the formal, officially sanctioned cult be withheld until the emperor's death, and Curtius' language echoes a *topos* of Roman literature from Horace's *serus in caelum redeas* onwards.[98] The best commentary is probably Tacitus' report of the proposal by Anicius Cerealis to build a temple at public expense for *divus Nero*. This he moved on the grounds that the emperor had exceeded mortal stature and deserved the worship of mankind, but, even so, the proposal failed because of its implications of premature decease: 'for divine honours are not paid to an emperor before he has ceased to live among men'.[99] That corresponds exactly to Curtius' formulation: *hominem consequitur aliquando, nunquam comitatur divinitas* (viii. 5. 16). It was a concept alien to the early Hellenistic world, in which the voting of divine honours (as opposed to a hero-cult, which might well be assigned to mortals after death[100]) took place within the lifetime of the person honoured. As the Athenian votes in honour of Antigonus and Demetrius show only too clearly,[101] it was the temporal power of the living ruler that was assimilated to the divine. Curtius' observations are cast in a different mode of thought, in a context where deification of the dead ruler was the norm.

Arrian's version of Callisthenes' speech is totally different in content and flavour. There is no indication that he would toler-

---

[98] Hor. *Odes* i. 2. 45. For the numerous parallels see the commentary *ad loc.* by Nisbet and Hubbard.

[99] Tac. *Ann.* xv. 74. 3. The same sentiment in Tertullian (*Apol.* 34. 4): *maledictum est ante apotheosin deum Caesarem nuncupari.*

[100] On the hero-cult and its distinction from divine honours see particularly C. Habicht, *Gottmenschentum und griechische Städte* (2nd edn.; Munich, 1970) 200–5; S. R. F. Price, *Rituals and Power* (Cambridge, 1984) 34. In the Roman period hero-cults are only attested for recently deceased princes, such as Lucius Caesar or Nero Drusus.

[101] The evidence is assembled in full by Habicht 44–58. The hymn composed for Demetrius in 291 is particularly significant: ἄλλοι μὲν ἢ μακρὰν γὰρ ἀπέχουσιν θεοί . . . σὲ δὲ παρόνθ' ὁρῶμεν (Duris, *FGrH* 76 F 13).

ate the cult of the living or dead Alexander in any form. The line of demarcation is drawn very fully and sharply. Temples, cult statues, sanctuaries, sacrifices, libations, hymns—all are proper to the gods, as is *proskynesis*. There are rigid barriers between the honours paid to gods and those of heroes, let alone between god and man. That is a different world from that of Curtius' speech. Divine honours are categorically distinguished from the cult of heroes and from secular homage to sovereigns. None the less, so it is argued, Callisthenes' speech in Arrian reflects the thought-patterns of the principate.[102] The language echoes the formula of polite refusal which had been evolved in Augustus' reign and becomes almost a litany in imperial despatches under Tiberius and Claudius. In particular Callisthenes' opening words strongly resemble Claudius' letter to Thasos rejecting the vote of a temple; he judges that appropriate to the gods alone and will envisage only honours suitable for princes.[103] That the formula of refusal existed is certain, but it should not be pressed too far. There is a world of difference between a ruler diplomatically refusing honours which he deemed excessive and a subject such as Callisthenes insisting on an absolute divide between god and man.

What is becoming increasingly clear is that there was almost total acceptance of the ruler-cult among the aristocracy of Arrian's day.[104] The honours paid to the emperor were wholly integrated with the honours paid to the gods. Nowhere is this more apparent than in Arrian's native Bithynia. In the trials of the Christians the emperor's statue stood with the *simulacra deorum* and received the same cult acts.[105] The Bithynian mysteries involved ceremonies for the reigning emperor. Inscrip-

---

[102] Cf. Habicht 248: 'für Arrian als einen Schüler Epiktets war die göttliche Verehrung eines Menschen lächerlich, für Arrian als römischen Senator ebenfalls'. See, however, Badian (above, n. 86) 29–30.

[103] Dunant–Pouilloux, *Recherches sur l'histoire et les cultes de Thasos* ii (1958) no. 179 ( = Smallwood, *Documents . . . Gaius, Claudius and Nero* 371), ll. 6–8. Cf. Arr. iv. 11. 2. For other examples of the formula see M. P. Charlesworth, *PBSR* 15 (1939) 1–8; C. Habicht, *Entretiens Hardt* 19 (1973) 76–85. The polite refusal did not, of course, indicate official disapproval of the voting of cult honours; cf. F. Millar, *Entretiens Hardt* 19 (1973) 155–6; Price (above, n. 100) 72 f.

[104] See now Price (above, n. 100) 114–17. There is no adequate evidence for intellectual scepticism about the cult in educated circles. Even in Epictetus (*Diss.* i. 19. 26–9) emperor worship is not criticized in itself, only excessive concern for the external trappings of the priesthood (cf. Millar, *JRS* 55 [1965] 145).

[105] Pliny *Ep.* x. 96. 5–6. See, however, Price 221–2.

tions attest a σεβαστοφάντης alongside the official hierophant,[106] and Arrian as priest of Demeter and Kore (and Eleusinian initiate) ought to have participated in the rites. There were also official hymnodes, attested mostly in Asia, who were devoted to the cult of Hadrian.[107] Arrian himself was no opponent of such institutions. In the *Periplus* we find him in the hills overlooking Trapezus, refurbishing the memorials of Hadrian's visit, which included a monumental statue of the emperor side by side with altars of white marble.[108] What is more, he is clearly sympathetic to the idea of Alexander's deification. He admits that the claim to be son of Zeus is pardonable, for Alexander was at least as distinguished a king as Minos, Aeacus, or Rhadamanthys,[109] whose divine lineage is unchallengeable. Here he is not far removed from the sentiments of the flatterers at Bactra and Maracanda. Indeed he is totally lacking in sympathy for Callisthenes, whom he indicts for crass insensitivity, insisting that he should have devoted himself to the king's service without compromising his personal dignity.[110] It was *hybris* for Alexander to insist upon *proskynesis*, but equally Callisthenes' opposition was arrogant stupidity. His own attitude is thoroughly conventional, expecting moderation in the monarch and due respect from the subject. The sentiments voiced by Callisthenes, still more the manner of their utterance, appear to have shocked him, and the absolute distinction between divine and mortal honours is not a theme which he is likely to have expounded without the inspiration of his sources.

It is, however, appropriate to the lifetime of Alexander, when the barrier between god and man was not lightly transcended. Much has been made of the famous passage in Aristotle's *Rhetoric* which defines the various components of honour and places the vote of sacrifices and sacred precincts alongside

---

[106] *Ath. Mitt.* 24 (1899) 429; Le Bas–Waddington 1178; cf. L. Robert, *Opera Minora Selecta* ii. 837–8; H. W. Pleket, *HTR* 58 (1965) 338–41.

[107] J. Keil, 'Zur Geschichte der Hymnoden in der Provinz Asiens', *JÖAI* 11 (1908) 101–10, esp. 107 ff.; Robert, *Opera Minora Selecta* ii. 832–40.

[108] Arr. *Peripl.* 1. 2–4. Cf. T. B. Mitford, *JRS* 64 (1974) 162 f.; Price (above, n. 100) 70–1.

[109] Arr. vii. 29. 3. See below, ch. 6.

[110] Arrian's account of Callisthenes begins with a strong statement of disapproval (iv. 10. 1) and concludes with a succinct exposition of his own philosophy (iv. 12. 6–7, cf. 8. 5).

purely secular honours, and includes *proskynesis* in the catalogue.[111] But the sacrifices are probably heroic sacrifices of the type standardly offered to city founders in the classical period.[112] There is nothing here to contradict the basic distinction between human and divine. On the other hand we may set against it a categorical statement in the *Ethics* that different things are appropriate for gods and men.[113] Indeed Aristotle's own prosecution for impiety is itself a commentary on the problem. Whatever the actual literary form of his encomium for Hermeias of Atarneus, his accuser, Demophilus, insisted that it was a paean, and a paean in honour of a mortal was nothing less than sacrilege.[114] The accusation may have been misdirected and malicious, but it must have been based on a widely held conviction. A little later we can see the same concepts behind the criticism levelled at the Athenian honours for Antigonus and Demetrius.[115] They were seen as both servile and a profanation. For our purposes the best text is Philippides' comic lampoon on Stratocles: he was responsible for the anger of the gods, causing the frost which withered the vines and the tearing of the sacred *peplos* by making the honours of the gods the preserve of men.[116] This is of course comic burlesque (and politically motivated at that), but underlying the satire is a conviction that there is a divide between human and divine

[111] Arist. *Rhet.* i. 1361ᵃ 34–7: μέρη δὲ τιμῆς θυσίαι, μνῆμαι ἐν μέτροις καὶ ἄνευ μέτρων, γέρα, τεμένη, προεδρίαι, τάφοι, εἰκόνες, τροφαὶ δημόσιαι, τὰ βαρβαρικά, οἷον προσκυνήσεις καὶ ἐκστάσεις. Cf. Habicht (above, n. 100) 211 for discussion and bibliography.

[112] Compare the heroic honours voted to Brasidas at Amphipolis, including a precinct and formal sacrifices (Thuc. v. 11. 1) and, perhaps even more pertinently, the annual sacrifices for the dead at Plataea (Plut. *Aristeid.* 21).

[113] Arist, *NE* iv. 1123ᵃ 9–10: οὐ γὰρ ταὐτὰ ἁρμόζει θεοῖς καὶ ἀνθρώποις. The context deals with the different manifestations of munificence, which must be varied according to circumstances.

[114] Athen. xv. 696A; Diog. Laert. v. 5. Cf. I. Düring, *Aristotle in the Ancient Biographical Tradition* (Göteborg, 1957) 343 f. and (on the literary form) R. Renehan, *GRBS* 23 (1982) 253–6.

[115] The evidence is reviewed by Habicht (above, n. 100) 213–16, arguing that the opposition was based on political considerations, not fundamental religious objections. See also Badian (above, n. 86) 29–30.

[116] Plut. *Demetr.* 12. 7–8 (τὰς τῶν θεῶν τιμὰς ποιοῦντ' ἀνθρωπίνας); cf. Arr. iv. 11. 5 (τοὺς θεοὺς δυσχεραίνειν ὅσοι ἄνθρωποι ἐς τὰς θείας τιμὰς σφᾶς εἰσποιοῦσι). There is a similar line of thought behind Theopompus' indictment of Harpalus for his deification of his deceased mistress Pythionice; it is an insult to the honours of Alexander and disregards the vengeance of the gods (τῆς ... παρὰ θεῶν τιμωρίας καταφρονῶν: Athen. xiii. 595C = *FGrH* 115 F 253). The attack is of course personally motivated, but some religious conviction must be there.

honours. Were there no such belief, there would be no point in
the comedy. There was a traditionalistic opposition to the cult
of living men which continued even after such cults had
become frequent, and the substance of Arrian's speech fits that
context well.

There is nothing that is demonstrably anachronistic. The
discussion of the apotheosis of Heracles fits a fourth-century
context quite comfortably. His translation to heaven was a subject familiar from Euripides' *Heracleidae* (910–16),[117] and would
have been discussed repeatedly at Alexander's court. The
oracle from Delphi (iv. 11. 7) is not attested in any fourth-
century context. Apart from Aelius Aristeides no other author
mentions it, and the worship is elsewhere treated as a spontaneous manifestation at Athens.[118] But an argument from
silence cannot be pressed. The story of the oracle may have had
an early pedigree in Athenian literary tradition. The same
applies to the eulogy of the Macedonian monarchy (iv. 11. 6).
Its Heraclid and Aeacid origins were stressed by Alexander
himself[119] and would have had a natural place in a contemporary paraenetic speech.

But there is something more. When Callisthenes turns to the
secular aspects of *proskynesis*, he makes an emphatic triple distinction between Greeks, Macedonians, and barbarians (iv. 11.
8–9). He first invokes the Hellenic pretext for the expedition
and asks whether Alexander will return to impose *proskynesis* on
the Greeks, the freest of mankind. Next he raises the possibility
of exemption for Greeks and conformity for Macedonians and
finally speaks of confining the barbarian practice to the barbarians who originated it. The Greeks are in a privileged category, as far as Callisthenes is concerned, whereas the
Macedonians occupy a strange middle ground, partly assimilated to the barbarians. The sentiment bears a striking resemblance to some of the principles enunciated in Isocrates' open

---

[117] The general picture of Heracles as hero on earth and god in heaven is also
familiar from Pindar (*Isthm.* iv. 61–6; *Nem.* i. 69–72, x. 17–18; at *Nem.* iii. 22 he is succinctly characterized as ἥρως θεός). Cf. H. A. Shapiro, 'Herōs Theos; the death and
apotheosis of Heracles', *CW* 77 (1983/4) 7–18.

[118] Aristid. 5 (Heracles) 14–15; cf. Parke, *Greek Oracles* no. 560. For other (late)
versions of the story see Diod. iv. 38. 5–39. 2; Lucian *Hermot.* 7.

[119] Strabo xiii. 1. 27 (594); Arr. ii. 5. 9. For an earlier political use by Perdiccas II of
his Heraclid origins see Thuc, v. 80. 2.

letter to Philip written in 346. That homily ends with an exhortation to treat Greeks as free agents, Macedonians as worthy subjects, and barbarians as virtual slaves.[120] Macedonians are clearly differentiated from Greeks, explicitly defined as non-Greeks whose very survival depended on an absolute government. They were an alien people under the benevolent rule of a Heraclid king. Callisthenes' speech displays the same climate of thought. It depicts a royal house of Hellenic extraction ruling over non-Greek subjects with the subjects' full consent (οὐ βίᾳ ἀλλὰ νόμῳ),[121] and there is an implicit ranking of humanity according to the criterion of freedom. There is also the same contrast between Macedonians and barbarians. Both peoples may be under monarchy, but they respond in different ways, and *proskynesis* is the quintessence of barbarian servility. Though it might appear right to tolerate it when offered by willing barbarian subjects, Alexander should still refuse it. To be so treated smacks of *hybris* and risks the same disaster as was visited upon successive Persian kings. The flavour of the admonition recalls the Attic dramatists, notably Agamemnon's horrified rejection of Clytemnestra's prostration,[122] and it surely reflects some of the sentiment at court.

There is a strong factual content in Arrian's report of the debate. That is not to say that it is wholly based on his sources, for the phraseology is his own and some of the material may be his own addition. The list of Persian kings humbled by poor but virtuous adversaries could well be a contribution of his. At least the fate of Cyrus is a theme that occupies him elsewhere. At v. 4. 5 he has a short excursus speculating on the reasons for defeat. Retribution for *hybris* is not one of the alternatives he canvasses there, but it is a rhetorical theme which might have presented itself to him. In any case his description of the Scyths (πένητες ἄνδρες καὶ αὐτόνομοι) exactly echoes his description a

---

[120] Isocr. 5. 154. A fuller exposition of the theme at 5. 106–8.

[121] This formula may be a rhetorical commonplace (it certainly has no constitutional significance), but there is a striking parallel which suggests that the wording was in vogue during the third quarter of the century. In his famous dedication at Delphi Daochus of Pharsalus honoured his grandfather who ruled over all Thessaly for 27 years οὐ βίαι ἀλλὰ νόμωι (*SIG*³ 274 no. 6) That is exactly contemporaneous with Alexander's accession.

[122] Aesch. *Agam.* 919–20; cf. Eur. *Orest.* 1507–8; Xen, *Hell.* iv. 1. 35. Aristotle (above, n. 111) emphasizes the peculiarly barbarian quality of *proskynesis*.

few chapters earlier of a virtuous Scythian tribe, the Abii.[123] That earlier passage possibly inspired the contrast between the simplicity of the eastern Scyths and the presumption of the Persian monarch. A clearer instance, perhaps, is the sentiment attributed to Anaxarchus, that it was better to honour a man in his lifetime than wait until he was dead and the honour profitless (iv. 10. 7). The cynicism is extreme and cast in the thought patterns of the principate that we have seen so clearly exemplified in Curtius Rufus. It is unlikely in the extreme that the fact of mortality would have been underscored in a debate of the fourth century BC. The original might have depicted Anaxarchus arguing that Alexander would achieve apotheosis (like Heracles) when he was ultimately translated to heaven,[124] in which case it was unreasonable not to acknowledge his present godhead. Arrian added his own rhetorical pointing, and, almost inevitably, his language assumed some of the colour of his own time. But that is exceptional in this debate. For the most part Arrian is remarkably dependent on his sources.

### THE HYPHASIS DEBATE

The most extensive passage of direct speech in Arrian is the debate on the banks of the Hyphasis between Alexander and Coenus (v. 25. 3–27. 9).[125] Despite its length it is easily handled and responds well to the application of our criteria. There is general agreement in the sources that Alexander intended to pursue his campaign across the Hyphasis and that the Macedonian troops, demoralized by the monsoon rains, protested vigorously. Diodorus (xvii. 94. 3–5) claims that the king attempted to mollify his men, allowing them to plunder the riverain lands, and then treated them to a prepared harangue in support of his new expedition.[126] He does not report the con-

---

[123] Arr. iv. 1. 1; cf. Curt. vii. 6. 11.

[124] The terminology (ἀπελθόντα ... ἐξ ἀνθρώπων) is consistent with the usage of the early Hellenistic period. Cf. *OGIS* 4. 5; Diod. xviii. 56. 2. For the general line of thought see Habicht (above, n. 100) 199–200.

[125] See in general Tarn *Alexander* ii. 287–90 (sceptical); Kornemann 148–51 (fundamentally Ptolemy, freely adapted by Arrian; see, however, Strasburger, *Studien* i. 130); Brunt. *Arrian* ii.534 (probably Aristobulus).

[126] διελθὼν δὲ λόγον πεφροντισμένον περὶ τῆς ἐπὶ τοὺς Γανδαρίδας στρατείας καὶ τῶν Μακεδόνων οὐδαμῶς συγκαταθεμένων ἀπέστη τῆς ἐπιβολῆς.

tent of the speech, noting only that it was unsuccessful. By contrast Curtius gives relatively little of the background to the debate, mentioning the exhausted state of the army in vague and rhetorical terms (ix. 2. 10–11), but he agrees that there was a general assembly which was convened and addressed by the king. The other sources are less explicit. Plutarch (*Al.* 62. 2–6) has a brief account of the army's dismay at the reports of the formidable resistance expected at the Ganges and the king's chagrin. He gives no hint of a debate on the matter, but his narrative is too compressed for the omission to have significance. Similarly Justin (xii. 8. 10–11) records the army appealing pathetically to their king but we cannot conclude from his silence on the matter that Trogus knew of no speech by Alexander. His account of the appeals of the troops is closely paralleled in Curtius,[127] and there was probably a common source which documented a formal debate culminating in spontaneous representations by the army.

The context in Arrian is roughly similar. He agrees that the reports of the country beyond the Hyphasis inspired Alexander to advance but discouraged his men. As the complaints grew in intensity, protest meetings began to be held and the king considered it prudent to stop the unrest. He therefore summoned the commanding officers and delivered his oration to them. The setting coheres largely with that in the rest of the tradition but differs in that the debate takes place not before a plenary assembly but in a restricted council. That is the forum for Arrian's battle-speeches before Issus and Gaugamela and for the oration urging the siege of Tyre,[128] and it is clear that one at least of his major sources considered that Alexander's oratory took place before a limited public. There is no reason to doubt the setting or the fact that a speech was made. How far we can accept its content is another matter.

Once again Arrian and Curtius are the only authorities to give verbatim accounts of the speeches and there is virtually no common ground.[129] They agree that Coenus represented the

---

[127] Curt. ix. 3. 16–17. The texts are printed in parallel columns by O. Seel, *Pompeii Trogi Fragmenta* F. 97.

[128] Arr. ii. 7. 3, 16. 8; iii. 9. 5.

[129] Arr. v. 25.3–27.9; Curt. ix. 2.12–3.15.

complaints of the army,[130] but there is practically nothing else that indicates a shared tradition. Curtius' speech for Alexander is much more closely related to the grounds of the discontent. It suggests that the dangers reported ahead are grossly and maliciously exaggerated. Even if the vast numbers of elephants do exist, they will be a liability to their own side, not a danger to the Macedonians who have long since ceased to count the enemy. The ocean is close and the march there will bring vast booty. It ends with an appeal not to desert him on the eve of his triumph, which will equal the achievement of Heracles and Dionysus. Arrian gives a more general exposition, praising the hardships which have brought empire, claiming that there is no end to hardship in prospect and that the hardships, like the rewards, are shared by king and army alike. The similarities with Curtius are incidental. Both state that the Ocean is at hand,[131] but in Arrian the gaining of the Ocean is merely the prelude to a vastly expanded programme of conquest. Arrian also mentions Dionysus and Heracles, but insists that their achievements are already surpassed.[132] Similarly he discounts the dangers ahead but without any reference to the elephants.[133] Two more dissimilar speeches could hardly have been composed for the situation.

The speech of Coenus shows slightly more similarity. Both versions stress the weariness and demoralization of the army, but Curtius again refers more directly to the immediate situation, stressing the blunted weapons and rotting of equipment, while Arrian adduces the more general factors of wounds, battle losses, and desire for home.[134] In both cases Coenus' speech is carefully phrased to take up points from Alexander's

[130] Arr. v. 25. 3–27. 9; Curt. ix. 3. 3–5 (cf. 3. 20). Coenus had been deputed to superintend the crossing of the Acesines, ensuring that the foraging parties made their way safely to the front (v. 21. 1). Like Hephaestion, who had a similar commission away from headquarters (Arr. v. 21. 5–6), he probably rejoined the army after the siege of Sangala (cf. Curt. ix. 1. 35). There is no reason to doubt that he was present at the Hyphasis (cf. Schachermeyr, *Innsbrucker Beitr. z. Kulturgeschichte* 3 (1955) 129–30; Badian, *JHS* 81 (1961) 20; *contra*, Tarn, *Alexander* ii. 287).

[131] *Pervenimus ad solis ortum et Oceanum* (Curt. ix. 2. 26); ἔστε ἐπὶ ποταμόν τε Γάγγην καὶ τὴν ἑῴαν θάλασσαν (Arr. v. 26. 1).

[132] Arr. v. 27. 5; cf. Curt. ix. 2. 29: *ne infregeritis in manibus meis palmam, qua Herculem Liberumque patrem, si invidia afuerit, aequabo.*

[133] Arr. v. 25. 6; contrast Curt. ix. 2. 14–21.

[134] Curt. ix. 3. 10 (details taken from his narrative source, repeated in Diod. xvii. 94. 2); Arr. v. 27. 6.

preceding oration. Curtius observes that the elephants, even if the numbers are exaggerated, will prove a formidable obstacle in the troops' present condition and points out that the Ocean is more clearly accessible to the south (ix. 3. 12–14). Arrian takes up the concepts of πέρας and πόνοι (cf. 26. 1) as well as the theme of world conquest. Unlike the parallel versions of the Opis speech there is no common nucleus of content and it seems that there was no generally accepted tradition of what was said at the Hyphasis.

There is one interesting exception. Curtius gives Alexander a second speech after his first is received with sullen silence. The king now protests that he will go on alone with his Bactrians and Scythians. The rest can go home rejoicing, leaving their king deserted (ix. 2. 31–4). This wretched rhetoric is clearly influenced by the peroration of the Opis speech,[135] but it is a more highly coloured version of what Arrian reports of a second council (v. 28. 2). This was called the day after the first abortive meeting, and the king in high wrath insisted that he would continue but would force no Macedonian to follow him. Those who were willing would join him and those who wished to return could do so and report that they had deserted their king in the face of the enemy. Now this speech is given in abbreviated form, in *oratio obliqua*, and there is every reason to think that its substance is taken from Arrian's source.[136] The material was reused later in the peroration to the Opis speech (vii. 10. 5–7), but the sentiment is different. At the Hyphasis Alexander dismisses any who wish to leave, confident that volunteers will remain, whereas at Opis he dismisses the whole army.[137] The difference in phrasing reflects the changed situation.[138] At Opis

---

[135] Cf. Curt. x. 2. 27–9; Arr. vii. 10. 5–7.

[136] An explicit citation from Ptolemy occurs in the immediate sequel (v. 28. 4). It is often argued that Ptolemy's contribution to Arrian's account of the affair is limited, and Jacoby (*FGrH* 138 F 23) began his extract after the report of the second meeting (cf. Brunt, *Arrian* ii. 532). But Arrian is clearly isolating a single detail which he found suspicious (the providentially unfavourable results of the sacrifice before the crossing), and the incident is integral to the context. It is not cited as a variant. Most probably the entire context of v. 28 comes from Ptolemy. It reads as a unified narrative and the report of Alexander's speech at the second council is embedded in it.

[137] Arr. vii. 10.5—ἄπιτε πάντες; Curt. x. 2. 27—*neminem teneo.*

[138] Cf. Brunt, *Arrian* ii. 92–3 n. 1.

he was openly coercing his Macedonians and threatening them with supersession by his oriental troops, whereas there was an element of bluff at the Hyphasis. Alexander grandiloquently made a free offer of discharge, in the expectation that his offer would be refused and the resistance would collapse. As the event proved, he was mistaken, but there is every reason to believe that he indulged his feelings in the way reported by Arrian. The substance is repeated, with crude rhetorical embellishments, in Curtius, and the agreement is evidence that some at least of Alexander's words were remembered and recorded. By contrast the complete divergence in content in the reports of the earlier oration suggests that there was no common tradition.

The impression is reinforced when one looks at the details of Arrian's speeches. They abound in *topoi*, which are easily paralleled in the literature of rhetoric. The most interesting material comes from the Elder Seneca, who records various attempts at the famous declamatory subject of Alexander deliberating whether to sail the Ocean.[139] L. Cestius Pius made a systematic division of the subject, beginning with the theme that Alexander had won enough glory and should pause to organize his conquests and moving to an appeal to consider first his army, exhausted by success, and secondly his mother.[140] The division is exactly that of Coenus' speech: Alexander and his men have achieved their glory and should put a term to it (27. 4). The army is demoralized and decimated and all desire their homes. The king should return to see his mother and settle the affairs of Greece (27. 7). That corresponds nicely to Cestius' scheme and opens the possibility that Arrian was more influenced by rhetorical practice in his own day than by any contemporary report of the speeches. Other elements from the declamatory tradition recur in Arrian. It was fashionable to speculate on the nature of the Ocean (*Suas.* 1. 4), and the enumeration *ad nauseam* of Macedonian victories was obviously a recurrent

---

[139] Sen. *Suas.* 1: *Deliberat Alexander an Oceanum naviget* (cf. Quint. *Inst.* iii. 8. 16). The debate had a direct influence on Curtius, who repeats some of the *topoi* (ix. 4. 16–22) just before his account of the southern Ocean.

[140] Sen. *Suas.* 1. 8: *satis gloriae quaesitum; regenda esse et disponenda quae in transitu vicisset; consulendum militi tot victoriis lasso: de matre illi cogitandum.*

feature of the debate.[141] Both subjects appear prominently in Alexander's speech (26. 1–2, 25. 4–5), as does the mandatory comparison with Heracles and Dionysus.[142]

Other themes, though not directly paralleled in Seneca, can also be given a rhetorical pedigree. The *Leitmotiv* of Alexander's speech, the insistence that there is no proper term to hardships which lead to fair accomplishments, recalls Thucydides' Corinthians reminding the Spartans that it was their tradition to acquire excellence through hardship or Xenophon's Cyrus proclaiming that hardships are a relish to good things, one's ultimate satisfaction being in direct proportion to the preceding endeavour.[143] The *topos* supports Arrian's flight of rhetoric in v. 26, which culminates in the proud claim that a life of hardship for virtuous ends is pleasant in itself and the guarantee of immortality. It was a grossly inappropriate theme to air before officers and men who were soaked, exhausted, and weary with the endless pursuit of glory.[144] Alexander may have been insensitive enough to enlarge upon it in such a bombastic fashion, but we cannot assume it. The evidence so far adduced suggests that the rhetoric is Arrian's and is more influenced by the declamations of the schools than by the immediate historical context.

As has been already documented, there is a large amount of thematic material in Alexander's Hyphasis speech which is elaborated and varied in the later Opis speech. But the great bulk of the speeches is closely linked to the surrounding narrative. Alexander's confident prediction that the Indians beyond the Hyphasis would submit or vacate their lands (25. 6) reflects the military situation described repeatedly in the previous chapters,[145] and the references to Nysa and Aornus clearly re-

---

[141] Sen. *Contr.* vii. 7. 19: *et alteri, cum descriptis Alexandri victoriis, gentibus perdomitis, novissime poneret 'quosque invicte?', exclamavit Cestius: 'tu autem quousque?'*

[142] Arr. v. 26. 5: cf. Sen. *Suas.* 1. 1. 2 (*ultra Liberi patris trophaea constitimus*); Curt. ix. 4. 21.

[143] Thuc. i. 123. 1 (πάτριον γὰρ ὑμῖν ἐκ τῶν πόνων τὰς ἀρετὰς κτᾶσθαι); cf. ii. 63. 1. Xen. *Cyrop.* vii. 5. 80 (ἐκεῖνο δεῖ καταμαθεῖν ὅτι τοσούτῳ τἀγαθὰ εὐφραίνει ὅσῳ ἂν μᾶλλον προπονήσας τις ἐπ' αὐτὰ ἴῃ· οἱ γὰρ πόνοι ὄψον τοῖς ἀγαθοῖς).

[144] According to Kornemann (150) the nucleus of the speech is calculated to suit the psyche of the common soldier.

[145] Cf. v. 20. 3–4, 21. 3 and 6. Note particularly Alexander's actions after the siege of Sangala (v. 24. 7–8), immediately before the army reached the Hyphasis.

capitulate the earlier narrative.[146] Two details in Coenus' speech
have been considered aberrant. The statement that the Thes-
salian cavalry were dismissed from Bactra (27. 5) conflicts at
first sight with Arrian's earlier account of the demobilization at
Ecbatana, and Krüger resorted to emendation to restore consistency.[147] But the reference is clearly to the later demobilization, at the Oxus, of the Thessalians who had re-enlisted
voluntarily at the Median capital.[148] Bactra was relatively close
to the Oxus, and in any case Arrian can use the name in a
broad sense, to denote the satrapy of Bactria in general (at vii.
16. 3, for instance, the Oxus itself is said to flow ἐκ Βάκτρων).[149]
There is no inaccuracy here, only a casual reference to an event
already recorded. Admittedly Arrian did not explain the discharge in his narrative[150] but the explanation is clearly imposed
by the rhetoric of the passage. It is necessary for the argument
that the Thessalians had lost their appetite for hardship. The
same applies to the following sentence. It is true that there is no
other explicit reference in Arrian to Greek unwillingness to remain in the newly founded cities, but there are several passages
where voluntary settlers are contrasted with conscripts,[151] and
it was not a complicated inference that many of them were dis-
enchanted with their new domicile. There is nothing as yet that
is inconsistent with the historical narrative and could not have
been suggested by it.

The most controversial passages are those which relate to the
last plans. In his speech in Arrian the king unveils a grandiose
scheme of conquest involving the entire world. The boundary
of empire will be the circumambient ocean which is the boundary of earth itself (v. 26. 1–2). Now the terminology in which

---

[146] v. 26. 5; cf. v. 1. 1–2; iv. 28. 1–2, 30. 4.

[147] Ct. Arr. iii. 19. 3. Krüger's emendation is implicitly approved by Abicht and
Roos. See also Kornemann 151 (an embellishment on an original reference to Ecbatana);
Tarn, *Alexander* ii. 290 (an error). See, however, C. A. Robinson, *AHR* 72 (1957) 335.

[148] Arr. iii. 29. 5; cf. Curt. vii. 5. 27; *HCArr.* i. 374.

[149] See also v. 12. 2: τοὺς ἐκ Βάκτρων καὶ Σογδιανῶν.

[150] Arrian notes that the Thessalians who were discharged had stayed on as volunteers; it was an easy inference that their morale had subsequently flagged. The Macedonian veterans discharged at the same time are explicitly termed ἀπόλεμοι.

[151] Cf. v. 29. 3; vii. 21. 7 (Greeks alone); iv. 4. 1; 22. 5; 24. 7. The inference was easy
for Arrian or for a contemporary of Alexander. There is no reason to think (*pace* Tarn,
*Alexander* ii. 290) that the passage was written in the knowledge of the later desertion of
the colonists (on which see, most recently, Badian [above, n. 82] 43).

that concept is dressed is unashamedly borrowed from Eratosthenes. The plan of the world adopted, the encircling ocean with its subsidiary gulfs, is exactly the plan which Strabo digests from Eratosthenes,[152] and it was anticipated by Arrian himself in his preliminary geography of India when, explicitly following Eratosthenes, he described the Caspian as a gulf of Ocean.[153] Now in the mouth of Alexander this geographical scheme is a demonstrable anachronism. Aristotle had followed Herodotus in describing the Caspian as a self-contained inland sea,[154] and the topic had become a subject of controversy in Alexander's camp, with Polycleitus of Larisa arguing that the Sea of Azov and the Caspian were interconnected.[155] By the end of the reign Heracleides had been given his famous commission to explore the Caspian and determine whether it was connected with the Euxine or formed a separate gulf of Ocean.[156] The matter was therefore still *sub iudice* in 323, and Alexander cannot have described the Caspian confidently as a gulf as early as 326.[157]

Nor is it likely that he would have referred to a world empire in terms of the surrounding ocean. Outside the speeches in Arrian and Curtius I can find no indication that Alexander considered the eastern ocean at all close. Other sources which

---

[152] Strabo ii. 5. 18 (121); Cf. Berger, *Die geogr. Fragmente des Eratosthenes* 91 ff. According to Plut. *Al.* 44. 2 (cf. *Mor.* 944B–C) the concept had an older pedigree, probably dating back to the Ionian geographers, but it had ceased to be prevalent in Alexander's time.

[153] Arr. v. 5. 4; cf. iii. 29. 2.

[154] Arist. *Met.* 354a 1–5 (cf. 351a 8–10). See now P. Daffinà, *Rivista degli Studi Orientali* 43 (1969) 370–3; P. Goukowsky, *Diodore de Sicile xviii* 114–15; *contra* Tarn, *Alexander* ii. 5–6.

[155] Strabo xi. 7. 4. (509 f.) = *FGrH* 128 F 7; cf. J. R. Hamilton, *CQ* 21 (1971) 108–10; *HCArr* i. 378. According to Plut. *Al.* 44. 1–2, this was the view that Alexander himself favoured.

[156] Arr. vii. 16. 2. The passage is usually ascribed to Aristobulus (*FGrH* 139 F 54), on insufficient grounds. vii. 16. 3 recapitulates iii. 29. 2, a passage certainly derived from Aristobulus (cf. *FGrH* 139 F 20), but the context may well be a contamination from both the major sources.

[157] Brunt, *Arrian* ii. 532, suggests that the material could have come from Aristobulus, who had forgotten Alexander's agnosticism on the Caspian question. That cannot be excluded but it is not likely. He *may* have written in his old age, under the impact of Patrocles' 'discovery' that the Caspian was a gulf of Ocean (cf. *FGrH* 712), but Strabo (xi. 7. 3 [509] = *FGrH* 139 F 20) suggests that he wrote independently of Patrocles. On the other hand the influence of Eratosthenes on Arrian is patent and explicit.

describe his plans in India mention only the Ganges and the kingdom of the Gandaridae.[158] There is no suggestion that he intended to continue his campaign to the mouth of the great river. Similarly, though it is amply attested that he had plans to expand his empire in the north, those plans were intimately connected with contemporary views of the world and depended on the identification of the European river Tanais (Don) and the Sogdian Tanais (Syr Darya).[159] It was a basic postulate that the Sea of Azov was relatively close to Macedonian conquests in Central Asia, and Heracleides' voyage of exploration was intended to elicit whether the geographical framework was based on fact. If it were discovered that the Caspian was a gulf of Ocean, the plans would be largely sabotaged, for the theory of the interconnection of Euxine and Caspian would be proved untenable. Alexander did intend to traverse the southern ocean and had already commissioned a fleet before he marched east from the Hydaspes; and the idea of the circumnavigation of Africa could have been forming in his mind as early as the Indian expedition (see below, ch. 8). But it is most unlikely that the ocean featured prominently in his thinking as a boundary of world empire. That seems more a Roman concept. Pompey is alleged by Plutarch to have had the ambition to reach the Ocean in every direction that his conquests took him, and that ambition depended on the identification of the Caspian as a gulf.[160] The same motivation is suggested for Caesar's final Parthian preparations. Fictitious it may have been, but it was retailed by the contemporary Nicolaus of Damascus;[161] and the Ocean as the boundary of empire became almost a commonplace of Augustan literature, used by Livy, by the Panegyrist of

---

[158] Diod. xvii. 93. 2–4 (cf. xviii. 6. 1; ii. 37. 2–3); Curt. ix. 2. 2–8; Plut *Al.* 62. 2–3; *Metz Epitome* 68. This is fortunately not the place to discuss the historicity of these reports. On the specific question of the Ocean see Kienast, *Historia* 14 (1965) 181 f.

[159] Arr. iv. 15. 6; cf. Curt. vii. 6. 12; viii. 1. 7.

[160] Plut. *Pomp* 38. 2–3 (cf. *Mor.* 324A): ὡς τῷ περιιόντι τὴν οἰκουμένην πανταχόθν 'Ωκεανῷ προσμίξειε νικῶν. On this passage see O. Weippert, *Alexander—imitatio und römische Politik in republikanischer Zeit* 87—9. It is usually taken as evidence of Alexander imitation by Pompey, but there is no reference to Alexander in the context and the only passages adduced for comparison are the rhetorical inserts in Arrian and Curtius which are under investigation.

[161] Plut. *Caes.* 58. 3; Nic. Dam, *FGrH* 90 F 130 (§95). Cf. Weippert, 171–5; Green, *AJAH* 3 (1978) 15.

Messalla, by Virgil, and by Augustus himself.[162] It was natural for contemporary rhetorical practice to transfer the same ambitions to Alexander and make the king deliberate whether to embark on the Ocean and leave the world he had conquered for another (Sen. *Suas.* I. I).

Against that background Arrian's procedure is easily understood. For him the debate at the Hyphasis was a debate on the limits of empire. His Alexander has no viable limits to his ambitions and conceives the Ocean as the only possible boundary. That is Arrian's own conception of the king's imperialistic endeavours—no end to conquest and, if no other rival remained, he would compete with himself.[163] He takes the sentiment and its context, the plans of conquest in the west, and grafts them onto the debate at the Hyphasis. Alexander announces his plans to circumnavigate Africa and annex the western Mediterranean but the plans are embedded in a still more grandiose context, the expansion of the empire to the Ocean in every direction. In reply to this *bravura* display of megalomania Arrian's Coenus adopts an appropriately respectful tone.[164] The king's achievements are unmatched and unmatchable but his men are of weaker stuff and must be replaced by new blood. There must be a temporary respite to the programme of conquest but then it can continue in whatever direction Alexander wishes. Arrian again anticipates his exposition of the western plans and his Coenus envisages campaigns against Carthage

---

[162] Livy xxxvi. 17. 15 (L. Valerius Flaccus in 191 BC); Pan. Mess. 148–52 (cf. Virg. *Catal.* 9. 54). Virgil's fullest statement is *Aen.* vii. 100–1 (*omnia sub pedibus, qua sol utrumque recurrens | aspicit Oceanum, vertique regique videbunt*), amplifying the brief announcement at *Aen.* i. 287. Ovid also invokes the concept of the eastern and western Ocean in his encomium of Augustus (*Met.* xv. 829–31: *quid tibi barbariem gentesque ab utroque iacentes | Oceano numerem? quodcumque habitabile tellus | sustinet huius erit*). For Augustus' own claims see *Res Gestae* 26. 2. For further examples see F. Christ, *Die römische Weltherrschaft in der antiken Dichtung* (Stuttgart/Berlin, 1938) 51–3.

[163] Arr. vii. 1. 3. The sentiment was clearly in the forefront of Arrian's mind when he described the scene at the Hyphasis. He introduces Alexander's scheme of conquest with the explanatory statement οὐδὲ ἐφαίνετο αὐτῷ πέρας τι τοῦ πολέμου ἔστε ὑπελείπετό τι πολέμιον (v. 24. 8). It is clearly Arrian's comment (so Jacoby, *FGrH* ii.D 508; Strasburger, *Studien* i. 130; *contra* Kornemann 78), and sets the stage for the debate, suggesting that the idea of unlimited empire was axiomatic for Alexander. The speech that follows enlarges on the theme.

[164] That corresponds to Cestius' prescription (Sen. *Suas.* 1. 5): *nihil dicendum aiebat nisi cum summa veneratione regis*. The speech of Alexander is also well suited to Cestius' characterization of the king: *Alexandrum ex iis esse quos superbissimos et supra mortalis animi modum inflatos accepimus*.

and the Euxine, both of which figure as targets for conquest in the later passage.[165] What we have cannot be described as anything other than rhetorical embroidery upon themes broached elsewhere in the work. It is a debate upon imperial ambition which has limited relevance to its historical context and is not likely to bear any resemblance to what was actually said at the Hyphasis. Admittedly one cannot state categorically that the general sentiments in Arrian cannot have been voiced by Alexander. He may have been as loftily indifferent to the feelings of his troops as Arrian suggests. But there is nothing in the context that is demonstrably not Arrian's invention, while there are demonstrable anachronisms and a considerable body of material adopted from other parts of the work.

We must conclude that Arrian's sources gave no detailed account of the address to the first meeting or of Coenus' reply. The remarks at the second meeting, quoted in *oratio obliqua*, do seem based on the source tradition and they in turn serve as a basis for further elaboration in the Opis speech. There was no comparable report of the first meeting, or, if there was, it was ignored by Arrian. Instead he has used the occasion for a stock debate on the advantages of empire, drawing heavily on the themes and practices of contemporary rhetoric, and the speeches sit uneasily in their context. Coenus' speech at least moves somewhat awkwardly from its setting in the council of officers to become an appeal for the army in its entirety (27. 2–3), while Alexander's is an unashamed encomium of conquest for conquest's sake, with no concessions made to the fact that he has a selected audience.[166] The debate at the Hyphasis, then, is the clearest example we have of a purely fictitious composition, independent of any report in Arrian's sources. The Opis speech and Callisthenes' speech on *proskynesis* differ in that they are both based in part on material taken from the sources. In the *proskynesis* debate the themes seem derived almost totally from Arrian's immediate sources. Here his technique is not unlike his normal method of creating a historical narrative. He rearranges and rephrases but does not add significantly new thematic material. In the Opis speech there are traces of an original digest of contents, but the great bulk of it is Arrian's

[165] v. 27. 7; cf. vii. 1. 3, iv. 15. 6.
[166] So Niese i. 138 n. 5; Kornemann 149, 151.

own composition, a re-embroidery of themes previously expounded but now given a different emphasis. Some of the explanation of these differences may be found in the sources themselves. The *proskynesis* debate was reported fully enough to provide Arrian with all the material he required to refute Anaxarchus' arguments. He made the best of the themes transmitted, although he found the tone, if not the content, of Callisthenes' intervention highly offensive. On the other hand, the speeches at Opis and the Hyphasis appear to have been sketchily reported, so that Arrian needed to introduce material of his own. The question of authenticity is always difficult. To some degree we can extricate the nucleus reported in the sources and indicate the encrustation of Arrian's rhetoric. But, even then, our reports are at best second-hand and it is a matter of guesswork how far even they conveyed the content of what was originally said.

# 6

## THE PERORATION
## ARRIAN'S VIEW OF ALEXANDER

ARRIAN'S work ends in a carefully contrived panegyric, extended and fulsome (vii. 28. 1–30. 3). In the ninth century AD Photius noted dryly that the author praises his hero for virtually every known virtue,[1] and the modern reader will concur heartily. After recording Alexander's death and the length of his reign Arrian embarks on a catalogue of the king's excellences, phrased consistently in the superlative. Qualities of mind balance bodily virtues (28. 1). In rapid succession Alexander is characterized as a brilliant, almost prophetic, strategist, an inspiring and successful commander, a ruler dependable in his compacts but perceptive of falsehood, who combined personal frugality with generosity to others (28. 2–3). From encomium Arrian proceeds to apology (29. 1–4), discounting various moral objections to the king's behaviour on a number of grounds, some of them highly sophistical. He ends with an almost impassioned demand that Alexander's actions be viewed in their totality, their greatness contrasted with the insignificance of the critic. His overwhelming achievement sets him apart from the rest of humanity,[2] proving that there was divine agency at work in his birth. There may be flaws in the diamond, but its size and brilliance are matchless, its value unimpaired.

This encomium has many peculiarities. It is extremely fulsome but at the same time strangely defensive. The chapter of apology is far longer and far more elaborate than the initial panegyric, and it is conceived in a strongly polemical vein, designed to counter criticisms of Alexander that were

---

[1] Phot. *Bibl.* cod. 91: ἐπαινεῖ δὲ αὐτὸν ἐπὶ πάσαις σχεδόν τι ταῖς ἀρεταῖς ἐς τὰ μάλιστα ὁ συγγραφεύς.

[2] vii. 30. 2 (ἀνὴρ οὐδενὶ ἄλλῳ ἀνθρώπων ἐοικώς); cf. i. 12. 4. The sentiment echoes (perhaps consciously) Theopompus' celebrated verdict on Philip II (Polyb. viii. 9. 1; 11. 1 = *FGrH* 115 F 27).

entrenched in popular thought and literature. Some of the same flavour can be traced in Curtius Rufus (x. 5. 26–36), who also gives a summary of Alexander's virtues as a commentary on the refusal of the queen mother, Sisygambis, to survive the death of her conqueror. There is a similar contrast of virtues and vices, but the apology is more conventional: the virtues come from Alexander's nature, the vices from his fortune and youth. The virtues of nature do bear a close relation to those in Arrian: *vis animi*, physical stamina, liberality, fearlessness, piety, sexual temperance. Similarly the faults of fortune are much the same as those discounted by Arrian: the encroachment on the divine, excessive irascibility, orientalizing in dress and policy (33). At first sight one is tempted to posit a common source, but there are too many divergences for that hypothesis to be sustained. Curtius' catalogue is a list of moral virtues: there is no appreciation of Alexander's qualities as a general, except for a perfunctory passing reference to his *consilium* and *sollertia* (x. 5. 31). Arrian's encomium is slanted towards the practical virtues which were responsible for his accomplishments. The moral virtues are less prominent. Some, in particular *clementia*, are notable for their absence. On the other hand Curtius is prepared to accept the vices for what they are and admits the degenerative role of fortune. He goes so far as to suggest that Alexander's irascibility and appetite for wine might have been mitigated by the advancing years (34), but that is the limit of it. There is none of Arrian's committed and sophistical apology, which comes close to claiming the vices as virtues and falling under his own censure.[3] The two passages are clearly independent elaborations of a common theme, and both authors draw upon a stock of approved virtues and criticisms which has little or nothing to do with the historical material they record.[4]

Arrian's catalogue of virtues stands in isolation. There is no attempt to connect it with the campaign narrative, and it is

[3] Cf. vii. 29. 2 (οἱ δὲ τῷ προηγορεῖν αὐτοῦ ... ἐπικρύψειν οἴονται τὴν ἁμαρτίαν); so, even more rhetorically, iv. 9. 6.

[4] On Curtius see S. Dosson, *Étude critique sur Quinte-Curce* (Paris, 1887) 203–6, reviewing other passages where Curtius gives positive or negative appreciations of Alexander's character. He admits that the final composite picture is more flattering and less complete than the earlier *aperçus*. Tarn, *Alexander* ii. 100, claimed that this final encomium 'stultifies nearly everything Curtius has said about Alexander'.

hard to see how it could be connected. Some motifs may admittedly be foreshadowed in the fuller narrative. The praise of
Alexander's talents of anticipation recalls episodes like the
march on Thebes, the advance into Uxian territory or the
stratagem used at Massaga,[5] while the description of his
creative generalship (vii. 28. 2) probably owes something to
Ptolemy's penchant for explaining Alexander's calculations in
advance and underlining how they were vindicated.[6] The
commendation of the king's temperate attitude to sensual grati-
fication also echoes the earlier encomiastic treatment of his
behaviour towards the royal captives (iv. 19. 6). There Arrian
praises Alexander's temperance in the face of all the entice-
ments of youth and good fortune and attributes it to a desire for
good repute. Two themes are linked together and are recapitulated in the final encomium, rhetorically juxtaposed.[7] But
other themes have no obvious counterparts. Arrian's narrative
certainly does not highlight Alexander's reliability in keeping
promises, and, as has been noted, the survivors of Massaga, on
Arrian's own account, had justifiable complaints against his
good faith.[8] Nor is Alexander's immunity from deception a
feature of the regular narrative.[9] Most striking of all is the
paradoxical claim that Alexander was sparing in the use of
money for his pleasures. This is at total variance with the
record of banqueting during the last years, which Arrian himself documents. I suspect that he has been influenced by his
own (and others') rhetoric. At Opis he had made Alexander
disclaim any wealth of his own and portray himself as the ser-
vant and benefactor of his subjects.[10] In general the qualities

---

[5] i. 7. 5–6; iii. 17. 4–5; iv. 26. 2–4; cf. vii. 28. 3 (προλαβεῖν δεινότατος).

[6] i. 1. 9 (καὶ οὕτω ξυνέβη ὅπως παρήνεσέ τε ᾿Αλέξανδρος καὶ εἴκασεν); cf. ii. 10. 3–4; iii. 18. 9; v. 23. 7–24. 2 ( = *FGrH* 138 F 35). Compare vii. 28. 2 (τὸ εἰκὸς ξυμβαλεῖν ἐπιτυχέστατος).

[7] σωφροσύνῃ τε πολλῇ χρώμενος καὶ δόξης ἅμα ἀγαθῆς οὐκ ἀτόπῳ ἐφέσει (iv. 19. 6); ἡδονῶν ... ἐγκρατέστατος ... ἐπαίνου μόνου ἀπληστότατος (vii. 28. 2). For the latter theme see further vii. 2. 2 (above p. 73).

[8] Cf. iv. 27. 3–4. Brunt's exclamation mark (*Arrian* ii. 298) is well placed.

[9] On Arrian's own account he was taken by surprise when the Sogdian revolt broke out, instigated by the very men he had pardoned (iv. 1. 5), and also when the Persian army cut across his rear at Issus (ii. 7. 1–2).

[10] See particularly vii. 9. 9 (above, p. 104). The rhetorical contrast between personal frugality and liberality to others also occurs in Plutarch, *de Al. f.* ii. 4 (337B). As we shall see, it was a common *topos*.

adduced by Arrian are imperfectly attested in his narrative. The inspiration for the encomium should be looked for outside his range of specifically historical material.

Some literary models spring immediately to mind. As most commentators note, the description of Alexander's skill in fore-telling the outcome of present actions is irresistibly reminiscent of Thucydides' famous characterization of Themistocles.[11] That passage, like so much of Thucydides, was deeply in-grained upon Arrian. He was to use it in a similar context in the *History of the Successors*[12] where he praises Demosthenes and fuses its terminology with echoes of another Thucydidean character-sketch, that of Antiphon.[13] But, important as Thucydides undoubtedly was, Xenophon was the greater in-spiration. One of the most impressive passages of the *Anabasis* is the sustained eulogy of Cyrus the Younger, which Xenophon places immediately after his report of that prince's death.[14] This begins like Arrian's encomium with a string of superlatives (βασιλικώτατός τε καὶ ἄρχειν ἀξιώτατος κτλ.) and proceeds with a catalogue of boyhood and adult virtues, consistently framed in the superlative. Many qualities stressed by Arrian reappear here: intrepidity, reliability in keeping promises, unsurpassed magnanimity to friends.[15] In fact Cyrus' behaviour in giving and receiving presents, as described by Xenophon,[16] could serve as a commentary on Arrian's final antithesis (at vii. 28. 3). But the praise of Cyrus is a simple catalogue of virtues exem-plified in action without the forced rhetorical antithesis of Arrian.

A closer parallel is furnished by Xenophon's most extended

---

[11] Thuc, i. 138. 3: τῶν μελλόντων ἐπὶ πλεῖστον τοῦ γενησομένου ἄριστος εἰκαστής ... ἐν τῷ ἀφανεῖ ἔτι προεώρα μάλιστα.

[12] 'Suda' s.v. Δημοσθένης = Arr. *Succ.* F 23 (Roos)—the fragment is not explicitly attributed to Arrian but it is stylistically impeccable (see, however, Stadter 236 n. 58).

[13] εἰπεῖν ὅσα ἐνθυμηθείη δυνατώτατος ... ἱκανώτατος τὸ ἀφανὲς εἰκάσαι καὶ τὸ γνωσθὲν ἐξηγήσασθαι. Cf. Thuc. viii. 68. 1, 4.

[14] Xen. *Anab.* i. 9. 1 ff. On the use of the encomium by Xenophon see G. Fraustadt, *Encomiorum in litteris graecis usque ad Romanam aetatem historia* (diss. Leipzig, 1909) 56–7, 67–70; A. Dihle, *Studien zur griechischen Biographie*[2] (Abh. der Ak. der Wiss. in Göttingen, 3. Folge, Nr. 39: 1970) 24–9. Dihle's conclusion ('Das Leben der dargestellten Personen ... interessiert die Autoren viel weniger als der Tugendkanon einer Idealgestalt', 28) applies as well to Arrian's encomium as it does to Xenophon and Isocrates.

[15] Cf. *Anab.* i. 9. 6, 9. 7.

[16] *Anab.* i. 9. 22–7.

encomium, his essay on the Spartan king Agesilaus. There Xenophon presents Agesilaus as a canon of moral virtue.[17] He expounds his hero's excellences in deliberate précis, to assist his readers' memory (11. 1), and he uses antithesis constantly, building up a climactic deluge of superlatives.[18] The similarities with Arrian both in form and in content are undeniable. In the body of the text there are successive eulogies of Agesilaus' restraint towards money and generosity to his friends (4. 1–6), his total temperance with regard to food, drink, and sex (5) and his inspirational leadership in battle (6. 4–8). All these elements have their brief counterpart in Arrian's characterization of Alexander. His catalogue of virtues amounts to a fusion of Thucydides' Themistocles with Xenophon's Agesilaus; the strategic foresight of the one is wedded to the moral excellence of the other. The form too was dictated by Xenophon. Arrian has refined the style, with more balanced antithesis and borrowings from Thucydides, but his immediate model is evident. One immediately recalls the famous passage of Book i where Arrian complains that, thanks to the genius of Xenophon, the achievements of Cyrus and the Ten Thousand are more celebrated than those of Alexander and explicitly sets up his own work in competition.[19] His Alexander could not be second to Xenophon's Cyrus or Clearchus, and his final encomium needed to surpass that of Xenophon. Surpass it it did, but only by superimposing moral virtues which had little support in the actions of Alexander that Arrian recorded.

The form of the encomium, based on antithesis and phrased in superlatives, is, as we have seen, borrowed from Xenophon. Other passages similar in style and sentiment but shorter in scope occur elsewhere in the Alexander history and were perhaps a feature of Arrian's mature historical writing.[20] If the relevant entries in the 'Suda' are correctly ascribed to him (and linguistically and stylistically they are difficult to fault), he gave shorter but comparable appreciations of Demosthenes and Craterus in the *History of the Successors* and of one of the early

---

[17] Xen. *Ages.* 10. 2: παράδειγμα ... τοῖς ἀνδραγαθίαν ἀσκεῖν βουλομένοις.

[18] e.g. *Ages.* 11. 12: βαρύτατος μὲν ἀνταγωνιστὴς ἦν, κουφότατος δὲ κρατήσας. ἐχθροῖς μὲν δυσεξαπάτητος, φίλοις δὲ εὐπαραπειστότατος.

[19] i. 12. 3–4. See above, ch. 2.

[20] Cf. vii. 22. 5 (on Seleucus).

Arsacid monarchs in the *Parthica*.[21] The latter passage is very
strikingly similar, echoing the vocabulary of vii. 28. 1–2 and
stressing similar virtues with similar (occasionally identical)
superlatives.[22] But there is something very different in the
appreciation of Alexander, and that is the defence or mitigation
of his vices. All the other examples in Arrian or, for that matter,
in Xenophon are undiluted encomia. There is no hint of anything which required apology. In the case of Alexander the
praise is emphatic in the extreme but it is outweighed by the
defence.

Is Arrian here borrowing from one of his sources, taking over
a brief already prepared? At first sight one might think so.[23]
The chapter ends with a famous citation of Aristobulus, in
which that author maintained that Alexander drank little wine
but sat up late out of courtesy to his friends.[24] Some of the
material which precedes it may also come from Aristobulus,
notably the observations on Alexander's motives for drafting
Persian troops into Macedonian units.[25] That passage takes up
two episodes recounted somewhat earlier: the admission of
selected nobles into the cavalry *agema* (vii. 6. 4–5) and the
drafting of native levies from Persis into the phalanx (vii. 23. 3–
4). The reference here is not simple recapitulation but reflects a
substantial shift of emphasis.[26] The Persian troops incorpor-
ated in the phalanx are the crack guards, the *melophoroi*, whereas
in the earlier narrative it is implied that the new levies from
Persis were simple tribesmen. More significantly Arrian terms

---

[21] Arr. *Succ.* F 23 (Demosthenes), 19 (Craterus); *Parth.* F 19 (Arsaces).

[22] The similarity was noted by A. von Gutschmid, *Philologus* 8 (1853) 439 ( = *Kl. Schr.* iii. 130) and endorsed by Roos. Note the repetition of τὸ σῶμα κάλλιστος at the be-
ginning of the character-sketch and the highly poetical δαημονέστατος, borrowed from
Xenophon (*Cyrop.* i. 2. 12) and used by Arrian in the most diverse contexts (*Ind.* 24. 5;
*Tact.* 12. 1, 35. 6).

[23] Kornemann 33–6 claimed that the last chapters were practically all derived from
Ptolemy. This 'surprising result', which he alleged was the most important of his investigation, has been unsurprisingly ignored.

[24] vii. 29. 4 = *FGrH* 139 F 62. The same tradition appears in Plut. *Al.* 23. 1, 6 (see
further, ch. 7 below).

[25] ἐφ' ὅτῳ (sc. to counter the insubordination of the Macedonians) δὴ καὶ
ἐγκαταμίξαί μοι δοκεῖ ταῖς τάξεσιν αὐτῶν τοὺς Πέρσας τοὺς μηλοφόρους καὶ τοῖς ἀγήμασι
τοὺς ὁμοτίμους.

[26] Unlike vii. 8. 2, which plainly recapitulates vii. 6. 4–5 and deliberately echoes the
earlier terminology.

the Persian nobles ὁμότιμοι, a designation which recurs only once in his work, in the context of the Persian ladies captured at Issus.[27] The word is obviously taken from one of his sources, and it was not the source for vii. 6. 4. There the Persian nobles were admitted into the cavalry *agema* alone: here both the cavalry and infantry *corps d'élite* (τοῖς ἀγήμασι[28]) are at issue. There the admission of the nobles was one of a number of Macedonian grievances; here it is interpreted as a conscious device to conciliate the barbarians and create a defence against the arrogance of the Macedonians. The latter motif occurred in the vulgate tradition[29] and may well have occurred in Aristobulus also. If that is so, Arrian used at least some material from his second source which he passed over in the earlier narrative, reserving it for his defence of Alexander.

Other themes in the chapter might also be attributed to Aristobulus, the defence on the score of youth and fortune or even (at a pinch) the crass mitigation of the murder of Cleitus. What seems to me impossible for Aristobulus is the blatantly cynical interpretation of Alexander's claims to divine sonship (vii. 29. 3). No contemporary of Alexander could view the great king's relation with Ammon as a mere *sophisma*; and there were obvious dangers in such an attitude while contemporary monarchs were making similar pretensions—Demetrius as son of Poseidon and Seleucus as son of Apollo.[30] On the other hand in Arrian's day the claim to be son of a deity was a historical curiosity, unrelated to the contemporary ruler-cult. He could discuss Alexander as son of Zeus/Ammon in an entirely neutral way, placing any interpretation he liked upon the relationship, whereas the worship of the living Alexander was a far more

---

[27] ii. 11. 9; cf. *HCArr.* i. 218.

[28] This is the only occasion in Arrian that the plural is used (the manuscript reading at i. 8. 3 is clearly false: see *HCArr.* i. 81–2).

[29] Diod. xvii. 108. 3, on which see P. Briant, *Rois, Tributs et Paysans* (Paris, 1982) 30–9; Bosworth, *JHS* 100 (1980) 17–18.

[30] For the Seleucid evidence (particularly *OGIS* 227 = Welles *RC* 22) see W. Günther, *Das Orakel von Didyma in hellenistischer Zeit* (Ist. Mitt. Beih. 4; Tübingen, 1971) 66 ff. On Demetrius see Athen. vi. 253E (Duris, *FGrH* 76 F 13). The coinage, which prominently features Poseidon, is particularly important. One series depicts Demetrius with the bull's horn of Poseidon exactly as contemporary Alexander heads display the ram's horn of Ammon. Cf. E. T. Newell, *The Coinages of Demetrius Poliorcetes* (London, 1927), esp. 65–73 (nos. 53–8).

perilous theme.[31] Criticism of the deification of the king came close to criticism of the living emperor. While such criticism might be embodied in a speech by the historical Callisthenes, to be implicitly disavowed,[32] it could hardly be voiced by Arrian in his own person.

Indeed Alexander's pretensions to divinity are rarely the subject of discussion during the early Empire. Seneca, the most persistent critic, never refers to them but selects other traits for denunciation.[33] On a less exalted level Lucian satirizes Alexander in his *Dialogues of the Dead* and contrasts the fact of his mortality with his claims to divinity. But those claims are based solely on his presumed relations with Ammon; it is not suggested that he demanded worship in his own right. And Lucian, like Arrian, is cynical about his motivation: 'I accepted the oracle for my own purposes . . . the barbarians thought they were fighting against a god, so I conquered them the more easily.'[34] That was neutral ground. Like the imposition of *proskynesis* the claim to divine sonship was remote from contemporary practice and could serve as a moral *exemplum*. That is how Arrian approaches the subject. He accepts that it was a defect in his hero to have referred his birth to the divine. He concedes the possibility that it was a trick to impose upon his subjects (which made it justifiable) and adds that Alexander had as much reason for his belief as had the heroes of antiquity. Once again Arrian seems keen to steer his argument away from deification proper. The examples that he chooses are not the familiar examples from Alexander's lifetime, Heracles, Dionysus, and the Dioscuri,[35] all of whom were in some sense deities. Instead he parades the two founding fathers of Athens and Ionia

---

[31] There are curious parallels in modern scholarship. Greek attitudes to Macedon in the fourth century are an uncontroversial subject—until one impinges on the question of the Hellenism (or otherwise) of the Macedonians. Then the debate acquires contemporary relevance and an element of hysteria obtrudes.

[32] See above, ch. 5.

[33] Cf. A. Heuss, *Antike und Abendland* 4 (1954) 88–9. Livy similarly avoids the subject of deification, castigating only the fraudulent arrogation of divine birth (ix. 18. 4). Valerius Maximus (ix. 5. *ext.* 1) talks vaguely about claims to divinity other than those as son of Ammon. His language, however, is opaque (*spreto mortali habitu divinum aemulatus est*) and need not be a criticism of cult honours *per se*.

[34] Luc. *Dial. Mort.* 12. 1, cf. 25. 2. The remarks on the 'deification' of Hephaestion (*de calum.* 17–18) are based on some intemediate source.

[35] Cf. iv. 8. 3, 10. 6—7 with my remarks (pp. 114 ff., above).

(Theseus and Ion), implicitly contrasting Alexander, the paradigm of the city founder. Somewhat more surprising is the selection of the three judges of the underworld, Minos, Aeacus, and Rhadamanthys. Arrian may be implicitly recalling his eulogy of Alexander's critical acumen and perception of deceit, suggesting that his hero is at least the equal of the infallible and incorruptible judges of the dead.[36] His preliminary researches for the *Bithyniaka* may have enlarged his acquaintance with the relevant myths. At least he was to write in detail about the family of Europe, claiming (somewhat eccentrically) that Aeacus and Minos were brothers,[37] and he may already have been predisposed to think of the underworld triad as a set of full brothers, sons of Zeus and Europe. At all events the selection of parallels must be Arrian's own, his aim to show Alexander as the equal and more than the equal of the most distinguished mythological heroes but not encroaching upon the territory of the gods.

The defence of Alexander is not plagiarism. It may, as we have seen, include material from Aristobulus, deliberately held in reserve for the peroration, but the disposition is original. The problem remains as to why Arrian is so strongly on the defensive and why he spoils the effect of the catalogue of virtues by appending an exculpation of avowed misdeeds. In this he is not unique. There is, for instance, a similar passage in Aelius Aristeides' *Panathenaic Oration*, where the speaker defends Athens against conventional criticisms of her destruction of Melos and Scione.[38] To some extent he follows traditional lines, almost echoing Isocrates in his insistence that the Athenians ruled more moderately than could have been expected of them, so that their aberrations—against men who were recognized enemies—were particularly noticeable.[39] But the main line of defence recalls Arrian's challenge to the critics of Alexander. The city should not be reproached for one or two faults but the totality of her actions must be examined. If one or two are alone reprehensible, it is an implicit encomium of the rest.[40]

---

[36] Isocrates (12. 205) suggests that the trio were a proverbial paradigm of virtue.

[37] *Bithyn.* F 29 (Roos); cf. Serv. *ad Aen.* vi. 566 (*Rhadamanthus Minos Aeacus filii Iovis et Europae fuerunt*). Aeacus was traditionally son of Zeus and Aegina.

[38] Aristid. 1. 302–12.

[39] Aristid. 1. 308–9; cf. Isocr. 4. 100–6; 12. 62–6.

[40] Aristid. 1. 304; cf. Arr. vii. 30. 1–2.

Aristeides ends the passage with an analogy that Arrian himself might have envied. Like the sun and moon Athens must be judged by the sum total of her actions, which eclipses the very few deeds of harm.[41] That could hardly be closer to Arrian's position in his final chapter. There is also a common stress on the virtue of remorse, Aristeides praising Athens for her annulment of the verdict of Mytilene (310). The coincidences strongly suggest a common stock of rhetorical *topoi* which both authors deployed to combat automatic objections to their laudation. No encomiast of fifth-century Athens could avoid confronting the atrocities of Melos and Scione, and no encomiast of Alexander could evade equally standard criticisms.

Now the conventional criticisms of Alexander view him as a classic instance of the corruption of power.[42] Whether his arrogance or immoderation was inbred or the effect of unbroken and good fortune,[43] it was manifested in a series of arbitrary and tyrannical acts. The best catalogue is probably given by Livy, in his indignant contrast of Roman virtue with the degeneracy of the Macedonian king. If he had crossed into Italy at the end of his reign, he would have been more like Darius than the original Alexander, now that he had been submerged in the flood of fortune: *referre in tanto rege piget superbam mutationem vestis et desideratas humi iacentium adulationes ... et foeda supplicia et inter vinum et epulas caedes amicorum et vanitatem ementiendae stirpis* (ix. 18. 4). Livy proceeds to stigmatize his addiction to wine and his increasingly intractable anger. These are precisely the allegations Arrian tries to defend: the crimes of irascibility, the claim to divine sonship, the assumption of Persian dress, and the propensity to heavy drinking. There was evidently a standard list of *exempla* which would be adduced to enlarge upon the theme of Alexander the immoderate despot. That

[41] Aristid. 1. 311.

[42] The evidence is fully compiled, if somewhat schematically arranged, in two German dissertations: W. Hoffmann, *Der literarische Porträt Alexanders des Grossen im griechischen und römischen Altertum* (diss. Leipzig, 1907) and F. Weber, *Alexander der Grosse im Urteil der Griechen und Römer bis in die konstantinische Zeit* (diss. Giessen, 1909). A brief but somewhat deeper survey is provided by A. Heuss, 'Alexander der Grosse und die politische Idealogie des Altertums', *Antike und Abendland* 4 (1954) 65–104.

[43] These views, often inaccurately labelled Stoic and Peripatetic, are multiply attested. See the critical essays of E. Badian, *CQ* 8 (1958) 144–7, E. Mensching, *Historia* 12 (1963) 274–82, and J. R. Fears, *Philologus* 118 (1974) 113–30 (with the comments of Brunt, *Athenaeum* 55 [1977] 39–44).

comes out clearly in the work of Dio of Prusa. In that author's
attractive second discourse on kingship (a dialogue between
Philip and Alexander) the young prince appears as a high-
minded and virtuous enthusiast of Homer. However, in the first
discourse, Alexander is briefly brought on scene as the traditional bundle of vices: he would punish with exceptional sever-
ity, rage at his friends and comrades, and disdain his mortal
and real parents.[44] Once it fitted his rhetorical purposes, Dio
would regurgitate the stock description; and the choice of
*exampla* was clearly determined by the subject-matter of the
discussion.

Rhetorical convention provided Arrian with a standard list
of vices, and his defence is deeply coloured by rhetorical practice. The acts of anger and despotism are admitted but discounted on three grounds. All had been foreshadowed in the
body of his narrative. As we have seen, the defence on the
grounds of youth and good fortune was anticipated in the encomium of Alexander's sexual restraint and it was obviously a
standard theme, echoed by Curtius.[45] The argument is
strengthened by an observation on the ill effects of flattery.
Once again the theme recurs in the narrative. Darius' fatal
error at Issus is attributed to the malign effects of flattery, that
inevitable evil of sovereignty, and, more significantly, the origins of the Cleitus tragedy are traced to unprincipled flattery
by Alexander's courtiers.[46] The sentiments and wording are
echoed in Arrian's defence and they must have been commonly
used in contemporary rhetoric. Plutarch also ascribes the ruin
of Callisthenes, Parmenion, and Philotas to the insidious
actions of flatterers, the gangrenes and cancers of the court.[47]
But Plutarch's picture is highly unflattering to Alexander, who
is said to have been 'worshipped, dressed up, and moulded like
a barbarian idol'; and Arrian himself must have been embar-
rassed by the argument, which implied that his hero had a pen-

---

[44] Dio Chrys. 1. 6–7. See also the pseudo-Dionic oration *On Fortune*, 64. 19–22.

[45] iv. 19. 6 (quoted above, n. 7); cf. Curt. x. 5. 29 (*ut iuveni et in tantis . . . rebus*).

[46] ii. 6. 4 (τῶν καθ'ἡδονὴν ξυνόντων τε καὶ ξυνεσομένων ἐπὶ κακῷ τοῖς ἀεὶ βασιλεύουσιν);
iv. 8. 3; cf. vii. 29. 1.

[47] Plut. *quom. adul. ab amico intern.* 24 (Mor. 65D); cf. *Al.* 23. 7. As Brunt notes, there is
a similar indictment of flattery in Seneca (*de Ben.* vi. 30. 4–31. 12), where Xerxes serves
as the example of the despot brought to ruin (vi. 31. 1–10 strongly recalls Arr. ii. 6.
4–6). See Plut. 18 (60B–C) for another instance of flattery at Alexander's court.

chant for self-deception. If he were a prey to flattery, it was perverse to claim simultaneously that he was invulnerable to deception.

Not surprisingly, Arrian moves to a stronger debating-point, Alexander's capacity for remorse. Once more this recalls his earlier narrative, where he reprehends Alexander's loss of control and his inebriâtion but praises his immediate admission of fault after Cleitus' death.[48] The theme is now developed as the basis of the defence. Remorse does not excuse the error but it makes it more tolerable.[49] Here Arrian is at his most rhetorical, far removed from the ethical teaching of Epictetus, which might be thought to have underpinned his appreciation of Alexander.[50] The Stoa had traditionally regarded repentance as a characteristic of the base individual ($\varphi a \hat{v} \lambda o s$), a typical manifestation of his emotional instability which was the polar opposite of the unchanging virtuous disposition of the sage.[51] Admittedly from the time of Aristotle and Epicurus there had been some concession that the consciousness of error was the beginning of virtue: *initium est salutis notitia peccati*.[52] But this was a long way from the acceptance of remorse as a moral virtue. It was a *sine qua non* of moral improvement, and, according to Seneca and Plutarch, one of the primary functions of philosophy was to inculcate a consciousness of error and desire for moral improvement. But remorse was not a virtue in itself; good cannot be generated from ill, any more than a fig-tree from an olive.[53] At best Alexander's remorse at Cleitus' death might be seen as a sign that he was not beyond redemption but had the capacity for improvement.[54] For Arrian, however, the

---

[48] iv. 9. 2, 5–6.

[49] vii. 29. 2: μόνη γὰρ ἔμοιγε δοκεῖ ἴασις ἁμαρτίας ὁμολογεῖν τε ἁμαρτάνοντα ...

[50] See, particularly, P. A. Brunt, 'From Epictetus to Arrian', *Athenaeum* 55 (1977) 19–48, esp. 38.

[51] Cf. Chrysippus, *SVF* iii. 548 (οὐδὲ μετανοεῖν δ' ὑπολαμβάνουσι τὸν νοῦν ἔχοντα), 563 (so 414). See also Sen. *Ep.* 90. 34.

[52] Sen. *Ep.* 28. 3 = Epicurus F 522 (Usener). Cf. Arist. *NE* vii. 1150ᵃ 21–2 (negatively phrased: without repentance one is irredeemable), with iii. 1110ᵇ 18 ff. See also Diog. Laert. v. 66 = Lycon F 23 (Wehrli).

[53] Sen. *Ep.* 87. 25. See further, P. Grimal, *Sénèque ou la conscience de l'Empire* (Paris, 1978) 193 ff.

[54] Plut. *quɔm. quis suos in virtute sentiat profectus* 11 (*Mor.* 82A–C): τὸ δ' ἑαυτὸν ἁμαρτάνοντα παρέχειν τοῖς ἐλέγχουσι ... οὐ φαῦλον εἴη προκοπῆς σημεῖον. See further, W. Schmidt, *Rh. M.* 100 (1957) 301–27, esp. 309 ff.

capacity for remorse is an actual virtue, and he does not seriously expect improvement. There would have been more rash acts had Alexander lived, and they would have been mitigated by more repentance. As far as I can see, Arrian had no precedent for this view. He contributed a new theme to literature. Julian later elaborated it, making his Alexander apologize for his harsher acts on the ground that they were followed by remorse, 'that altogether temperate spirit which is the saviour of wrongdoing'.[55] It is, however, a highly sophisticated argument, which only the converted could entertain. Cleitus and the other victims of Alexander gained no consolation from his regrets.

Arrian's defence, despite its recapitulation of earlier themes, sits very uneasily with what went before. Most of his material was tackled in the great excursus in Book iv (7. 4–14. 4), and Arrian's moral attitudes are significantly different in that context. In the peroration he accepts Aristobulus' view that Alexander did not drink heavily, whereas in the prelude to Cleitus' death he emphasizes that his drinking was becoming more barbaric (iv. 8. 2). The two statements are irreconcilable. More interesting is Arrian's attitude to the assumption of Persian court dress. This is an episode which is not mentioned at its correct chronological place in 330. Instead Arrian uses it as a moral *exemplum*, to be reprobated or explained away. In the peroration it is a political device to conciliate the barbarians and neutralize the Macedonians, and Arrian goes some way towards Plutarch's interpretation of court dress as a symbol of political fusion.[56] In the earlier passage (iv. 7. 4) it is simply the standard illustration of degeneration into autocracy.

Arrian's attitude is interesting at a more general level. His condemnation of court dress comes in the wider context of condemnation of barbarian excess, seen at its worst in the mutilation of Bessus. Arrian was clearly shocked by what he read. One of his most appealing features is revulsion against cruelty. Though a passionate huntsman, he was distressed by the death

[55] Julian *Caes.* 325A–C.
[56] Arr. vii. 29. 4; cf. Plut. *de Al. f.* i. 8 (*Mor.* 330A) = *FGrH* 241 F30. For the development of the *topos* see *JHS* 100 (1980) 3–6. For the historical dating (autumn 330) see Plut. *Al.* 45. 1; Diod. xvii. 74. 4; Curt. vi. 6. 1; Justin xii. 3. 8.

of his quarry, and he takes Xenophon to task for his exultation in the kill.[57] The mutilation of Bessus revolted him and he reacted strongly, condemning it as an act of oriental extravagance. He appends another example of the same trait (Persian dress) and concludes with a quasi-philosophical homily: Alexander's entire career is an object-lesson that the greatest good fortune is no guarantee of happiness ($εὐδαιμονία$) unless its recipient is also endowed with moderation (iv. 7. 5–6). That comes close to the moral position taken by Epictetus, who stated forthrightly that happiness was to be found in none of the externals, not in wealth, in office, or in kingship.[58] The poverty of a Diogenes is infinitely preferable in terms of happiness to the pomp of the Great King. For Arrian also, when he comments on Bessus' punishment, Alexander is the antithesis of the sage, the type of barbarian arrogance, and his assumption of Persian court dress is one of the most notable symptoms of immoderation.

The same moral stance is evident when Arrian focuses upon Alexander's lust for conquest. He was insatiable and, if there were no other rival, he would have competed with himself (vii. 1. 4). This note of reluctant admiration is then stifled by an approving reference ($ἐπὶ τῷδε ἐπαινῶ$) to the virtuous admonition of the Indian gymnosophists who reminded Alexander of his mortality and stressed the futility of conquest as an end in itself. Arrian then remarks that the king praised the sentiments but ignored the advice, just as he had ignored the virtuous example of Diogenes.[59] Once more the passage reflects Epictetan scorn for externals. The attitude of the gymnosophists is the attitude of the sage typified by Diogenes, who treats as slaves the powerful and feared of this world—'who on seeing me does not imagine that he sees his king and master'.[60] Arrian's conclusion is conventional. The episode proves that Alexander was to some degree capable of seeing the better but was marred by his desire for glory. His appetite for fame becomes a besetting vice, marring his acquisition of true virtue. Once again there is

---

[57] Arr. *Cyneget.* 16. 5–8; cf. Xen. *Cyneget.* 5. 33.
[58] See particularly Epict. *Diss.* iii. 22. 26–30, 60–1 (this is explicit Cynic doctrine).
[59] vii. 1. 5–2. 2. On this passage and its Cynic inspiration see above, pp. 72 ff.
[60] Epict. *Diss.* iii. 22. 45–9.

a contradiction of the rhetoric of the peroration,[61] where Alexander is approvingly dubbed φιλοτιμότατος and his unshakeable desire for praise is singled out as laudable (vii. 28. 2). The canons of the rhetorical encomium were substantially different from those of popular moral philosophy.

This oscillation of values can be seen in the various works of the emperor Julian, more than two centuries later. When the context is an overt panegyric of Macedon, Alexander is the paradigm of virtue, excelling in generalship as in everything else, and his military achievement is the crown of his success.[62] Elsewhere, when the aim is to praise the virtues of philosophy, the emphasis changes and the conquests are discounted: 'Who has ever found salvation through Alexander's victories? What city was ever more wisely governed because of them? What individual improved? Many indeed you might find whom those conquests enriched, but not one whom they made wiser or more temperate.'[63] The king's lust for fame also leads to perplexity. According to one's intentions, whether praise or blame, it could be interpreted as innate greatness of virtue or excess leading to empty vainglory.[64] By this time the rhetoric is predetermined. The centuries of literary, rhetorical, and philosophical debate have produced admitted clichés, and the conventional picture of Alexander is divorced from the detailed record of his reign. This type of rhetorical moralizing is a minor but significant element in Arrian's writing. Its direction is determined by the immediate context. In particular, when he criticizes Alexander's desire for fame, his language inevitably echoes the platitudes of Stoic and Cynic moral philosophy.

A philosophical basis to Arrian's moral criticisms is less evident elsewhere, but it does leave its traces, notably in the excursus in Book iv, where the more extravagant features of the tradition are treated together. The picture of the king is at its most adverse: the indictment for barbarian arrogance is re-

---

[61] Cf. Brunt (above, n. 50) 44: 'In these passages ... he did embrace the Stoic view, but only to forget it when it came to the final appreciation of his hero'.

[62] Julian *Pan. ad Eusebiam* 106D–107C.

[63] Julian, *Ep. ad Themistium* 264D. In a different context compare *Pan. ad Constantium* 45D–46A, where Alexander's arrogance and pretensions to divine sonship are contrasted with the mildness and filial piety of Constantius. For Alexander in the familiar role of the slave of fortune see 257A–B.

[64] Julian, *ad Sallustium* 251B–C.

peated, the malign influence of the flatterers underscored.[65]
There is no denying the fact that he acted repeatedly out of
*hybris*, and Arrian regards his subjection to wine and intoxication as pitiable (iv. 9. 1). That is not far from Epictetus' observations on tyranny: it is not the victim of despotic violence who
is harmed; rather it is the person who inflicts the violence who is
in the most pitiable state.[66] Arrian does praise Alexander for
his repentance after Cleitus' murder, but he does not (as in the
peroration) claim the capacity for remorse as a moral virtue. It
is rather a sign of his capacity for improvement, in the same
category as his appreciation of the gymnosophists. Arrian, at
least in this restricted context, was not inconsistent with the old
Stoic view that the *need* for repentance is an evil, the characteristic of an unhappy and unstable *psyche*. Alexander's disposition
may have been reprehensible but it contained the ingredients
for improvement.

On the other hand Arrian is severely critical of other actors
in the drama. Anaxarchus was a moral disaster, urging that
justice was a totally relative concept, the whim of the ruler.[67]
Cleitus was to blame for his insulting remarks (iv. 8. 5, 9. 1), as,
most emphatically, was Callisthenes. Now at first sight this censure of free criticism seems a total contradiction of Epictetus'
practice of *parrhesia*, which Arrian himself praises in his prefa-
tory *Letter to Gellius*,[68] and the virtuous behaviour of men like
Helvidius Priscus and Paconius Agrippinus, who would not
compromise their ideals of the duties of their station by comply-
ing with tyranny.[69] But the moral situation is not altogether
clear-cut. Arrian has nothing against plain speaking in itself.
The edifying reproofs of the gymnosophists are retailed very
favourably, and the frankness of Coenus at the Hyphasis,
though displeasing to Alexander (v. 28. 1), is documented
without adverse comment, indeed with implicit approval.
What was wrong with Callisthenes' criticism was that it was

---

[65] iv. 8. 3–4, 9. 9.

[66] *Epict. Diss.* iv. 1. 127: ἐκεῖνος δὲ (sc. the tyrant) ὁ βλαπτόμενός ἐστιν ὁ τὰ οἰκτρότατα πάσχων καὶ αἴσχιστα. So Chrysippus, *SVF* iii. 289. It was common Stoic doctrine.

[67] iv. 9. 7–8; cf. Plut. *Al.* 52. 3–7, *ad princ. inerudit.* 4 (781A–B).

[68] *Ep. ad Gell* 2. A good example of this trait in action is the dialogue with the *corrector* Maximus (*Diss.* iii. 7; cf. Millar, *JRS* 55 [1965] 145; Stadter 25–6).

[69] Cf. Epict. *Diss.* i. 1. 26–32, 2. 12–24.

misplaced (ἄκαιρος), an act of gratuitous stupidity.[70] It is clear that Arrian regarded Callisthenes' behaviour as blatant self-advertisement. He exalted himself at the king's expense and had no concern for the moral improvement of his royal master. Arrian had recorded Epictetus' recommendation that a man should not assume a *persona* beyond his powers,[71] and no doubt felt that Callisthenes was monstrously ill equipped to take on the role of a sage at court. His motives were not virtue but self-gratification, rather like Epictetus' convert to Cynicism who considered the career of the sage a licence for promiscuous abuse.[72] Cleitus' actions were worse, *hybris* and drunken *hybris* at that (iv. 8. 7), incompatible with any concept of the duty of a subject. The correct action was to preserve one's own dignity and attempt quietly to promote the king's fortunes (iv. 12. 6). There is a flavour of Epictetan thought here. If one has assumed the role of courtier, one must play that role, not shaming oneself by flattery but without undermining the regime by ostentatious public opposition. Silence may often be the best policy (iv. 8. 5). Now, even in his most critical moments, Arrian never thought of Alexander as depraved or lacking virtue and, on his interpretation, the most punctilious Stoic would not wash his hands of him. The general attitude is reminiscent of Thrasea Paetus in the early years of Nero's reign: *silentio vel brevi adsensu priores adulationes transmittere solitus*.[73] Thrasea only publicized his objections after the crowning enormity of the murder of Agrippina, Previously he was prepared to compromise with the regime, not stooping to flattery but offering no overt opposition. That was close to the ideal praised by Arrian.

Elsewhere the moral comment has no philosophical content. The criticism of the burning of Persepolis is based on common sense, as is the shocked reaction to the letter to Cleomenes (vii. 23. 8): any man in his right senses would think the same. Similarly he endorses the general censure of Alexander's recklessness at the Malli town (vi. 13. 4), commenting that he could see the

---

[70] iv. 12. 7: ἐπὶ τῇ ἀκαίρῳ τε παρρησίᾳ καὶ ὑπερόγκῳ ἀβελτερίᾳ. For a highly unpleasant picture of Callisthenes' self-advertisement see iv. 10. 1–2.

[71] Epict. *Ench.* 37; cf. Panaetius, *SVF* i. 111–14 (quoted by Brunt, *PBSR* 30 [1975] 14).

[72] Epict. *Diss.* iii. 22. 9–12.

[73] Tac. *Ann.* xiv. 12. 1. For Thrasea's role in the first years of the reign see Brunt, *PBSR* 30 (1975) 26; M. Griffin, *Seneca: a Philosopher in Politics* (Oxford, 1976) 100–3.

merits of prudence but was carried away by the excitement of battle and desire for glory.[74] Once again the obsessive search for fame is represented as Alexander's besetting sin, a positively harmful characteristic, and Epictetus with his repeated insistence that glory is external and desire for it futile could only have agreed.[75] But there is no strong or consistent philosophical underpinning. When Arrian is moved to criticism, he assumes modes of thought that find parallels in Epictetus. The bulk of his narrative is devoid of moral judgements for good or ill. The tone of the peroration, however, is remarkable for its total absence of Stoic thought and almost revels in Alexander's devoted pursuit of glory. It reflects the values of the rhetorical schools, and the contradictions, as we have seen, are many and blatant.

The inconsistency of judgement betrays a certain inconsistency of purpose. In Arrian's work panegyric and moral criticism blend together in an uneasy union. Other writers insisted on a distinction of genres. Polybius, for instance, distinguishes his early encomiastic biography of Philopoemen from a history proper. The former, being panegyrical, demanded a brief report, designed to enhance the actions, whereas history, which contains praise and blame alike, requires a true statement, clearly put, with the considerations that accompanied each action.[76] The contrast is highly pertinent to Arrian. At one level his work is avowed panegyric. He claims to give an account of Alexander's achievements which will do them credit and is explicit that his work is a literary tribute. On the other hand there were facets of his sources' picture which he could not accept, and it was his duty as a conscientious historian to single them out for criticism. That was a commonplace of historical thinking, whether voiced by a professed Stoic such as

---

[74] This comment is foreshadowed in the narrative of the siege, where Alexander's yearning for fame, even posthumous fame, is adduced as a motive (vi. 9. 5—the sentiment is often ascribed to Ptolemy, who certainly provided the details of the account).

[75] Cf. *Diss.* ii. 9. 15, 19. 32, iii. 22. 29.

[76] Polyb. x. 21. 8. The thought is echoed (and trivialized) by Lucian *hist. conscr.* 7. On these passages see Avenarius 13–16, 157–62. On Polybius' biography see R. M. Errington, *Philopoemen* (Oxford, 1969) 232 ff.

Poseidonius or an eclectic like Tacitus;[77] and it is hardly surprising that Arrian felt it incumbent upon him to reprove some of Alexander's actions in the interests of truth and utility (vii. 30. 3). But the greater aim was the encomium of Alexander, and the peroration marks its climax. The string of excellences eclipses the virtues of a Cyrus or an Agesilaus, and the conventional criticisms are placed in perspective, flaws but not detracting from the total picture. In the last analysis Alexander's greatness depends on his conquests, for it was as a conqueror that his name had penetrated to every race and city of mankind (vii. 30. 2). Viewed in that light his desire for fame and the military qualities that achieved his fame are elevated into primary virtues. Yet earlier, when the focus of discussion was different, those ambitions could be stigmatized as supererogatory and inimical to true happiness. The emphasis and indeed the whole hierarchy of values changes with the context of discussion.

Arrian was not, of course, alone in his dilemma. Curtius Rufus' inconsistencies are no less blatant and far more numerous,[78] given his greater penchant for interlarding his narrative with moral comment. But any historian who had historical favourites and a modicum of honesty was forced into inconsistency. A particularly good example is provided by Tacitus, whose comparison between Germanicus and Alexander could almost serve as a commentary upon these final chapters of Arrian. Tacitus' portrait of Germanicus, like Arrian's of Alexander, was in general highly favourable, although there is an occasional hint of criticism.[79] Germanicus' death is the occasion for a brilliant eulogy, characteristically phrased in *oratio obliqua*, in the guise of remarks by bystanders at the funeral

---

[77] Poseidonius, *FGrH* 87 F 108u and w; Tac. *Ann.* iv. 33. 2 (cf. iii. 65. 1). Other passages are adduced by Avenarius 158–9. On Poseidonius see Brunt (above, n. 50) 35 f.; Strasburger, *JRS* 55 (1965) 47.

[78] This was strongly emphasized by Tarn, *Alexander* ii. 96–100, who thought that Curtius used two separate and inconsistent portraits of the king. Contrast the reasoned discussion of Atkinson (above, ch. 1, n. 2) 70–3, esp. 72: 'the individual story generates its own picture of the characters involved and inconsistencies may then occur between different episodes'.

[79] See particularly *Ann.* i. 78. 2; ii. 8. 2 with the commentary of Goodyear (below, n. 81).

(*Ann.* ii. 73. 1–3). The deceased prince is compared with Alexander on the superficial basis of age and fashion of death: both were physically handsome, of distinguished lineage, and died in their early thirties. But Tacitus then embarks on a *deterior comparatio*,[80] using all the standard criticisms of Alexander's immoderation and treating him solely as a foil to Germanicus. Unlike Alexander, the type of irascibility, Germanicus was mild with his friends; and he was the paradigm of moral virtue, moderate in his pleasures, content with a single marriage and with children of determinate parentage.[81] Next the historian has to face the inevitable criticism. How could Germanicus, whose military achievements were insignificant, be compared favourably with Alexander? The answer is that he had been prevented from following up his victories and reducing Germany to servitude. If, like Alexander, he had been a free agent and had enjoyed regal power, he would easily have overhauled his military glory, just as he eclipsed him in moral virtue, notably temperance and clemency.

Tacitus sustains the comparison by concentrating on his hero's undoubted uprightness. The defects of strategy are forgotten. The record in Germany was one of victory, and the only reason why no permanent conquests accrued was the malicious obstructiveness of Tiberius.[82] What emerges is a caricature of the earlier narrative,[83] an implicit denial of military error or military reverses, and Germanicus is seen resplendent as a potential world conqueror frustrated by the political limitations of his command. Tacitus of course avoids direct responsibility for the comparison, which is placed in the mouths of unnamed commentators, and it is quite possible that his sources reported comparisons with Alexander, whom Germanicus did

---

[80] The technique was not Tacitus' invention. Note Velleius' short comparison of Caesar and Alexander, *magno illi Alexandro (sed sobrio neque iracundo) simillimus* (Vell. ii. 41. 1) and (at a much later date) Julian's extended panegyric of Constantius (45D–46C).

[81] 73. 2: *sed hunc mitem erga amicos, modicum voluptatum, uno matrimonio, certis liberis egisse.* The reference to children is problematic. It may be a hit at the illegitimacy of Heracles, son of Barsine or even an insinuation against the virtue of Rhoxane (cf. Goodyear, *The Annals of Tacitus* ii. 419). Perhaps Tacitus is focusing on the notorious marital chastity of Germanicus and Agrippina, leaving his readers to entertain what conclusions they wished about Alexander.

[82] 73. 3: *praepeditusque sit perculsas tot victoriis Germanias servitio premere.*

[83] Syme, *Tacitus* 492: 'The artifice is patent, the laudation gross in disproportion— and the historian evades responsibility.'

apparently emulate.[84] But the reported comment is entirely favourable. There is no attempt to balance it with saner criticism (as was done so effectively in the report of Augustus' funeral).[85] There can be no doubt that Tacitus was favourably disposed to the views he reports, but he was sensitive enough to state them indirectly. There is no such artifice in Arrian. He operates openly, focusing upon Alexander's undoubted military achievements and his universal reputation. The moral strictures were then neutralized by a sophistical two-pronged approach. Arrian denies the validity of the individual criticisms when viewed against the totality of Alexander's achievement and he actually claims some of the purported vices as virtues. The effect and the intention is not historical appreciation, but rhetorical encomium.

Arrian saw himself in two lights, as panegyrist for Alexander and as moral critic, serving both the posthumous reputation of the king and the edification of his readers. In his earlier monographs on Dion and Timoleon there was probably no conflict, for both men were generally acknowledged as standard types of virtue and no apology would have been needed.[86] In Alexander's case there was a whole literature of invective and, while it was possible for him to discount the criticism in the rhetorical passion of the peroration, Arrian was honest enough to reflect the common sentiment in his historical exposition. In the finale, however, he speaks as enthusiast and apologist, and the Alexander he creates is as fictitious as the philosopher in action of Plutarch's first treatise *On the Fortune of Alexander*. As rhetoric it is impressive. It would not have appealed to Epictetus, in whose eyes all epideictic rhetoric was futile. Nobody listening to such performances, he claimed, is troubled about his moral welfare or moved to self-examination. Even if the speaker is at the height of his reputation, the comments go no deeper than 'a

---

[84] The question posed by Syme, *Tacitus* 771; cf. Goodyear (above, n. 81) ii. 417. The recent essay by M. L. Paladini, in *Alessandro Magno tra storia e mito* (ed. M. Sordi; Milan, 1984) 179–93, is not particularly helpful. For Germanicus' emulation of Alexander see *POxy*. 2435r. 20–1 (*EJ*³ 379), with G. J. D. Aalders, *Historia* 10 (1961) 382–4; Weippert (ch. 4, n. 96) 257–8.

[85] Tac. *Ann.* i. 9. 1–10. 7.

[86] Timoleon, however, suffers when Plutarch compares him adversely with Aemilius Paulus (*Comp. Tim. Aem.* 2).

pretty talk, that one about Xerxes',[87] Intellectually the record
of Alexander's campaigns was trivial, the classic example of the
glorification of externals, and a committed disciple of Epictetus
should have scorned the theme.[88] But Arrian had a thoroughly
conventional view of the desirability and glory of conquest. It
was better if accomplished with the Stoic qualities of moderation and temperance but it was still an eminently worthy end in
itself. In that respect Alexander was the great exemplar, the
standing challenge to all future empire-builders, and his
achievement deserved to be commemorated in literature with
the appropriate meed of praise. Moral criticism was not out of
place but subordinated to the greater end of encomium. Inconsistency was the inevitable result. Each passage when viewed in
isolation may appear logical and effective, but the total work is
a farrago of conflicting commonplaces.

[87] Epict. *Diss.* iii. 23. 33–8.
[88] So Brunt (above, n. 50) 37–9, 47–8. Stadter 110–14 is more indulgent ('Arrian,
always a philosopher . . .').

# THE *EPHEMERIDES*
# THE TRADITION OF THE KING'S DEATH

W E can now move to a problem of historiography which is at the same time a historical conundrum of major importance: the nature and authenticity of the so-called *Ephemerides* or 'Royal Diaries'.[1] Quoted explicitly by Arrian and Plutarch, this source provides a day-by-day description of Alexander's last illness in Babylon. Another extract, relating to earlier transactions in the Macedonian month of Dios, is selectively reproduced by Aelian. The details transmitted are meagre, yet for generations they were assumed to derive from an official court journal, kept by the chief secretary, Eumenes of Cardia, and drawn upon by Ptolemy as the major source of his history of Alexander. This theory was fully enunciated by Ulrich Wilcken in a masterly article published in 1894 and endorsed by successive scholars in the German-speaking world. It was reiterated in Kaerst's influential Pauly article and in Jacoby's standard commentary on the historical fragments.[2] In English scholarship Sir William Tarn insisted on the primacy of Ptolemy and the archival basis of his narrative, and this classical view has been repeatedly restated in recent years by N. G. L. Hammond.[3]

Superficially attractive with its bonus of an 'official' documentary source at the core of Arrian's narrative, Wilcken's

---

[1] The fragments are conveniently assembled by Jacoby, *FGrH* 117. For bibliography, see Seibert, *Alexander der Grosse* 5–6 (to 1970) and P. Högemann, *Alexander und Arabien* (Munich, 1985) 112–15.

[2] U. Wilcken, 'Hypomnematismoi', *Philologus* 53 (1894) 84–126; cf. J. Kaerst, *RE* v. 2749–53; Jacoby, *FGrH* ii.d 403–4. The fullest elaboration of Wilcken's doctrine was to be provided by the American scholar, C. A. Robinson (*The Ephemerides of Alexander's Expedition*, Brown University Studies 1; Providence, RI, 1932). The most recent statement of the traditional view is P. Pédech, *Historiens compagnons d'Alexandre* 246–51.

[3] e.g. Tarn, *Alexander* ii. 1, 263, 331, 374. For Hammond's views see *JHS* 94 (1974) 77–8; *KCS* 1; *Three Historians* 4–11. His arguments are criticized in detail by E. Badian, 'The Ring and the Book', to appear in a forthcoming Festschrift for G. Wirth.

theory was unchallenged for decades. Then, some thirty years ago, Lionel Pearson argued that the *Ephemerides* as reproduced in the extant texts could not derive from a contemporary journal and were a fabrication of the Hellenistic period, fraudulently issued under the name of Eumenes.[4] In this he has been recently supported by the weighty authority of P. A. Brunt.[5] There have been other approaches, notably A. E. Samuel's ill-fated attempt to prove that the *Ephemerides* were extracts from Babylonian documents[6] and my own argument that they were probably the work of Eumenes but published with limited propagandist aims.[7] The fundamental divergence of opinion fully justifies a new investigation of the problem.

## ARRIAN AND PLUTARCH ON ALEXANDER'S DEATH

By far the most important issue is the account which the *Ephemerides* give of Alexander's death. Two versions survive, those of Plutarch and Arrian.[8] They are summarized in the table on pp. 160–1, and, as we shall see, they are not only different but formally inconsistent. Plutarch's version is the more straightforward. He begins his account of the last illness with a brief notice of the festivities for Nearchus' men at Babylon and the ensuing invitation to the feast of Medeius of Larisa.[9] After a sceptical reference to the common stories of carousing and sudden illness at the feast, he records Aristobulus' disclaimer that the king only took to drink when he was already in high fever.[10] Next Plutarch gives an account of the illness, which he

---

[4] L. Pearson, 'The Diary and Letters of Alexander the Great', *Historia* 3 (1955) 429–39. F. Altheim, *Weltgeschichte Asiens im griechischen Zeitalter* i (Halle, 1947) 115–17, had already expressed some scepticism.

[5] Brunt, *Arrian* ii. 288–93 cf. i. xxiv–vi. The conclusions of Badian (above, n. 3) are not dissimilar. For a somewhat different approach see now G. Wirth, 'Ephemeridenspekulationen', *Studien zur alten Geschichte* (Festschrift S. Lauffer: ed. H. Kalcyk, B. Gullath, A. Graeber; Rome, 1986) iii. 1051–75.

[6] A. E. Samuel, 'Alexander's Royal Journals', *Historia* 14 (1965) 1–12.

[7] A. B. Bosworth, *CQ* 21 (1971) 117–23; cf. *Entretiens Hardt* 22 (1976) 3–6.

[8] Arr. vii. 25. 1–26. 3; Plut. *Al.* 76. 1–77. 1 (*FGrH* 117 F 3a–b).

[9] Plut. *Al.* 75. 3. The occasion for the festivities is the receipt of oracular confirmation of the hero cult for Hephaestion; that is recorded by Arrian vii. 23. 6 at much the same time.

[10] Plut, *Al.* 75. 5 = *FGrH* 139 F 59.

takes from the *Ephemerides* (explicitly named as his source). Beginning with the night of 18 Daesios, he gives a day-by-day report of the progress of the fever, culminating with the king's death on 28 Daesios (10 June). He adds that the bulk of the narrative is taken verbatim from the *Ephemerides*.[11] There is no reason to doubt what he says. Plutarch does not often claim direct citation. Most of the instances come from his philosophical works, where he quotes explicitly from Chrysippus and Epicurus.[12] Where the original is lost there are no criteria for assessing his accuracy, but fortunately we have a useful test case in the treatise *On the Malice of Herodotus*. There Plutarch claims to quote Herodotus verbatim, and he does indeed follow his original word for word, the few variants attributable to the textual transmission.[13] In all probability his version of the *Ephemerides* is a similar selective excerpt. It is internally consistent, labelling the days of the illness by the days of the Macedonian month, and the illness displays a regular progression. Plutarch clearly excerpted a single document, produced in book form, which he used on two other occasions as a source of information on court life.[14]

Arrian's version is far less straightforward. He introduces the illness in much the same way as Plutarch with festivities, distributions of food and wine to the army, and finally Medeius' invitation to the fateful banquet (vii. 26. 4). Next Arrian refers explicitly to the 'royal' *Ephemerides* (vii. 25. 1), recording the progress of the illness each day (but without any indication of the Macedonian month). At vii. 26. 1 he repeats that he is using the *Ephemerides* and takes two more detailed episodes from them, the march-past of the army and the visit paid by senior officers to the temple of 'Sarapis'. Arrian reaches Alexander's death at vii. 26. 3 and adds an enigmatic note contrasting Aristobulus and Ptolemy with the (unnamed) sources which purported to record the king's last words. Now the wording of the passage has evoked considerable controversy. The key phrase

---

[11] τὰ πλεῖστα κατὰ λέξιν: Plut. *Al.* 77. 1.

[12] Plut, *de Stoic. repugn.* 9 (1035A) = *SVF* ii. 42; 10 (1036A—αὐταῖς λέξεσι) = *SVF* ii. 127; *adv. Colot.* 7 (1110C–D) = Epicurus F 29 (Usener).

[13] Plut, *de Hdt. mal.* 37 (869D–E), citing (κατὰ λέξιν) Hdt. viii. 57–8. The text is quoted selectively but accurately.

[14] Plut. *Al.* 23. 4 (*FGrH* 117 F 1); *Quaest. conv.* i. 6 (623E = F 2c).

## The Accounts of Alexander's Illness in Arrian and Plutarch

| Plutarch *Alexander* 75. 4–76. 9 | Arrian vii. 24. 4–26. 3 | |
| --- | --- | --- |
| | (i) Aristobulus (?) | (ii) Ptolemy (?) |
| 75. 4 Al. feasts Nearchus' men. Before he retires, Medeius invites him to a party, where he drinks for the whole of the following day. The fever begins. | | 24. 4 Al. feasts his army. Medeius invites him to a party when he is about to retire. Reference to *Ephemerides* (25. 1) Al. drinks with Medeius and retires to sleep (day 1) Al. dines with Medeius and drinks far into the night (day 2) He sleeps in the bedroom because *the fever is already present.* |
| 76. 1 Account of *Ephemerides* introduced. Al. sleeps in the bathroom *because of the fever* (18 Daesios). | | |
| | 25. 2 Al. is carried to sacrifice. He lies in the men's room until dark, instructing his officers to begin the journey by land after three days, by river after four (25. 3). He crosses the river to a paradise, bathes and rests (day 3). | |
| 76.2 Al. spends the day with Medeius playing dice. He bathes, sacrifices and after eating is in fever all night (19 Daesios). | | Al. spends the day in conversation with Medeius, instructing his officers to meet at dawn. Fever the whole night (day 4). |
| | Bathes and sacrifices. Instructs Nearchus and the other officers to have the fleet ready in two days (day 5). | |
| 76. 3 Bathes and sacrifices. Talks with Nearchus, hearing about the voyage and the outer sea (20 Daesios). | | Bathes and sacrifices. Decides to be active despite the fever. He instructs his officers to have everything ready for the voyage. After the bath he is in a bad way (day 6). |

The Accounts of Alexander's Illness in Arrian and Plutarch—*continued*

| *Plutarch Alexander* 75. 4–76. 9 | Arrian vii. 24. 4–26. 3 | |
| --- | --- | --- |
| | (i) Aristobulus (?) | (ii) Ptolemy (?) |
| 76. 4 The previous day's routine again, in higher fever (21 Daesios). A bad night and high fever the following day (22 Daesios) | | |
| 67. 5 Al. is carried to the great pool where he discusses vacant commands with his officers (23 Daesios). | | 25. 5 Al. is carried to the house near the pool, sacrifices, and summons his officers for more instruction (day 7). |
| | Al. is carried out with difficulty to sacrifice. Even so, he gives instructions to his officers (day 8). | |
| 76. 6 Al. is carried out to sacrifice and instructs his officers (high command, taxiarchs and pentakosiarchs) to keep vigil (24 Daesios). | | 25. 6 Though in a bad way Al. performs sacrifices; he instructs his officers (generals, chiliarchs, pentakosiarchs) to keep attendance (day 9). |
| 76. 7 Al. crosses to the far palace, sleeps a little, and loses his voice (25 Daesios). The same as the previous day (26 Daesios). | | In a desperate condition Al. is transferred to the palace. He recognizes the officers but is speechless (day 10). Al. is in fever two nights and two days (days 11–12). |
| 76. 8 The troops force entry and march past their king. | | 26. 1 The *Ephemerides* cited* for the troops pressing in and filing past. |
| 76. 9 On the same day comes the visitation of the Sarapeum (27 Daesios). | | 26. 2 The *Ephemerides* again cited for the incubation in the temple of Sarapis. |
| Al. dies towards evening on 28 Daesios. | | 26. 3 'Not long afterwards' Al. dies. |

* In vii. 26 Arrian does not assign the events to days. From Plutarch it would appear that the two episodes there described belong to the second day of terminal fever (day 12).

has been translated in two very different ways.[15] On one interpretation one reads 'neither Aristobulus nor Ptolemy gives an account that is far [different] from this', and it is usually assumed that Arrian contrasted the *Ephemerides* with Ptolemy and Aristobulus. In other words there were three separate versions of Alexander's death which Arrian knew and used. On the other hand the sentence has been translated as follows: 'neither Aristobulus nor Ptolemy takes the record further than this [Alexander's death].' Proponents of this latter interpretation have tended to argue that Arrian cited the *Ephemerides* indirectly through references in his two major sources.

The question cannot be settled on philological grounds. Parallels may at a pinch be provided for either interpretation, but Arrian's general usage tells against understanding πόρρω in any comparative sense (i.e. 'further').[16] Plutarch and Dio Chrysostom, authors nearly contemporaneous with Arrian, supply close parallels for the first interpretation,[17] which must be regarded as the more plausible. But the meaning is still ambiguous. What precisely is Arrian contrasting with the accounts of Ptolemy and Aristobulus? One possibility of course is the record of the *Ephemerides* but it is not the only possibility. Arrian could be referring to *his own* account of the king's death, the entire passage from vii. 24. 4 onwards. That passage, he alleges, is based on both Aristobulus and Ptolemy; he has taken material from both authors but his composite narrative does not diverge much from either. In contrast the reports of Alexander's last words are quite distinct, unrelated to material in his main sources. If this interpretation is accepted, Arrian is not comparing the *Ephemerides* with his narrative sources but is characterizing the previous passage as an amalgam of Ptolemy and

[15] οὐ πόρρω δὲ τούτων οὔτε ᾿Αριστοβούλῳ οὔτε Πτολεμαίῳ ἀναγέγραπται. For a summary of the controversy see Pearson (above, n. 4) 437–8. Most recently Brunt (*Arrian* ii. 294–5) and I (*HCArr* i. 23–4) have opted for the second interpretation, Hammond (*Three Historians* 4 n. 9) for the first.

[16] The nearest parallel is iv. 11. 5 (πόρρω τοῦ ἱκανοῦ—'far beyond what is sufficient'). Elsewhere (*Ind.* 34. 4; *Cyneget.* 8. 4) Arrian uses the explicit comparative πορρωτέρω, and πόρρω (occurring about three dozen times) is used in a simple spatial sense.

[17] Plut. *Quaest. conv.* vii. 9 (714C): οὐ πόρρω δὲ τούτων ὁ νυκτερινὸς σύλλογος παρὰ Πλάτωνι ('Plato's night council operates in a way similar to these [*sc.* the *phiditia* at Sparta]'). Dio Chrys. 36. 27: οὐ πόρρω τοῦ ῾Ομήρου φθέγγεται.

Aristobulus and contrasting it with the less reliable reports of
the secondary tradition.

This is at first sight an extreme position, but there are
demonstrable parallels in the *Indike*, where Arrian refers by
name to Ctesias, Nearchus, and Onesicritus.[18] There the citations do not come from the original authors but from the
intermediary text of Eratosthenes. Cross-comparison with
Strabo proves that the references are second-hand. The same
may be the case with the *Ephemerides*. Arrian names them
because they were named by Ptolemy, and the passage is based
in the first instance upon Ptolemy and supplemented from Aristobulus. That impression is strengthened by Arrian's wording
when he first refers to the *Ephemerides*. The preceding narrative
is explicitly continued with the source reference.[19] It begins
with the connective καί, which elsewhere introduces additional
material from the source exploited in the immediate context.[20]
I know of no instance where it marks a transition to a new
source. The reference to the *Ephemerides* continues the narrative
begun in the previous paragraph. In theory it might be a
delayed introduction, where Arrian finally identifies the source
he has been using for the last few sentences, but the content of
his narrative makes it impossible that he is using the *Ephemerides*
directly, certainly not the version quoted by Plutarch.

The fact that the two accounts diverge has long been
known,[21] but the divergences have tended to be minimized.
Arrian, for instance, speaks generally about briefing sessions
with the senior commanders in preparation for the Arabian expedition, and he repeats the notice in what amounts to a formu-
laic pattern.[22] Plutarch is much more precise, claiming that
one meeting was a report by Nearchus on his voyage in the
Indian Ocean (76. 3) and another a discussion on the filling of
vacant commands (76. 5). In this case it could be argued that
Arrian gave the fact of the meeting while Plutarch supplied a
synopsis of the agenda. It remains true, however, that one
would never infer from Plutarch that a great expedition was on

---

[18] *Ind.* 3. 6, 6. 8. See above, ch. 2.
[19] καὶ οἱ βασίλειοι Ἐφημερίδες ὧδε ἔχουσιν: vii. 25. 1.
[20] Cf. iv. 25. 4 (καὶ λέγει Πτολεμαῖος); vi. 29. 10; *Ind.* 30. 2.
[21] See, for instance, Tarn, *Alexander* ii. 41 n. 5, 307 n. 4; Bosworth, *CQ* 21 (1971)
120–1; Brunt, *Arrian* i. xxv (retracted at ii. 289 n. 1, 'their versions are congruent').
[22] vii. 25. 2, 4 (twice), 5 (twice).

the point of departure. To be sure, Nearchus' information about the coastline around the Musandam peninsula would bear repetition on the eve of embarkation from the Persian Gulf, but Plutarch does not place the meeting in its context. Nothing indicates that the document he cites contained any explicit detail about the imminent departure of the naval and land forces, which is the chief recurrent theme of Arrian's account.

Other discrepancies are even more serious. The more closely one compares the two versions, the more obvious it becomes that their chronology is different. The illness according to Arrian occupies more days than it does in Plutarch.[23] Consider the onset of the infection. Plutarch says that on 18 Daesios the king spent the night in his bathroom because of the fever. The following day he passed with Medeius playing dice; and on 20 Daesios he bathed, performed the customary sacrifices, and spent the day in discussion with Nearchus.[24] That report is internally consistent and precisely dated. Arrian, however, has an extra day. He duly reports the night in the bathroom after Medeius' banquet (vii. 25. 1) but then inserts a day for which there is no parallel in Plutarch. The king is carried to sacrifice, meets with his commanders until dark, instructing the army to be ready for departure after three days, the fleet after four. He is then transported across the river to the paradise, where he spends the night (25. 2–3). Next day he converses with Medeius, suffers high fever overnight, and spends the following day in conference with Nearchus and other senior officers (25. 3). An additional day has clearly been inserted between the banquet of Medeius and the day of dice and relaxation, a day during which Alexander is totally incapacitated and carried to sacrifice.

The same phenomenon recurs a little later in the illness. Plutarch records a meeting by the great swimming pool on 23 Daesios at which the vacant commands were discussed. On the following day, 24 Daesios, Alexander was carried to sacrifice and ordered his senior officers to spend the night about his person (76. 5–6). Arrian has a similar sequence, but again with an

---

[23] His account is followed by Schachermeyr, *Alexander der Grosse* 560–5 with superb rhetoric but without any comparison with Plutarch's version.

[24] Plut, *Al.* 76. 3. The material is presented synoptically in the accompanying table.

extra day. He notes the meeting by the swimming pool, describing it as yet another briefing session (vii. 25. 5), and claims that the same programme was followed the next day. The day after that brought the instructions to the senior officers to stay close to his person (25. 6). Where Plutarch has two days of activities, Arrian has three. On the other hand there is one day in Plutarch that has no counterpart in Arrian, the day of high fever on 22 Daesios, which comes between the second conference with Nearchus and the staff meeting by the great pool (76. 4).

These differences are (to put it mildly) radical, and there is a limited range of explanations. It is theoretically possible that the *Ephemerides* existed in two redactions, a shorter one used by Plutarch and a longer one used by Arrian.[25] In that case it would be virtually inescapable that one version, at least, was bogus. But there is also a wide measure of agreement, particularly in the final report of the farewell of the army and the consultation of Sarapis.[26] It is also difficult to see why Arrian's version added non-existent days of illness or why Plutarch's version should have shortened its course. Given the considerable degree of overlap, it is most implausible that we have two independent forgeries. In my view the simplest, indeed the only viable, explanation is that we are dealing with an incompetent contamination by Arrian. Both his primary sources gave a report of the intensifying illness and he combined them, occasionally giving two versions of the same transaction.

The hypothesis is supported by a degree of internal inconsistency in Arrian's account. We have noted that he has Alexander incapacitated by the second day of the illness, unlike Plutarch, who represents the king apparently on his feet until 23 Daesios. But there is a hint of Plutarch's tradition in Arrian. On the sixth day of the illness Arrian notes: καὶ τὰ ἱερὰ ἐπιθέντα οὐκ ἐλινύειν πυρέσσοντα (25. 4). The wording is important. It does not, as most translations imply, refer to the absence of intermission in the fever ('he no longer had any respite from the

---

[25] As I argued in *CQ* 21 (1971) 121 and is now propounded by Badian (above, n. 3).

[26] Cf. Pearson (above, n. 4) 433. There are minor variants (one of which, Python in Plutarch for Peithon in Arrian, is probably due to manuscript error: cf. Arr. *Succ.* F 1. 2 with Roos's textual notes), but the substance of the reports is practically identical.

fever').[27] It seems agreed that the fever did not slacken at any time after its onset at Medeius' banquet. Arrian's use of the verb ἐλινύειν is constant elsewhere in the sense of 'rest', 'slacken activity'.[28] His meaning is surely: 'he no longer rested in his fever'. But the king's activities that day are a carbon copy of the previous day. What his source presumably had in mind was the day of relaxation with Medeius, which Alexander hoped would make the fever abate. When that failed, he reverted to his normal schedule and summoned the commanders for briefing. That connection is broken in Arrian's account and an extraneous day is inserted, presumably from a different source.

There are, I think, two clear strands in the narrative, one with a close affinity to Plutarch's version of the *Ephemerides* and the other a substantially different version. The related source began with the fever after Medeius' banquet, moved to the abortive day of convalescence with Medeius, then to the meeting by the pool and the vigil of the commanders. From vii. 25. 6 the narrative runs exactly parallel to Plutarch and is presumably extracted from a single source. Now the interwoven thread is one which reiterates the report of briefing sessions and indicates that the departure for Arabia was imminent.[29] I assume that this secondary account moved from Medeius' banquet to the briefing sessions which occurred some days later. Arrian inferred that they came immediately after the banquet and inserted them before the day of relaxation which he took from his other source. It is a perfect instance of variant reports of the same event being wrongly assumed to be different episodes.

If there are two strands combined in Arrian's narrative, it is safe to assume that only one purported to give the version of the *Ephemerides*. The other was roughly similar in outline but omitted the detailed description of the intensification of the illness.

[27] So Brunt, *Arrian* ii. 291 (modifying Robson). Other recent renderings are 'la fièvre ne l'avait plus laissé un instant en repos' (Savinel), 'begann er stark zu fiebern' (Wirth, in the Artemis edition). The traditional Latin rendering (e.g. in Blancardus and Raphelius) is *febrim non cessasse*.

[28] Cf. iii. 15. 5, iv. 30. 1; *Ind.* 29. 7, 36. 9; *Parth./Succ.* F 10 (Roos). There is no parallel in Arrian for the verb used with a participle, but the usage occurs in Herodotus (viii. 71. 2: ἐλίνυον ... ἐργαζόμενοι = 'they rested in their labours'). In medical writings the word had an almost technical sense, rest as opposed to exercise. Galen (xvii. A 838κ) commenting on the Hippocratic *Epidemiae* (ἐλινύειν οὐ συμφέρει ἀλλὰ γυμνάσια) glosses the word ἡσυχίαν ἄγειν.

[29] See the synoptic table for detailed analysis.

That source, I think can be confidently identified as Aristobulus, whose version of Alexander's death certainly did not cohere with that of the *Ephemerides*. He argued that Alexander drank only after the onset of the fever, whereas the *Ephemerides* made it clear that the fever supervened after two solid days of potation.[30] He also dated Alexander's death to Daesios 30 (probably giving a round figure), whereas the *Ephemerides* gave a precise dating to 28 Daesios. Aristobulus will have recorded the illness in somewhat vague terms, stressing Alexander's devotion to duty as manifested in the repeated briefing sessions but largely ignoring the detailed account of the *Ephemerides*. In that case it was Ptolemy who used and cited the document. This is preferable to the other view, that Arrian used the *Ephemerides* independently and noted retrospectively that Ptolemy's version of events was much the same. There are two strands in the narrative which Arrian has worked together and presented (in indirect speech) as the report of the *Ephemerides*. He could not have been more misleading.

### THE PROBLEM OF SARAPIS

It follows that Ptolemy used the *Ephemerides* for his report of Alexander's death and also that his text of the document was similar to that used by Plutarch. In that case it was not a late forgery. This conclusion, however, runs headlong against what at first sight appears to be a glaring anachronism. Both Arrian and Plutarch refer to a temple of Sarapis,[31] where senior Macedonian officers consulted the god, asking whether the sick king should be transferred to his protection. Now it seems impossible that the Hellenistic cult of Sarapis was foreshadowed in Babylon. Sarapis, as he was known in the Graeco-Roman world, was a syncretistic creation of Ptolemy I, and *a fortiori* the Sarapis of the *Ephemerides* cannot have been that deity.[32]

---

[30] Plut. *Al.* 75. 6 = *FGrH* 139 F 59. For the *Ephemerides* see Arr. vii. 25. 1 with Plut. *Al.* 76. 1.

[31] Plut. *Al.* 76. 9: εἰς τὸ Σαραπεῖον; Arr. vii. 26. 2: ἐν τοῦ Σαράπιδος τῷ ἱερῷ.

[32] This has been, to my mind, established by P. M. Fraser, 'Current problems concerning the cult of Sarapis', *Opuscula Atheniensia* 7 (1967) 23–45, arguing against C. B. Welles, *Historia* 11 (1962) 272–89 and R. Stiehl, *History of Religion* 3 (1963) 21–33. See also Fraser's *Ptolemaic Alexandria* i. 246–50. The theory of anachronism was pressed hard by Pearson (above, n. 4) 438–9 and is accepted now by Brunt, *Arrian* ii. 293 n. 2 and Wirth (above, n. 5) 1070–1.

What, then, are the alternatives? Could the deity have been native Babylonian? If so, the form of the name would need to be practically identical to Sarapis, so that it became assimilated to the Greek name in the course of the centuries of textual transmission. Various alternatives have been suggested, none remotely possible.[33] The closest in form appears to be the consort of Marduk, Zarpanitum, who was worshipped with Marduk in the state temple of Esagila and had at least one chapel of her own in the great hieratic complex.[34] It is not impossible that the companions of Alexander solicited a deity who might be viewed as a direct beneficiary of the king. The Queen of Esagila[35] would have been assumed to have some propensity for Alexander, who had announced the restoration of her sanctuary and started building operations. Whatever form the Greeks chose for her name it was close enough to Sarapis for assimilation to occur automatically in the course of transmission. But there are two strong objections. Both versions of the *Ephemerides* state explicitly that the deity was masculine, which would be a curious error in a contemporary source, and secondly Zarpanitum is not familiar as a goddess of healing. One would expect the approach to have been made to one of the primary gods of healing.[36] This line of attack does not seem particularly promising, and one should look for a more attractive alternative.

The other approach to the problem is to concentrate on the Egyptian origins of the cult of Sarapis. It is now accepted that

[33] e.g. C. F. Lehmann-Haupt, *Z.f.A.* 12 (1877) 112 (Šar-apsi 'king of the ocean', a cult title of Ea) and, recently, A. H. D. Bivar, in *Mysteria Mithraica a cura di U. Bianchi* (Leiden, 1979) 747–8 (an Iranian counterpart of Apollo, named as Ḫsatrapati in the new Lycian trilingual [*CRAI* 1974, 146–7] ).

[34] E. Dhorme, *Les Religions de Babylonie et d'Assyrie* (Paris, 1945), 146; E. Unger, in *Reallexikon der Assyriologie*, i. 358 (99g, 8), 355 (99b, 1).

[35] Cf. *Spätbabylonische Texte aus Uruk II* (ed. E. von Weiher): Ausgraben des deutsch. Forschungsgemeinschaft in Uruk-Warka 10 (Berlin, 1983), No. 13, iv. 16, No. 22, iv. 40, No. 38. 35. See also *Les Religions du Proche-Orient asiatique* (ed. R. Labat; Paris, 1970) 340–1.

[36] Strongly emphasized by I. Lévy, 'Sarapis', *Revue le l'histoire des religions* 67 (1913) 308–17, who like many subsequent scholars (below, n. 40) insisted that the deity consulted in 323 was the city god, Marduk. One might attempt to save the theory by arguing that the god consulted was indeed Marduk but that the consultation took place in the chapel of his consort, Zarpanitum. Given the ruined state of Esagila and the desolation of the central sanctuary (cf. Hdt. i. 183. 3–4), consultations may have taken place in a subsidiary shrine. But the hypothesis is too elaborate to carry conviction.

the Ptolemaic cult of Sarapis was a development of the much earlier cult of the deceased Apis bulls at Memphis.[37] The worship of Apis was fused with that of Osiris and a new deity emerged, Osiris-Apis (*Wsir-Ḥp*), the lord of the underworld. The cult was popular at the time of the Macedonian conquest, and it was adopted by the Hellenic community of Memphis, who named the god Oserapis.[38] It is not impossible, indeed more than likely, that Egyptian immigrants had transported the cult to Babylon. Thanks to the vicissitudes of war and the inducements of trade, there was a substantial community of Egyptians in the Babylonian capital, not only prisoners of war but landowners of some substance. As early as the reign of Cambyses there was an 'assembly of the elders of the Egyptians' which had some legal standing, at least in the transfer of real estate.[39] It would not be surprising if the underworld god of Memphis had established a subsidiary shrine in Babylon, perhaps on the periphery of Esagila itself.[40] Once more one must ask why Alexander's officers approached what was inevitably a minor sanctuary and not one of the great healing centres of Babylon. The answer can only be that Osiris-Apis had established a local vogue and was renowned for efficacy in healing. The sanctuary may even have been specially recommended by Egyptian residents. At all events one cannot deny the existence of a cult of Osiris-Apis at Babylon, a deity which Alexander's men may well have termed Sarapis. If that is so, the events at Babylon probably influenced the origins of the later Sarapis cult. Ptolemy knew of the underworld god in a healing aspect and knew the god under the name Sarapis. Both the attribute and the name were later absorbed into his new creation. Far

---

[37] See Wilcken, *UPZ* i. 77–88; Fraser, *Op.Ath.* (above, n. 32) 23–4.

[38] A prayer to Oserapis by the Hellenomemphite lady Artemisia survives from the mid-4th cent. BC (Wilcken, *UPZ* i. 97–104).

[39] I. Eph'al, *Orientalia* 47 (1978) 76–80; see also D. J. Wiseman, *Iraq* 28 (1966) 154–8.

[40] Suggested briefly by P. Goukowsky, *Essai sur les origines du mythe d'Alexandre* i. 199–200. Early scholars had argued that Alexander's men knew of the cult of Oserapis but saw him as an Egyptian manifestation of Marduk, the bull-god of Babylon (Lévy [above, n. 36] 315; Wilcken, *UPZ* i. 79–82; Kornemann 37–9). I myself (*CQ* 21 [1971] 120) accepted that Sarapis was an *interpretatio Graeca* of Marduk, but I would now agree that the argument is unnecessarily forced and elaborate. In this context I should like to express my appreciation to Dr S. Dalley for guidance in the esoteric field of Babylonian theology.

from being a forgery, the *Ephemerides* may have anticipated and in part inspired the later cult.

There is no Ariadne's thread to deliver us from the labyrinth. We must remain in the maze of probabilities and attempt to balance them. It is not inherently impossible (or improbable) that a deity, Babylonian or Egyptian, was visited by Alexander's officers shortly before his death and that its name was reproduced by Greek speakers in the form Sarapis. On the other hand it is hard to see why a forger should have invented a bogus and anachronistic cult of Sarapis unless he were totally ignorant of Babylonian institutions.[41] Nor can it be said that the list of officers consulting the god shows signs of fabrication. The only name really celebrated in later history is that of Seleucus. Otherwise it is a fairly random selection: the bodyguards, Peithon and Peucestas, the phalanx commander Attalus, the seer Demophon,[42] the newly arrived Menidas,[43] and the otherwise unknown Cleomenes. They are not the most distinguished or familiar names, but on the other hand they are undeniably historical personages who might well have invoked divine help for their king. So far there is nothing to refute the general conclusion that Arrian used the *Ephemerides* only as they were transmitted by Ptolemy. The original compilation must therefore be dated to the first generation after the king's death.

## OTHER EXTRACTS FROM THE EPHEMERIDES

There is another substantial extract from the *Ephemerides*, preserved in Aelian's *Varia Historia*.[44] This is a record of Alexander's intemperance, set against his military achievements, the discreditable balancing the glory. It is a diary of the Macedonian month of Dios, attributed to a number of authors,

---

[41] That tells against the once fashionable theory (cf. Tarn, *Alexander* i. 120 n. 2., ii. 70; Fraser, *Op. Ath.* [above, n. 32] 33) that Ptolemy deliberately introduced propaganda for his new cult, associating it with the great Alexander. In any case Plutarch's version, which seems independent of Ptolemy, also has the reference to Sarapis. And, since the god did nothing to help the dying king, the story cannot have been very effective as propaganda.

[42] Diod. xvii. 98. 3; Curt. ix. 4. 28; cf. Berve ii. no. 264.

[43] Arr. vii. 23. 1. On his career see now *JHS* 106 (1986) 7 n. 46.

[44] Ael. *VH* iii. 23 = *FGrH* 117 F 2a.

one of whom was Eumenes of Cardia.[45] The reports are attached to specific days, and in content they correlate with explicit citations of the *Ephemerides* in Plutarch and Athenaeus.[46] All this makes it quite certain that we are dealing with the same document that recorded Alexander's death. But the details relate to a rather earlier phase of the reign and have nothing to do with the king's last days. The extract in Aelian begins with the king on a journey. On the fifth of the month he drank with 'Eumaeus';[47] on the sixth he slept after drinking, reviving only enough to discuss the next day's march with his commanders. On the seventh he feasted with Perdiccas and drank again, and on the eighth he slept again. The pattern recurred on the fifteenth and the sixteenth. On the twenty-fourth he dined with Bagoas, whose house was ten stades distant from the palace, and he was still sleeping two days later.

This peculiar record of excess is not dated to any particular year or assigned to any particular stage of the expedition. Three indications combine to suggest a historical context: the extract is taken from the month of Dios (October/November),[48] it begins with Alexander on the march, and it ends with him in some capital where there was a royal palace. There would seem to be two possibilities only. After Gaugamela (*c.* 1 October, 333 BC) Alexander marched rapidly to Babylon and was in the capital roughly a month.[49] The events recorded in Aelian's extract might be assigned to this period. A rather more attractive possibility, I think, is the autumn of 324 BC. In the high summer of that year Alexander had left the plains of Mesopotamia and travelled via Bisutun to the Median capital of Ecbatana. There, after a protracted bout of carousing, Hephaestion died. We have no explicit date for his death,

[45] Aelian mentions a collaborator, whose name is unfortunately corrupted to ἐκεῖνος. Whoever he was, he was presumably different from the Diodotus of Erythrae whom Athenaeus (x. 434B) names as co-author with Eumenes.

[46] Plut. *Quaest. conv.* i. 6. 1 (623E); Athen. x. 434B (*FGrH* 117 F 2b–c).

[47] The name is not otherwise attested and may be corrupt; but none of the emendations suggested carry conviction (e.g., Eumenes, Medeius, Ptolemy).

[48] That is the only feasible interpretation of the manuscript reading δι' οὗ μηνός, Scheffer's emendation Δαισίου presupposes that the record concerns Alexander's last days.

[49] Diod. xvii. 64. 4; Curt v. 1. 36. This dating would support Samuel's view (above, n. 6) that the *Ephemerides* are derived from Babylonian records, but Samuel himself argued that the document only covered the last months of Alexander's life.

but it was followed by a long period of mourning and a campaign in midwinter against the Cossaeans of the Zagros.[50] On general grounds it is usually placed somewhere in October,[51] but I can see no cogent reason against its dating as late as November. In that case we have a report of the last stage of the journey through Media, followed by the first part of the residence in Ecbatana. The extract would begin with the seven-day march from Bisutun to Ecbatana[52] and continue with the drinking bouts with the Companions, which all sources agree to have been the principal feature of the celebrations there.[53] Alexander's host, Bagoas, was presumably the son of Pharnuches, the sole Persian trierarch named at the Indus and clearly a man who ranked as the equal of the Macedonian Companions.[54] Once more there is nothing inherently implausible in the record of fact.

What is surprising, however, is the emphasis on drinking and its aftermath. That symposia were a regular feature of court life is certain,[55] as is the fact that they entailed quite epic feats of toping. But the *Ephemerides* seem to harp upon the theme and underline the king's subsequent incapacitation. It might be argued that the drinking-sessions recorded by Aelian were uncharacteristic and that the month of Dios 324 was selected because its entries were exceptionally sensational.[56] That does not seem to be the case. Admittedly Athenaeus (x. 434B) might be basing his remarks on the same passage when he comments on the two-day periods of convalescent sleep, but it is difficult to discount Plutarch, who obviously knew the *Ephemerides* and used them directly. He claims that the entry that the king slept

[50] For the winter campaign against the Cossaei, lasting forty days, see Nearchus, *ap.* Arr. *Ind.* 40. 7–8; Strabo xi. 13. 6 (524); Arr. vii. 15. 3; Diod. xvii. 111. 4–6; Plut. *Al.* 72. 4. The next event was his return to Mesopotamia in spring 323. There is nothing in the events of summer 324 that can be precisely dated (at least as regards Alexander).

[51] Following Berve ii. 173 (no. 357); cf. Badian, *JHS* 81 (1961) 34 n. 137 (the *theoroi* sent to Siwah needed seven or eight months for their journey).

[52] Diod. xvii. 110. 6; cf. P. Bernard, *Studia Iranica* 9 (1980) 315.

[53] Arr. vii. 14. 1; Diod. xvii. 110. 7 (πότους συνεχεῖς).

[54] Arr. *Ind.* 18. 8. On this individual see *JHS* 100 (1980) 13. Berve ii. no. 195 preferred an identification with the well-known eunuch and favourite of Alexander. That is perfectly possible (cf. Badian, *CQ* 8 [1958] 156).

[55] See now E. N. Borza, 'The Symposium at Alexander's Court', in *Ancient Macedonia* 3 (Thessaloniki 1983) 45–55, cf. 55 'the symposium itself may have served as the means by which Alexander's inner court was defined'. See also Berve i. 13–15.

[56] As recently argued by Hammond, *KCS* 298–9.

after his potations was extremely frequent.[57] I do not see how one can avoid the superlative. The conjunction of sleeping and drinking must have been an immediately obvious feature of the document. That is to some extent corroborated by another passage of Plutarch. Reporting on Alexander's restless energy, he observes that he often held play hunts in pursuit of foxes and birds — that one may infer from the *Ephemerides*.[58] The discussion then moves from hunting to food and drink, changing in tone from positive to negative. Alexander was too prone to flattery and spent days in sleep; 'after drinking he bathed and would often sleep until midday: sometimes he would even spend the day asleep'.[59] The *Ephemerides* had been explicitly cited a few sentences before and it is reasonable to suppose that Plutarch continued to use them. No doubt he had in mind the type of entry that he quotes in the *Quaestiones conviviales*.

### THE NATURE OF THE EPHEMERIDES

The document is extremely strange. It is not as it stands an unedited extract from a court journal, for it shows none of the characteristics we should expect from such a compilation. The Achaemenid 'memorials of the king's days' with which Artaxerxes I beguiled his sleepless hours were a full report of all events concerning the king.[60] Similarly the daybook of Ptolemy Philadelphus, cited by Pseudo-Aristeas, was a complete account of all the king's actions and utterances during the day, and the author supposedly draws upon it for a verbatim transcript of the king's edifying conversations with the Jewish translators of the Septuagint.[61] The *Ephemerides* of Alexander have a very different complexion. Far from being a complete record of the king's day, they are restricted to laconic and highly general notes. Plutarch, who purports to give a literal, if selective, transcript, has only short statements of the principal

[57] συνεχέστατα γέγραπται καὶ πλειστάκις: Plut. *Quaest. conv.* i. 6. 1 (623E) = *FGrH* 117 F 2c. Aelian also claims that his extracts are a typical sample of the work.

[58] Plut. *Al.* 23. 4 = *FGrH* 117 F 1.

[59] Plut. *Al.* 23. 8. Jacoby, *FGrH* ii.D. 405 accepts that the sentence comes from the *Ephemerides* but posits an intermediate source.

[60] *Esther* 6. 1; cf. 12. 4

[61] Aristeas *ad Philocr.* 298–300. See further E. J. Bickerman, 'Notes sur la chancellerie des Lagides', *RIDA* 2 (1953) 251–67, esp. 262–3.

events of the day. No single utterance of the king is preserved, and there is only the sketchiest suggestion of the matter of the briefing sessions during those last days in Babylon. The notices may be derived from the royal secretariat and be ultimately based upon a complete journal, but, as they stand, they are at best extracts and the picture they give is highly selective. That the focus is so sharply concentrated on the king's drinking is surely significant. To note that the king slept for a day might be justified if there were no other court business, but to add the qualification 'after drinking'[62] is excessively pointed, well outside the bounds of secretarial discretion. I see no alternative to the conclusion that the authors of the *Ephemerides* had an interest in stressing the legendary intemperance of Alexander's court.

The drinking-sessions recorded in the *Ephemerides* were hardly exaggerated. The royal chamberlain, Chares of Mytilene, left a lurid account of the banquet which celebrated the self-immolation of the Indian sage, Calanus.[63] A competition ensued in drinking unmixed wine which aroused such collective enthusiasm that thirty-five of the participants expired in their cups. The winner Promachus, who consumed three gallons of the lethal brew, enjoyed his prize for a mere four days before going the way of his fellow competitors.[64] Some of the details may be exaggerated or even apocryphal, but it is patent that the enormous consumption of undiluted wine was a feature of court symposia.[65] It culminated in the notorious banquet of Medeius. The details of that carouse were soon promulgated in memoirs and pamphlets. According to Ephippus of Olynthus, who stigmatized the Macedonian predilection for huge aperitifs,[66] there was an informal exchange of bumpers between

---

[62] ἐκ τοῦ πότου: twice in Aelian, also (explicitly) in Plutarch. Athenaeus reads ἀπὸ τῆς μέθης. Cf. Arr. vii. 25. 1: αὖθις πίνειν πόρρω τῶν νυκτῶν.

[63] Calanus himself had exhorted his Macedonian audience to make his death an occasion of joyous intoxication (Plut. *Al.* 69. 6).

[64] Athen. x. 437A–B; Plut. *Al.* 70. 2 = *FGrH* 125 F 19; cf. Ael. *VH* ii. 41.

[65] Cf. Borza (above, n. 55) 48–50, arguing speculatively that the Macedonian wine was of a quality that did not require dilution. That may be. What cannot be denied, however, is that drunkenness was traditional and encouraged at the Macedonian court. Theopompus was explicit (Polyb. viii. 9. 7 = *FGrH* 115 F 225a, cf. 163, 236, 282), and Philip's feast celebrating the marriage to Cleopatra was obviously not an occasion when the participants were sober (Plut. *Al.* 9. 7–10).

[66] Athen. iii. 120C–D = *FGrH* 126 F 1.

Alexander and the well-known toper, Proteas.[67] The king collapsed and sank into his fatal illness, thanks to the enmity of Dionysus.[68] Ephippus was no friend of Alexander or, it seems, of Macedonians in general. He insinuated that the king had drunk himself to death, with the willing collaboration of Dionysus. The same bias occurs in the mysterious pamphlet of Nicobule, which alleged that Alexander toasted not only Proteas but all twenty of the guests at Medeius' banquet.[69] However exaggerated the details, they cohere with what is known of Macedonian symposia. The drinking at Medeius' feast was clearly substantial enough to encourage the suggestion that the king died from his excesses.

Uglier suggestions could be and were made. If Alexander died as the result of drink, could not that drink have been poisoned? The vulgate tradition, represented by Diodorus and Justin and criticized by Plutarch and Arrian, has a picturesque story of Alexander convulsed by a spasm of pain after drinking a toast to Heracles.[70] The illness immediately supervened in full strength and death came rapidly. The scenario was ominous and encouraged the worst insinuations: Alexander was poisoned by his cup-bearer, Iollas, whose father, Antipater, was under threat, aided and abetted by Medeius and his fellow guests. The story is expanded in the early versions of the Alexander Romance, where the whole gamut of supposed accomplices is named and it is stated that the contemporary Onesicritus spoke openly of poisoning.[71] The rumours without doubt go back to the period of the king's death. In Athens at least Hypereides moved honours for Iollas, the supposed murderer,[72] and his proposal can only have come in the immediate aftermath of Alexander's death, before the battle of Crannon in August 322, which brought the city under the sway of Antipater. In Babylon the rumours may have been widely broad-

---

[67] Ironically a nephew of Cleitus the Black (Berve no. 665).

[68] Athen. x. 434B = *FGrH* 126 F 3.

[69] Athen. x. 434C = *FGrH* 127 F 1. Cf. Athen. xii. 537D (F 2).

[70] Diod. xvii. 117. 2; Justin xii. 13. 8–9; cf. Plut. *Al* 75. 5; Arr. vii. 27. 2. For discussion see *CQ* 21 (1971) 114–15.

[71] For texts and discussion see R. Merkelbach, *Die Quellen des griechischen Alexanderromans* 164–92, 253–83. The reference to Onesicritus is *Metz Epit.* 97–8 (*FGrH* 134 F 37).

[72] [Plut.] *Vit. X Orat.* 849F. *Pace* Hammond (*Three Historians* 187–8 n. 55), the notice concerns a decree and is probably based on documentary evidence.

cast in the ugly period of mutiny when cavalry and infantry were at loggerheads, Meleager standing virtually alone against the rest of the officer corps. The king, it was probably alleged, had been treacherously and secretly murdered by his staff. The guests at Medeius' banquet were particularly vulnerable to the innuendo.[73]

The report of the *Ephemerides* is remote from the hysterical and rhetorically pointed atmosphere of the rest of the tradition. There is no attempt to gloss over the fact that the king spent two days drinking with Medeius, but he is reported leaving the feast on his own two feet, eating, and then sleeping in the bathroom.[74] There was no unseemly accident at the feast, and the fever occurred as the direct consequence of the drinking. From then on Alexander's condition deteriorated, but he was able until the last to discharge the sacral duties of kingship and to conduct business meetings with his staff.[75] Nothing could be more different from the vulgate story of convulsions in the act of drinking and a precipitate and swift demise. There were ten full days between the banquet and the king's death, days of comparative activity until the last decline on 25 Daesios. The story is of a natural illness, gradually intensifying. It is indeed preceded by a drinking-bout, but the symptoms are fever, not intestinal pain. The reader might ascribe Alexander's death to intemperance; he would not readily think of poison.

As we have seen, the *Ephemerides* laid particular emphasis on the court symposia and their after-effects. Aelian noted a particular concentration in the month of Dios, probably in the year 324. Now the autumn of 324 was the season of Hephaestion's death, a death which is ascribed to excessive drinking.[76] That cannot be the whole story. Hephaestion's death was unexpected. His sudden decline took Alexander by surprise,[77] and

---

[73] The nucleus of the tradition of the Alexander Romance probably derives from propaganda issued by Perdiccas in 322/1, designed to attack Antipater and his other adversaries in the civil war (Merkelbach [above, n. 71] 171–4; *CQ* 21 [1971] 115–16). The rumours were presumably in circulation already, and Perdiccas slanted them as his own interests dictated.

[74] Arr. vii. 25. 1; cf. Plut. *Al.* 75. 4–5.

[75] Cf. Arr. vii. 25. 4–6; Plut. *Al.* 76. 3–6.

[76] Diod. xvii. 110. 8; Plut. *Al.* 72. 2. Arrian vii. 14. 1 correlates Hephaestion's illness with the celebrations and symposia at Ecbatana.

[77] Arr. vii. 14. 1.

there was a story that his final illness (like Alexander's) came after he had downed a large bumper of wine.[78] The circumstances were suspicious, as Alexander showed when he crucified the unfortunate doctor Glaucias. Whether the grounds were professional neglect of the inebriated or administration of the wrong drug,[79] there must have been allegations of foul play, allegations which were naturally damaging to Hephaestion's enemies. Now Eumenes was the most notorious opponent of Hephaestion. His quarrel with the court favourite was resolved only through Alexander's intervention, and the enforced reconciliation came a matter of weeks before the stay at Ecbatana.[80] As a result his position became extremely delicate, and he retrieved the king's favour only through an excess of zeal in proposing honours for the dead favourite. Eumenes secured his position and was even promoted to command the vacant hipparchy of Perdiccas,[81] but the innuendo that he had colluded in Hephaestion's death would have been hard to escape. That helps explain the stress on the frequency and intensity of the drinking-sessions. If Alexander himself was forced to spend up to two days in convalescence, his favourite might easily lose his resistance to the infection that killed him. The presumption is also made that Alexander's own constitution was weakened. That was not stated, but the weight of documentation imposed the conclusion. As Aelian observed, 'we must suppose one of two things: either Alexander inflicted damage on himself through the wine for all those days of the month or the compilers of the record are lying.'[82] Aelian was hardly the only reader to draw that inference, and the inference was intended to be made. If the king regularly abused his system, it would

---

[78] Plut. *Al.* 72. 2.; cf. Arr. vii. 14. 4.

[79] Both variants are given by Arrian vii. 14. 4 (cf. Plut. *Al.* 72. 3). As the story of Philip the Acarnanian shows only too well (Berve no. 788), a court physician was peculiarly vulnerable to allegations of poisoning—Philip was lucky that his patient recovered.

[80] Arr. vii. 12. 7, 13. 1; Plut. *Eum.* 2. Plutarch's version of the quarrel (not in Nepos' *Life of Eumenes*) shows the secretary in an invidious light, and the episode was presumably exploited by his enemies. Cf. Kaerst, *RE* vi. 1083–4; J. Hornblower, *Hieronymus of Cardia* 154.

[81] Plut. *Eum.* 1. 5 (cf. 2. 9–10); Nepos *Eum.* 1. 6.

[82] Ael. *VH* iii. 23. Plutarch in a similar context (*Quaest. conv.* i. 6. 1) used the entries in the *Ephemerides* to refute Aristobulus' allegation that the king attended symposia for the sake of conversation and drank moderately.

not be surprising that he, like Hephaestion, was unable to shake off the fatal illness.

Contemporary medical theory was certainly suspicious of the ultimate effects of alcoholic indulgence. The Athenian doctor, Mnesitheus, though eulogistic of the occasional drinking-bout (it will ultimately purge the body and clear the mind), has no illusions that the result of drinking large quantities of unmixed wine is severe mental and physical injury.[83] More pertinently, the Hippocratic *Epidemiae*, dating from the fifth century BC, list a number of cases in which the onset of fever is associated with drinking and sexual excess.[84] In many instances the symptoms, described on a daily basis, strongly resemble those of Alexander. In particular, a certain Silenus, twenty years old, was overtaken by fever after drinking and untimely exercise (*Epid.* i. 26β′). The illness began with pains in the lower back, heaviness in the head, and persistent sleeplessness. From the sixth day there was acute fever. From the seventh day the patient was speechless and on the eighth he lapsed into a coma, dying on the eleventh day of the illness. The connection between drinking and fever was axiomatic and repeated throughout antiquity. Galen commented that over-indulgence in eating and drinking makes one prone to quartan fever;[85] and one of his patients, Eudemus the Peripatetic, insisted that an attack of fever had been caused by his drinking old wine (his regular doctors concurred in the diagnosis).[86] The report of the *Ephemerides* could only reinforce such prejudices: Alexander's death was due to natural causes, exacerbated by intemperance.[87]

Eumenes was vulnerable to rumours about Hephaestion's death. He was also named as one of the guests at Medeius' banquet. The source for that is the document on Alexander's death (the *Liber de Morte*) which concludes some versions of the Alexander Romance, and, though it is undoubtedly distorted by

---

[83] Athen. xi. 483F–484B. Compare the sentiments of the cautious and pedestrian Eryximachus (Plat. *Symp.* 176C–D).

[84] Hipp. *Epid.* iii. 1ε′, 17ι′, ιϛ′. Cf. *Aff.* 12 (winter fevers are induced by wine, fatigue, or some other cause).

[85] Galen *de med. meth.* i. 7 (xi. 23K); cf. i. 9 (xi. 28K).

[86] Galen *de progn.* 2. 10 (76. 19 ff. Nutton = xiv. 608K).

[87] Cf. Justin xii. 13. 10: *amici causas morbi intemperiem ebrietatis disseminaverunt.*

propaganda, the propaganda is early and, to some extent, based on fact.[88] Indeed Eumenes' rank made it inherently likely that he was at the banquet or at any rate close enough to Alexander's person to have been sensitive to rumours about poisoning. He had every reason to issue his version of events, a short day-by-day record of the last year or so of the king's life, stressing the factors which might have contributed to his early death. No doubt he claimed to have compiled that record from documents which he as chief secretary had in his possession. Those could have included the notebooks of the royal doctors, which must have documented the course of the illness, but they would have been at most one of the sources. Eumenes was close enough to his dying king to record the symptoms himself—and perceptive enough to select those that were consistent with a malarial attack. I am not suggesting that Eumenes produced a forgery.[89] He provided an account of the king's doings which was based on fact—that was necessary if the work was to gain acceptance. But the facts were carefully edited to convey a very definite impression.

What we cannot trace is an original court journal, a daybook retailing all official acts of the king. The bare title *Ephemerides* cannot be enlisted as proof that the work was an official diary. Long ago Wilcken drew attention to a series of documents from Roman Egypt which record the daily round of a minor official, the *strategos*.[90] These records (termed ὑπομνηματισμοί, not *ephemerides*) are not dissimilar in form to the notes on Alexander. The daily activities of the *strategos* are duly recorded, his supervision of tax-collectors and market officials, and the public sacrifices he performed, notably those to celebrate the emperor's birthday. But these records are exclusively public; the private life of the *strategos* receives no documentation. Even the similarities present problems. Why in both cases is the record so unin-

---

[88] *Metz Epit.* 97–8; Ps. Call. iii. 31. 8–10. For the propaganda see above, n. 73.

[89] I need to stress this point after Hammond's recent remarks (*Three Historians* 8–9 with notes). I do not argue (and have never done so) that Eumenes wrote a 'fake Journal'. He wrote an account in diary style of the king's last months, but nothing suggests that he published it as an official extract from the archives.

[90] Wilcken, *Philologus* 53 (1894) 81–6 (cf. *Chrestomathie* 41). For more recent examples see *POxy* 3072–4; *PSI* xiv. 1444 (with J. Rea, *CdE* 47 [1972] 236–42).

formative, so devoid of detail about any of the transactions at issue? A bare record that the *strategos* held an audience was of no administrative use,[91] unless it was a report provided by the *strategos*, authentication that he was fulfilling his official duties.[92] As reports to superior authority they make excellent sense,[93] but the explanation cannot of course be transferred to the *Ephemerides*. Different factors were at work. Like the compilers of the Egyptian records, the authors were uninterested in administrative minutiae but focus on the overt actions of the king. Their audience was presumed to be interested in what the king did but unconcerned about the details of the transactions. The work was in no sense an archive. The title, *Ephemerides*, is neutral and uninformative, applied both to documents and to literary works, to private account books and to Caesar's *Commentarii*.[94] In the context of history Sempronius Asellio objected to the type of work which was a mere diary or ἐφημερίς, and Gellius indicated that there was a specific genre of writing, where events were recorded not by the year but by the day.[95] Eumenes' work may have been an instance—a report of Alexander's doings arranged on a daily schema. We need not go back to some 'Urquelle', an entire archive, also labelled *Ephemerides*, which provided fuller documentation.

Nothing unfortunately can be deduced of the work of Strattis of Olynthus, who is usually accredited with a five-book commentary on the *Ephemerides* of Alexander. This author and his work are known from a single entry in the 'Suda' which is

[91] There were in addition full official reports which gave transcripts of speeches (in précis at least) and duly recorded decisions made (cf. *PFam. Tebt.* 19, 24 etc.). These records were lodged in the official archives and were immensely more informative than the laconic notes of the 'daybooks': a complete roll might contain the transactions of less than a month (*PLeipz.* 123 = Preisigke, *Girowesen* 409–10; N. Hohlwein, *Le stratège du nome* [Brussels 1962] 101–2).

[92] This has been pointed out to me in conversation by Professor Brunt.

[93] Such reports are already found in late Ptolemaic Egypt and must go back to an early period. Cf. *BGU* 1767–8 with the comments of D. J. Crawford, 'The Good Official of Ptolemaic Egypt', in *Das ptolemäische Ägypten* (Mainz, 1978) 195–202, esp. 197: 'such reports have the ring of model behaviour rather than reality. One would like to know how the στρατηγός actually spent his day.'

[94] For instances see Samuel (above, n. 6) 1–3. For Caesar's *Commentarii* see Plut. *Caes.* 22. 2.

[95] Gell. v. 18. 7–8 ( = Asellio F 1, Peter *HRR* i. 179). Gellius' introductory comment is *cum vero non per annos sed per dies singulos res gestae scribuntur, ea historia Graeco vocabulo* ἐφημερίς *dicitur.*

plagued by manuscript variants.[96] Even if we read the text authorized by Jacoby and Adler (περὶ τῶν ᾿Αλεξάνδρου ἐφημερίδων βιβλία ε′.), it remains problematic. Pearson once argued that the wording is ambiguous; we could translate 'five books about the *Ephemerides* of Alexander' or 'five books of *Ephemerides* about the affairs of Alexander'.[97] The second interpretation is forced and the parallels cited are not exact. The word order compels the first interpretation—if the phrase is read as an entity.[98] But there lies the crux. We cannot be certain about the punctuation in the 'Suda'. There may be two works at issue not one, a book on the career of Alexander and five books of *Ephemerides*.[99] In that case the *Ephemerides* of Strattis may have nothing to do with Alexander or his royal journals.

The entire entry concerning Strattis is enigmatic. The 'Suda' reports other works, a treatise on rivers, springs, and lakes[100] and a discussion of the death of Alexander. All are attributed to Strattis, but there are many demonstrable examples in the 'Suda' of works wrongly accredited to authors. Equally, when the attribution is correct, the works cited may be bogus. A pertinent case is the egregious *Ephemeris* of Dictys of Crete, which the 'Suda' presents as an account of the events of the siege of Troy, written by a contemporary.[101] That of course was a blatant forgery. A Latin version is extant, a circumstantial and tedious soap opera of life in Troy, which provides a nice illustration of what might be termed an *ephemeris* in late antiquity. The works of Strattis may be similar concoctions based on the period of Alexander and foisted on a fictitious author whose

---

[96] 'Suda' s.v. Στράττις ᾿Ολύνθιος, reprinted as *FGrH* 118 T 1. The most reliable manuscript (A) omitted the entry, which a later hand has added as a marginal note, with no reference to the *Ephemerides* and transferring the book number to the work on Alexander's death. The published texts have the readings of the *deteriores*.

[97] Pearson (above, n. 4) 437, criticized by Hammond, *Three Historians* 172 n. 21 and Badian (above, n. 3).

[98] The entry on Philochorus (*FGrH* 328 T 1) includes a treatise περὶ τῶν Σοφοκλέους μύθων βιβλία ε′., which can hardly mean 'five books of myths about the affairs of Sophocles'.

[99] For the form of the entry see 'Suda' s.v. Φύλαρχος (*FGrH* 81 T 1): περὶ εὑρημάτων, Παρεκβάσεων (?) βιβλία θ′. There are clearly two works at issue.

[100] This may have been a handbook of examples compiled for rhetorical purposes. Cf. Men. Rh. περὶ ἐπιδεικτικῆς i. 349. 25 ff., where the general concept of water is divided into springs, rivers, and lakes.

[101] 'Suda' s.v. Δικτύς = *FGrH* 49 T 1. See Jacoby's commentary for discussion of the date of composition.

ethnic was deliberately chosen to suggest a contemporary. Indeed the *Ephemerides*, like the treatise on rivers, springs, and lakes, need not be a work on Alexander, merely a series of fictitious diaries. It may be extreme to dismiss Strattis as a 'Schwindelautor', but it is equally extreme to infer that he was a near contemporary of Alexander who wrote a long and involved commentary on the *Ephemerides* of Eumenes.[102] Nothing of any substance can be based on an uncorroborated and textually uncertain entry in the 'Suda'.

CONCLUSIONS

What evidence we have suggests that Eumenes' record was limited in scope, providing brief notes on Alexander's daily activity. They may have been produced at Babylon in the months before he moved to Asia Minor to assume his satrapy.[103] It would have been a hasty compilation, to provide an acceptable record of the king's last days and months in a literary form that would be widely read. In this Eumenes was probably acting in the interests of the entire staff at Babylon, all of whom must have found the rumours of poisoning disturbing and distasteful. From the outset it was probably regarded as an authorized version. This literary propaganda accompanied more repressive attempts to scotch the rumours. Antipater, who had Hypereides' tongue torn out,[104] discouraged their promulgation in his own dominions, but, even so, scandal persisted. In 317 Olympias exploited the rumours in her vendetta against the family of her old enemy, executing Nicanor and desecrating the tomb of Iollas.[105] Few people, however, had her interest in the matter, least of all Ptolemy, who had shared Medeius' hospitality in the fateful carouse. As the self-proclaimed beneficiary of Alexander and guardian of the king's body, he was naturally disposed to exclude all suggestions of poisoning. Eumenes' account of the last days was congenial to him, and he cited the *Ephemerides*

---

[102] If we accept the hypothesis, one needs to ask (as does Badian) why a supposedly straightforward record of fact required a commentary of such scope. It would suggest that its content and even authorship was a matter of controversy.

[103] For Eumenes' position after Alexander's death see Plut. *Eum.* 3. See also *CQ* 21 (1971) 122–3.

[104] [Plut.] *Vit. X Orat.* 849B (with variants); Plut. *Dem.* 28 fin.

[105] Diod, xix. 11. 8; Plut. *Al.* 77. 2.

explicitly. He may have used the work elsewhere, but there is no evidence (and little probability) that he based his narrative upon it.[106] The recorded extracts are too jejune and uninformative and, at least in the passages known to use, devoid of military detail. What is more, it is only in the record of the last illness that Arrian shows any trace of a narrative arranged by days.[107]

In general the *Ephemerides* seem to have been little used. Either the material was regarded as too commonplace or the circumstances of their composition were seen as suspicious. Aristobulus had nothing to do with them. He ignored the explicit date for the king's death[108] and reacted violently against the insinuations that the fever was accelerated by excessive drinking. On the contrary, his Alexander was temperate. He stayed late for companionship and not for drink,[109] and at the fatal feast he drank only to slake his thirst when the fever was already raging.[110] It is apologetic and sadly unconvincing at that, a desperate and rather pathetic attempt to rebut a universal criticism enshrined in the *Ephemerides*. Faced with a choice between poison and inebriation, he rejected both and was forced to create a temperate Alexander, who existed only in his own wishful thinking.[111]

The *Ephemerides*, then, are not in any sense a full archive or extracts from an archive. Nor are they a deliberate forgery, purporting to be something other than what they are. They are memoirs of the king, with the peculiarity that they are written on a day-to-day basis. But they hardly provide an unbiased factual record. Eumenes had his interests to protect and selected his material accordingly. The facts as they stand are probably

[106] Attempts to prove a diary-like style in Arrian have been frequent (cf. *Entretiens Hardt* 22 [1976] 6–7), but Arrian's style is unitary and there is nothing in the Alexander history that cannot be paralleled in other works.

[107] Some campaign reports do from time to time give an account of events in successive days (e.g. iii. 21. 3–9; iv. 2. 4–3. 1), but the details are usually striking enough to have been vividly remembered by participants in the drama.

[108] Plut. *Al.* 75. 6. See above, p. 167.

[109] Arr. vii. 29. 4; Plut. *Al.* 23. 6; cf. *Quaest. conv.* i. 6. 1.

[110] Plut. *Al.* 75. 5. Cf. Arr. vii. 25. 1, where the fever begins only after two successive nights of drinking.

[111] His picture, however, has commended itself to latter-day enthusiasts of Alexander. See Tarn, *Alexander* ii. 41, 48; Hammond, *KCS* 297–8 (who elevates Aristobulus into a close friend of the king).

correct. The most brilliant political tactician of his age will hardly have introduced demonstrable falsehoods into his work. On the other hand we cannot expect to have anything like the whole truth. Eumenes emphasized the events which suited the interpretation he wished to impose: the protracted, almost continuous, drinking bouts, the subsequent onset of fever, and its gradual intensification through ten days of illness. Behind that façade there is scope for all manner of machination, even conspiracy against the king's life. The *Ephemerides* gives us what was public and verifiable, but their description is too vague and disjointed to support a diagnosis of the illness, let alone a reconstruction of the political subcurrents at court. The serious modern historian is enmeshed in two very different strands of evidence, on the one hand a tradition which emphasized the sensational elements, the gargantuan feats of drinking and the rumours of poison, and on the other a report which is deliberately edited to lull any suspicion of foul play. The truth lies beyond both and will probably be elusive for all time.

# 8

## ALEXANDER'S LAST PLANS

THE discussion of the *Ephemerides* leads naturally to the consideration of other supposedly documentary evidence. Undoubtedly the most interesting and controversial example is provided by Diodorus.[1] After Alexander's death, he claims, the regent Perdiccas made it one of his first tasks to quash a number of projects which he found in the royal archives.[2] Diodorus describes the most striking and memorable: the provision of 1,000 warships, all above trireme size, for a campaign against Carthage and the inhabitants of the western Mediterranean, the construction of a military road across north Africa and the establishment of appropriate harbours and arsenals. There were also gigantic building-projects: the completion of Hephaestion's pyre, the erection of six colossal temples in Greece and Macedonia,[3] and a tomb for Philip to rival the Great Pyramid of Gizeh. Finally there were to be new city foundations and transplanting of populations from Europe to Asia and vice versa. A Macedonian assembly formally annulled

---

[1] Diod. xviii. 4. 2–6. For surveys of modern literature see Seibert, *Alexander der Grosse* 7–10; *Das Zeitalter der Diadochen* 91. In what follows I shall confine myself to citing what I regard as the most important and instructive treatments of the subject.

[2] ἐν τοῖς ὑπομνήμασι τοῦ βασιλέως (4. 2). The terminology, as usual in Diodorus, is very lax. Elsewhere he uses ὑπομνήματα to designate documents in the royal Ptolemaic archives (iii. 38. 1) or even written records in general (v. 57. 3). 'In the records of the king' seems a reasonably neutral translation.

[3] There is probably some manuscript dislocation. In Diodorus' text the provision concerning the temples occurs between the military road and the building of harbours. Fischer's transposition is accepted in the most recent editions and may well be correct. It is not, however, necessary. The temple constructions could be interpreted as a preliminary to the war in the west, to ensure the support and succour of the gods. K. Rosen's attempt (*Acta Classica* 10 [1967] 50) to prove inconsistency must be adjudged a failure. The phrasing at 4. 4 (ἀκολούθως δὲ τῷ τηλικούτῳ στόλῳ) certainly does not suggest a digression. Diodorus simply underscores the scale of the harbours and arsenals, consistent with the vast scope of the expedition (cf. xvii. 115. 6, xviii. 28. 2 for similar phrasing).

these proposals, declaring them excessively ambitious and impracticable.

Diodorus' report has evoked very different reactions among modern scholars. Schachermeyr, for instance, has had no hesitation in accepting it as authentic in every detail, the most illuminating evidence for Alexander's imperial aims.[4] On the other hand Tarn followed Droysen and Kaerst and dismissed the entire story as a late fabrication, foisting on Alexander wholly unhistorical ambitions of world conquest.[5] Between these extremes comes Badian's interpretation, which views the episode as a purely political manœuvre within the context of the Succession. Alexander's plans needed to be rejected in their totality, so Perdiccas presented material that made rejection inevitable. If there was forgery, it was contemporary forgery, and the projects were ones that Alexander might have conceived.[6] That is a theory strongly resembling the interpretation of the *Ephemerides* propounded in the last chapter and it has obvious attractions. But there is always a strong element of subjectivity in the discussion, depending on one's prejudices about what Alexander could or could not have planned.[7] One particular danger should be avoided. Too often the discussion has revolved exclusively around Diodorus, to ascribe his material to the contemporary Hieronymus of Cardia or to a later, less reliable, secondary source. That leads to stalemate. Even if the report comes from Hieronymus in its entirety, it is not necessarily authentic. On Badian's interpretation he could still have been bamboozled by a contemporary forgery by Perdiccas.

---

[4] 'Die letzten Pläne Alexanders', *JÖAI* 41 (1954) 118–40; *Alexander in Babylon* 187–94; *Alexander der Grosse* 547–56. Schachermeyr reacted strongly against the scepticism of Tarn, just as, in an earlier age, Wilcken had rejected the first exposition of Tarn's views (*SB. Berlin* 1937, 192–207 = *Berliner Akademieschriften* ii. 369–84) in what is probably the classic defence of the authenticity of Diodorus' report. See now Hammond, *KCS* 302–4.

[5] 'Alexander's Hypomnemata and the World Kingdom', *JHS* 41 (1921) 3–17; *Alexander* ii 378–98. For more recent sceptical positions see F. Hampl, 'Alexanders des Grossen Hypomnemata', *Robinson Studies* ii. 816–29; K. Kraft, *Der 'rationale' Alexander* 119–28; Wirth, *Studien* 74–5; Hornblower, *Hieronymus of Cardia* 94–6 (on which see below, p. 209.

[6] E. Badian, 'A King's Notebooks', *HSCP* 72 (1968) 183–204 (see now *CH Iran* ii [1985] 490–1).

[7] See, for instance, the *obiter dicta* of H. Hauben, *Ancient Society* 7 (1976) 98: 'one's opinion of the *hypomnemata* will be strongly conditioned by one's own idea of Alexander, while precisely those *hypomnemata*, if authentic, are of primary importance to one's judgement of the king's personality'.

Discussion of individual detail is equally inconclusive.[8] The most one can say is that the particular items in the report are not inconsistent with what is known of Alexander. What we need is confirmation from the rest of the tradition. It is (or should be) axiomatic that the wider the attestation of an episode, the more diverse the range of independent authorities, the more likely it is to have a historical basis. It is the extent of common ground that I wish to investigate here. The tradition outside Diodorus may provide a matrix against which we may assess his report.

### MILITARY PLANS

#### (i)  *The Persian Gulf*

Most of the specific projects mentioned by Diodorus are auxiliary, means to a greater end. He registers the fleet, the harbours, the military road, but gives no background explaining the war for which they were intended. It is simply '*the* campaign against the Carthaginians and the rest of the inhabitants of the coast of Libya and Spain as far as Sicily' (xviii. 4. 4). The campaign is described as an established fact, with the definite article, and the emphasis is upon the gigantic scale of the preparations. Diodorus himself may be responsible for the omission of the background, but there is a possibility that it was an omission already present in his source. Whoever provided the information perhaps considered the general plan of Mediterranean conquest too well known to require additional explanation. If so, there ought to be documentation elsewhere.

The most unambiguous evidence comes from Aristobulus. As reported by Arrian and Strabo, he gave a detailed description of Alexander's naval preparations for his projected Arabian expedition.[9] In the early summer of 323 his fleet was massing in Babylon. Nearchus' fleet from the Ocean was joined by new vessels which had been prefabricated in Phoenicia, assembled

---

[8] Cf. Badian 189–90: 'the reasonable connections of attested events that form the web of history can disintegrate into a bundle of threads'. His entire article is an excellent essay in the contextual analysis of evidence. So, in its day, was Wilcken's (above, n. 4), attempting a synthesis of all evidence to Alexander's imperial ambitions. The investigation, however, can be continued further.

[9] Arr. vii. 19. 3–5; Strabo xvi. 1. 11 (741) = *FGrH* 139 F 55–6.

at Thapsacus,[10] and floated down the Euphrates to Babylon. A harbour was being built near the capital to accommodate 1,000 warships,[11] and there was a large campaign to recruit manpower, free and slave, from the Levantine coast. To some degree this echoes the provisions of the plans in Diodorus. There are naval preparations on a vast scale. Shipbuilding is highly organized around Phoenicia. There is massive recruitment, with the specific intention of providing a maritime population for new foundations on the Persian Gulf.[12] The twin motives of military conquest and transfer of population are both evident in Aristobulus.

But there are some discordant elements. The shipbuilding is not on the massive scale of Diodorus' plans. Far from all being above the size of a trireme, the ships described by Aristobulus are relatively small. Only two quinqueremes and three quadriremes are mentioned; the rest are triremes and triaconters, and a meagre total at that, no more than forty-seven vessels. What is more, the Mediterranean coast was not the sole source of ships. More were commissioned from Babylonia by ruthlessly felling the cypress groves of the satrapy.[13] Much worse, there is no hint of ambitions outside Arabia. The whole context in Aristobulus concerns a campaign of discovery and annexation in the Persian Gulf. Alexander's motives are expounded in detail: conquest for its own sake, desire to exploit the legendary wealth of spices, and the vision of new foundations, particularly on Falaika and Bahrain.[14] There are no implications of a wider scheme of conquest. For Arabia the ambitions were real enough. The first wave at least of the invasion force was ready to move by sea and land when Alexander was struck down with

[10] The techniques were well developed by Alexander's day. Transport of ships in sections is attested in Pharaonic days (cf. L. Casson, *Ships and Seamanship in the Ancient World* 136), and Alexander himself had had experience in India hauling triaconters (in three sections) from the Indus to the Hydaspes (Arr. v. 8. 5; Curt. viii. 10. 3). The warships transported to the Euphrates were on a larger scale, but the techniques to shift them in sections certainly existed. Trajan, nearly half a millennium later, built his entire war fleet in sections in the forests of Nisibis and transported it by wagon to the Tigris (Dio lxvii. 26. 1).

[11] Arr. vii. 19. 4, 21. 1; Strabo xvi. 1. 11.

[12] Arr. vii. 19.5: τήν τε γὰρ παραλίαν τὴν πρὸς τῷ κόλπῳ τῷ Περσικῷ κατοικίζειν ἐπενόει.

[13] Arr. vii. 19. 4; Strabo xvi. i. 11.

[14] Arr. vii. 19. 5–20. 2; Strabo xvi. 1. 11. For exhaustive discussion see P. Högemann, *Alexander der Grosse und Arabien* 120–35.

his last illness,[15] and some of his plans for Arabia were carried through. Falaika at least received Greek settlers and some distinctly Greek institutions in the early Seleucid period.[16] But there is as yet no evidence which points beyond Arabia to a general war of conquest in the Mediterranean litoral.

This apparent silence may be misleading. As we have seen,[17] Arrian's narrative technique tends to make episodes more cohesive and self-contained than they were in the original. The focus on the Arabian expedition may be artificially precise. What is clear is that a whole complex of arrangements made over a wide span of time is placed together for narrative convenience. The voyages of discovery, which had taken place by the summer of 323 and which saw the islands of the Persian Gulf at their most verdant (i.e. in January or February),[18] had obviously been commissioned long before, hardly later than the summer of 324.[19] The same applies to the shipbuilding in Phoenicia. Arrian has concentrated all these preliminaries at a single point of the narrative and restricted the context to the Arabian expedition. Aristobulus may have spoken of other plans, just as he described engineering works on canals other than the Pallacotta. There is at least one hint of wider schemes. The harbour for 1,000 ships was clearly meant as a permanent installation in Babylon and designed for a larger armada than the original invasion fleet.[20] Other fleets would obviously

[15] Arr. vii. 25. 2–4 (on which see above, ch. 7). See now Högemann 189–97, who argues for three phases in the invasion plan.

[16] Cf. K. Jeppesen and O. Mørkholm, *KUML* 1960, 153–297; Mørkholm, *KUML* 1972, 193–202; *KUML* 1979, 219–30; G. M. Cohen, *The Seleucid Colonies* (Historia Einzelschr. 30: 1978) 42–4. For texts and detailed discussion of the important Greek inscriptions see now C. Roueché and S. Sherwin-White, *Chiron* 15 (1985) 1–39.

[17] See ch. 3 *passim*.

[18] It is clear from Theophrastus that Androsthenes' report on Bahrain was almost rhapsodic (Theophr. *HP* iv. 7. 7–8; v. 4. 7; *FGrH* 711 F 3–5). Högemann 92 calculates that Androsthenes' voyage took place over winter 324/3 (so Berve ii. no. 80) and suggests, perhaps correctly, that Hieron's voyage, which penetrated further (Arr. vii. 20. 7–8), began earlier. According to Arrian he reported to the living Alexander and he had clearly completed a voyage of several months in each direction.

[19] Another voyage of discovery, mentioned by Eratosthenes, apparently explored the east coast of Arabia from Heroonpolis to the mouth of the Red Sea (Strabo xvi. 4. 4 [768–9]; cf. Theophr. *HP* ix. 4. 4, 9; Högemann 80–7). If Arrian knew of this expedition, he consciously omitted it, focusing his narrative exclusively on the Persian Gulf and its islands.

[20] It was barely completed before Alexander's death (Arr. vii. 21. 1) and was certainly not intended to house the first invasion fleet (cf. Högemann 158).

follow, which would *inter alia* convey the colonists recruited by Miccalus and supply a naval defence force for the new cities.[21] If, then, Alexander's projects in Arabia were larger than Arrian suggests, there is some reason for supposing plans of conquest outside the Persian Gulf and justification for examining other evidence.

## (ii)  *Africa and the Mediterranean*

The most interesting and controversial material comes from Arrian. Book vii begins with Alexander's desire to explore the mouths of the Tigris and Euphrates. The story continues with reports in unnamed sources that Alexander intended to circumnavigate Arabia and Africa as far as Cadiz and to conquer Carthage and north Africa. After that Arrian reports two divergent traditions, one a plan to push around the Black Sea to Lake Maeotis and the other ambitions of conquest in Sicily and south Italy, inspired by the growing power of Rome (vii. 1. 1–3). Apart from Schachermeyr, who sees the report as a genuine echo of Alexander's original, undiluted plans of world conquest,[22] recent scholars have been unanimous in dismissing the passage as late fiction, derived from Arrian's secondary sources. Badian in particular has characterized it as 'a ragbag of recollected reports in various authors', thrown together to form a narrative bridge introducing the meeting with the Indian gymosophists.[23] This has the great merit (rare at the time Badian wrote) of drawing attention to Arrian's historical techniques. They are indeed of fundamental importance, but I think in this instance they have been a little misrepresented. That there is a narrative bridge is indubitable. As has been shown already,[24] the episode of the gymnosophists was carefully tailored to continue the theme of military aspiration and to introduce the story of the self-immolation of Calanus, which Arrian's sources located in Persis (vii. 3. 1), the general setting of the first chapters of Book vii. The theme of the gymnosophists

---

[21]  Arr. vi. 19. 5, 20. 2.

[22]  See particularly *Alexander der Grosse* 539 ('Im ganzen gesehen, war das nicht mehr als die Impression eines freudetrunkenen Augenblicks'); cf. *JÖAI* 41 (1954) 137–8.

[23]  Above, n. 6, 193. Cf. Kornemann 158; Brunt *Arrian* ii. 501.

[24]  See the detailed analysis presented above, pp. 72 ff.

and their reprobation of martial glory was clearly held back
and reserved for comment on this occasion. But were Alexander's plans of western conquest also presented anachronistic-
ally, to continue the bridge passage? I would suggest not.
Plutarch reports the same ambitions, to sail down the
Euphrates, to circumnavigate Arabia and Libya, and to penetrate the Mediterranean through the Pillars of Heracles. The
project is dated to the stay in Carmania and is said to have been
inspired by Nearchus' report of his experiences in the southern
Ocean.[25] That is not far from the setting in Arrian. It seems
that at least one of his sources referred in general to Alexander's
ambitions of conquest and mentioned them in the context of
the stay in Persepolis, listing his immediate designs to explore
the mouths of the Tigris and the Euphrates (which were partly
realized in 324 and 323) and then his more grandiose schemes
in Arabia.

But where does this report originate? There is consensus that
it comes from Arrian's subsidiary sources. The narrative formula he uses (οἱ δὲ καὶ τάδε ἀνέγραψαν) certainly does break the
exposition. It signals new and sensational material, the authenticity of which Arrian will not guarantee. Does it also mark a
change of sources? As we have often seen, a turn of phrase such
as 'they say' or 'there is a report' may merely signify the introduction of striking or suspicious material from his principal
sources, and the same may be the case here. The specific formula used recurs quite often. In some cases Arrian does employ
it to introduce subsidiary material which he personally discounts, the Bacchic revels and the rumours of poisoning, but he
makes it plain that he is giving a variant and underlines his disagreement.[26] Other cases are much less clear-cut, and there
are apparent instances where Arrian uses the formula with his
principal sources.[27] There is a good example at vii. 24. 4,
where he singles out a particular detail of the narrative
(Medeius' invitation to his banquet) using it as a link with the

---

[25] Plut. *Al.* 68. 1. The same setting in Curt. x. 1. 17–19.

[26] e.g. v. 2. 7; vi. 28. 1 (see above, pp. 67 ff); vii. 26. 3, 27. 1.

[27] There is a parallel case at vi. 11. 1, in the sequel to Alexander's wounding at the
Malli town, a passage generally excerpted from Ptolemy. Arrian introduces a variant
report (οἱ μὲν Κριτόδημον ἀνέγραψαν ... οἱ δὲ Περδίκκαν), clearly distinguishing Ptolemy
(who ignored Perdiccas) from another source, Aristobulus or Nearchus.

next narrative segment (the reports from the *Ephemerides*).[28]
The passage we are examining is not dissimilar. Arrian singles
out material from his sources which enables him to develop the
theme of Alexander's military ambitions and to move smoothly
to the next episode.

Two sources are at issue, as the internal variant (vii. 1. 3)
shows. Arrian declares himself unable to decide between them,
claiming that a decision is irrelevant, given the notoriety of
Alexander's imperial aspirations. That is a not uncommon
practice with him, whether the variants come from his principal or subsidiary sources.[29] In this case one at least of the variants seems late. The report of Alexander's designs on south
Italy and Sicily is connected with growing Roman power.
Unless that is Arrian's own comment, we must assume that his
informant was writing with the knowledge of hindsight in the
days of Roman supremacy.[30] But the project of invading the
Black Sea is a different matter. It is reported in embryonic form
at iv. 15. 6, where Alexander rejects an invitation by the Chorasmian king to strike westwards from central Asia towards the
Black Sea. He foreshadows a future campaign from the Helles-
pont into the Black Sea but defers it until the conquest of Asia is
complete. There is no doubt that the information here comes
from one of the major sources, Ptolemy or Aristobulus;[31] and
either might have referred to the plans formulated in 328. At all
events Alexander did express ambitions of conquest around the
Black Sea; and the wider project of the circumnavigation may
well be contemporary also. Any historian of the reign might
have described Alexander's undoubtedly true ambition, soon
fulfilled, of exploring the Tigris and Euphrates and then dis-
coursed on the long-term plans of empire. The primary report
may well come from a contemporary, perhaps Aristobulus,
who had no illusions about Alexander's appetite for conquest.

[28] The report is matched in Plutarch (*Al.* 75. 4), who continues with details of
Medeius' banquet that are repeated in Arrian's version of the *Ephemerides* (vii. 25. 1). I
have no doubt that Medeius' invitation at Arr. vii. 24. 4 is taken from Ptolemy and that
Ptolemy continued with an explicit reference to the *Ephemerides* (echoed by Arr. vii.
25. 1).

[29] Cf. iii. 3. 6 (Ptolemy against Aristobulus); ii. 3. 8 (Aristobulus against unnamed
authorities); iv. 28. 2.

[30] See above, ch. 4.

[31] It is usually ascribed to Aristobulus (cf. Strasburger, *Studien* i. 127; Pearson, *LHA*
164) on no very specific grounds. Ptolemy certainly cannot be excluded.

There are traces of this tradition elsewhere, and in my opinion the problematic final chapter of Arrian's *Indike* can only be explained by reference to it. The chapter deals with the Arabian coast and the impossibility of circumnavigation. It is based largely on sources later than the Alexander period,[32] but refers briefly to the voyages of discovery of 324/3, recapitulating material already expounded.[33] Next Arrian (or his source) offers the opinion that, if the Arabian coastline had been navigable, it would have been discovered by the energies of Alexander. But then there is a perplexing jump to the voyage of Hanno from Carthage to the south of the Straits of Gibraltar and an equally perplexing note that Cyrene forms a fertile oasis in the most desert part of Libya (*Ind.* 43. 11–13). What had been a careful and logical exposition degenerates into apparent lunacy.[34] Either Arrian suffered a form of mental breakdown or the text is defective. The latter is surely the case. The transmission of Arrian's work is notoriously plagued by lacunae, and I believe that there is a break in the text at the end of *Ind.* 43. 10 (after βαδιστὰ ἐόντα). There is a fairly substantial omission, and what has dropped out can only be a comparison of the Arabian coastline with that of Africa.

If my supposition is accepted, one can restore some semblance of sense to Arrian's exposition. Arrian passed from the possibility of circumnavigating Arabia to the wider plan for Africa, discussing their feasibility. The main problems Alexander would have faced were the increasing heat and the difficulties of provisioning. That combination had proved intractable for Hanno, who turned back soon after his course verged southwards. Cyrene, however, provided a counter-instance; even in the most desert recesses of Africa there were oases of fertility and plenty. Supplies should never have failed totally. This is admittedly a speculative reconstruction, but it does restore some logic and give the *Indike* a more impressive ending, specifically related to Alexander. Had he lived, the great king would have established the possibility of traversing

[32] *Ind.* 43. 4–5 refers briefly to a crossing of Arabia by troops of Ptolemy I (dated by Högemann [above, n. 14] 16 n. 20 to 312/11; cf. Tarn, *CR* 40 [1926] 13–15).

[33] *Ind.* 43. 8–10 = vii. 20. 7–9.

[34] Cf. Brunt, *Arrian* ii. 433 n. 5: 'What has an inaccurately reported voyage on the west coast of Africa, or the fertility of Cyrene, to do with the circumnavigation of Arabia?'

the Arabian peninsula and even attempted to sail round
Africa.[35] Successful or not, the enterprise would have eclipsed
even the triumphs of discovery in India. These, I think, are the
main outlines of the argument, and the details come from his
immediate source, Eratosthenes, who found a natural illustration in his homeland, Cyrene.[36] In that case Alexander's ambitions of African exploration were still of interest a century after
his death.

Now, as it appears in Arrian, there is an element of fantasy in
the project. It passes belief that, after his bitter experience of
the political and administrative chaos caused by his absence in
India, Alexander planned to remove himself even further from
the centres of civilization on a far longer and more hazar-
dous journey. But was that his plan? Plutarch expresses no
doubt, claiming that Alexander intended to participate personally in the voyage, at least in that down the Euphrates.[37]
Arrian, both in his main exposition and in his earlier proleptic
reference (where he accepts the intended circumnavigation as a
fact),[38] talks as though Alexander himself was to do the circumnavigation. Elsewhere he is less certain. Alexander's speech
at the Hyphasis mentions a circumnavigation of Africa but
only part of the force appears to be involved.[39] He expresses
himself impersonally, as may be intended at vii. 1. 2 ('he
intended a circumnavigation'). What is more, the plan as
Arrian expounds it at the opening of Book vii falls into two
parts: a circumnavigation of Africa and the conquest of the
southern Mediterranean. The two projects could have been
completed simultaneously, not sequentially. Alexander would
have started with the Arabian campaign and after its completion returned to the north Syrian coast, leaving a portion of
the fleet to continue around the south of the continent. That is
what happened in south India when Alexander abandoned the

---

[35] This is suggested by Stadter 131, but he maintains (n. 70) that Hanno's attempted
circumnavigation was another proof of the impossibility of the Arabian journey. If so,
the connection is at best implicit. Nothing in the text *as it stands* suggests a comparison
between Arabia and Africa.

[36] Cf. Berger, *Die geogr. Fragmente des Eratosthenes* 93–4, arguing that Eratosthenes
intended to prove by historical examples that the south-west coast of the Oekumene
was not navigable.

[37] Plut. *Al.* 68. 1 (αὐτὸς πλεύσας).

[38] vii. 1. 2: ἐπενόει ... περιπλεῦσαι; iv. 7. 5.

[39] v. 26. 2: ἀπὸ τοῦ Περσικοῦ εἰς Λιβύην περιπλευσθήσεται στόλῳ ἡμετέρῳ.

command of the fleet to Nearchus.[40] In any case Alexander's notorious curiosity about the unknown would naturally have impelled him to discover the truth about the African coast. Herodotus, whose account he surely knew, had given a tantalizing description of voyages of discovery in the Achaemenid period,[41] and it would be natural enough for him to take steps to improve the state of knowledge—in the same way that he sent Heracleides to discover the facts about the northern Caspian coast.[42] In both cases the voyage had a military function (Heracleides had a fleet of warships) and might prefigure conquest and annexation. I see no problem in Alexander planning a circumnavigation of Africa, but it was of secondary importance, subsidiary to the main work of conquest in the Mediterranean.

There is near-confirmation in the vulgate tradition. As we have seen, Plutarch follows the report in Arrian, writing of an expedition down the Euphrates to Arabia and Libya and then through the Straits of Gibraltar. To that end boats were constructed near Thapsacus and sailors and helmsmen recruited from all quarters.[43] Plutarch speaks only of naval activity, not of plans of conquest. Fortunately those plans are explicit in Curtius Rufus (x. 1. 17–19). His discussion comes at exactly the same point of the narrative as it does in Plutarch, in the context of Nearchus' report (in Carmania) of his voyage in the Indian Ocean. Some of it parallels Plutarch (the report of shipbuilding at Thapsacus and the widespread preparations) but Curtius adds specific plans of conquest. After conquering the maritime coast of the east Alexander intended to leave Syria for Africa,

[40] *Ind.* 20. 1–3. The description may well be slanted to enhance Nearchus' merits (Badian, *YCS* 24 [1975] 154–6), but Alexander's general considerations seem correctly stated. The passage incidentally supplies a good example of a demonstrably impersonal reference to circumnavigation. πόθον μὲν εἶναι . . . ἐκπεριπλῶσαι (20. 1) parallels ἐπενόει . . . περιπλεῦσαι at vii. 1. 2, but here there is no suggestion that Alexander ever intended to sail in person.

[41] Hdt. iv. 42–4. There is an obvious contemporary instance of the direct influence of Herodotus in Alexander's desire to be worshipped as the third of the Arabian pantheon. The motive, attested by Aristobulus, can only have been inspired by Herodotus' report of the Arab cult of Dionysus and Urania (Hdt. iii. 8. 3; cf. Arr. vii. 20. 1; Strabo xvi. 1. 11 [741]; Högemann [above, n. 14] 131, 139–41).

[42] Arr. vii. 16. 1–2. See ch. 5, n. 156.

[43] Plut. *Al.* 68. 1–2. Wilcken, *Berliner Akademieschriften* ii. 381, 383, had seen that Plutarch was directly relevant to the tradition of the Last Plans, but he regarded the material about the circumnavigation of Africa as a late, apocryphal addition.

attack Carthage, penetrate the deserts to the Straits of Gibraltar, and return by way of the Spanish and Italian coasts.[44] There is nothing explicit about the Arabian expedition; but the instructions for concentrating a fleet at Babylon only make sense if its objective was the Persian Gulf and, as Wilcken saw, the text presupposes plans of conquest in Arabia.[45] Curtius' source, which has close affinities with Plutarch's, knew of impending campaigns in north Africa complementing the naval expedition to the south. Curtius, as so often, has only partially digested his original and reduced the first part of the plans, the coastal voyage, to near-incomprehensibility.

There is a wide measure of agreement. All sources agree that there were grandiose plans formulated in the winter of 325/4, after the king's return from India. Those plans involved a war of conquest in the north and a voyage of discovery to the south. Aristobulus confirms that the first stage, the preparation for the invasion of Arabia, was virtually complete by the summer of 323. What is more, the plan of conquest in Curtius largely coheres with the details of Diodorus' report, The main divergence, of which Tarn made much, concerns the number and size of the warships. Diodorus speaks of 1,000 vessels larger than a trireme, whereas Curtius apparently mentions 700 ships, all septiremes, to be concentrated at Babylon. This is not as complete a contradiction as Tarn implied. The warships mentioned by Curtius are earmarked for the Euphrates fleet, those in Diodorus for war in the west.[46] The figures are complementary not contradictory. Even so, Curtius' total of seven hundred seems high, if only the invasion fleet for Arabia is at issue. Provided that the figure is correctly restored (which is far from certain),[47] it may refer to the sum total of vessels earmarked for

---

[44] Tarn's attempts to show the points of detail anachronistic were adequately refuted by Schachermeyr, *JÖAI* 41 (1956) 132.

[45] Wilcken ii. 382–3, arguing that the introductory phrase (*omni ad orientem maritima regione perdomita*) refers to the Arabian expedition.

[46] Correctly emphasized by Badian (above, n. 6) 192.

[47] The manuscript reading at x. 1. 19 is *Thapsagas et ingentarumque*. Long ago Heinsius saw that the corruption concealed a numeral ('Leg. *Quingentarumque*'). Zumpt's *septingentarum* is the most attractive emendation to date, but it does not explain the ungrammatical intrusion of -*que*. Professor J. A. Willis has suggested to me that the corruption may be more complex: an original reading such as *septuaginta ducentarumque* could have been progressively contracted into the garbled nonsense of the manuscripts. We simply cannot say what was the primary figure.

the campaign: Nearchus' fleet and the vessels built in Babylonia as well as those assembled at Thapsacus. Alexander's harbour installations at Babylon, we may recall, were designed for 1,000 warships, and in that context Curtius' figure is not outrageous. The dimensions of the vessels are another matter. Alexander may have projected the construction of warships of superior size,[48] but there is no evidence that anything larger than a quinquereme eventuated in his reign. But, once again, the problem may be unreal. In Curtius' text there is a certain amount of numerical contraction. The septiremes are presented in abbreviated form (*VIIremis*), and there is a real possibility that some of the *hastae* have been conflated under the influence of the preceding numeral.[49] Curtius may originally have written of quadriremes (*IIIIremis*), a size of warship perfectly compatible with Diodorus.

## (iii) *Preparations in Phoenicia*

Alexander had conceived plans of western conquest by 324, if not before. Preparations were well under way by the time of his death. As we have seen, the fleet which assembled in Babylon was only part of the armament. Further naval forces were to be committed to the Arabian adventure, but the mass of the preparations was reserved for the campaign in the Mediterranean. If Diodorus is correct, 1,000 ships would ultimately participate in that grand design. Now the shipyards of Phoenicia and Cilicia were operating at full capacity in the last months of Alexander's reign. The effects can be seen clearly in the naval operations of the Lamian War, where it can be shown that the Macedonian fleet was wholly dependent on vessels transferred from the eastern Mediterranean. When hostilities began in Greece, in the summer of 323, Antipater's fleet comprised 110 ships, 'which Alexander had sent to convey a mass of bullion from the royal treasury to Macedonia'.[50] There is no evidence

[48] So Pliny *NH* vii. 208, adduced by Schachermeyr (above, n. 44) 133.

[49] Modius reported that some *libri antiqui* did actually have *quadriremes*, misreading the manuscript tradition.

[50] Diod. xviii. 12. 2. Goukowsky (*Diodore xviii* 124) suggests the connection with Harpalus. It is equally possible that Alexander was reacting to the news of resistance to the Exiles' Decree. By the autumn of 324 he was close to war with Athens (Ephippus, *FGrH* 126 F 5; cf Justin xiii. 5. 7; *mille naves longas sociis imperari praeceperat*; Curt. x. 2. 2). The crisis slackened, but Alexander would be justified in diverting a large navy to Greece *pro tempore*.

when or why this fleet was sent (a connection with the flight of
Harpalus is possible but not provable), but it had most certainly been despatched from the north-east Mediterranean
coast. It had also arrived in the relatively recent past. Those
110 ships were all that Antipater had in 323.

The following year saw a dramatic change. Diodorus speaks
of a Macedonian thalassocracy, and the numbers quoted are
formidable. The Macedonian admiral Cleitus commanded 240
ships against 170 under the Athenian Euetion for the decisive
battle near Amorgos.[51] These forces were a fraction of the total.
Before Amorgos the Athenians had 49 of their 50 quadriremes
out at sea and as many as 234 triremes.[52] Other squadrons than
Euetion's were operating in the Aegean and facing Macedonian fleets other than that commanded by Cleitus.[53] The
warships at the disposal of the Macedonian admirals had increased enormously, and there is only one plausible explanation. The commander-in-chief, Cleitus the White, was one of
Craterus' lieutenants, a senior officer attached to the great
column of veterans dismissed from Opis in the summer of 324.[54]
He was with Craterus in Cilicia and, when Craterus moved by
land to give his decisive assistance to Antipater, it was clearly
Cleitus who took a naval force into the Aegean and tipped the
balance of power there. The Athenian fleet was outnumbered
and outmatched.

Cleitus probably brought from Cilicia the entire fleet of 240
which fought at Amorgos. Over a hundred ships had previously
been transferred from the Levant in 324. That was not the
whole story. In the spring of 321 the regent Perdiccas launched
his invasion of Egypt, and he had with him a considerable fleet,
commanded by Attalus.[55] There is no time in which Cleitus

---

[51] Diod. xviii. 15. 8–9.

[52] *IG* ii². 1631, ll. 167–74. On the reading and interpretation see N. G. Ashton,
*ABSA* 72 (1977) 4–8. The figure for the quadriremes is certain, that of the triremes less
so. The total number of triremes available was 315 (l. 171), and clearly the bare mini-
mum of unseaworthy ships will have been retained in the dockyards. The 170 ships of
Diod. xviii. 15. 8 I take to be the contingent under Euetion, not the entirety of the
Athenian navy.

[53] See T. Walek, *Rev. Phil.* 48 (1924) 23–30, who assumes independent operations
against Antipater in the Malian Gulf.

[54] Justin xii. 12. 8; cf. Berve ii. no. 428.

[55] Diod. xviii. 37. 2–3; 41. 7. The size of the fleet is not given, but it was clearly substantial. When Attalus reappeared near Rhodes he had 10,000 infantry and 800
cavalry (Arr. *Succ.* F 1. 39).

could have returned from the Aegean (in fact he remained a staunch partisan of Craterus and Antipater),[56] and it was hardly feasible to collapse the old war fleet on the Euphrates and transport it laboriously back to the Mediterranean coast. In all probability Perdiccas had a fleet awaiting him in the harbours of Cilicia and Phoenicia. He had enough ships to detach a modest squadron to escort Aristonous' invasion of Cyprus.[57] That squadron, it happens to be attested, came from Phoenicia, and there is every reason to suppose that the main invasion fleet came from the same source. If that is true, the shipbuilding around the Levant had been prodigious, enough for three substantial fleets, and the numbers may have been close to Alexander's target of 1,000

Large though this figure may be, it is certainly not fantastic, given what Alexander knew of the naval capacity of Carthage and the western Greeks.[58] The forces of Dionysius I in 399 were estimated at 400 warships,[59] some of which were quadriremes and quinqueremes, and the great fleet sent out from Carthage in 396 is said to have comprised 400 warships with 600 trans-

---

[56] *Pace* P. Briant (*Antigone le Borgne* [Paris, 1973] 212 ff), Justin xiii. 6. 16 is muddled when he says that Cleitus was given command of Perdiccas' fleet. The fact that he was rewarded at Triparadeisus (Arr. *Succ.* F 1. 37; Diod. xviii. 39. 6) suggests that he had no Perdiccan connection (Briant is forced to assume a double defection back to Antipater). It is much more likely that Justin has garbled his original and mistaken the command of Perdiccas' fleet for Antipater's. H. Hauben, *Het Vlootbevelhebberschap in de vroege diadochentijd* (Verhandelingen van de kon. acad. v. Wetenschappen van België: Kl. der Letteren No. 77: Brussels, 1975) 46–7, also accepts Justin, arguing for a temporary *rapprochement* between Antipater and Perdiccas in late 322. The citizenship decree from Ephesus (*JÖAI* 16 [1913] 235, IIn = *Inschr. v. Ephesos* iv. 1435) is not as decisive as he and Briant think. Both Cleitus and Perdiccas' brother, Alcetas, are honoured in the same vote of citizenship, but that does not imply that they were in the same camp. The decree (not precisely datable) probably comes in the period before the outbreak of civil war, when the Ephesians might have felt inclined to conciliate both sides. In 322 Alcetas was relatively close, sent by his brother to intercept Cynane (Arr. *Succ.* F. 1. 22; Polyaen. viii. 60; Diod. xix. 52. 5) at roughly the same time as Cleitus' naval operations in the Aegean. If the two were in relative proximity to Ephesus, they might have been honoured by the city. It did not preclude their operating on different sides the following year.

[57] Arr. *Succ.* F 24. 6.

[58] Emphasized by Schachermeyr, *JÖAI* 41 (1954) 134–5; Badian (above, n. 6) 192; Hauben, *Ancient Society* 7 (1976) 99.

[59] Diod. ii. 5. 6; cf. xiv. 42. 4–5 (ship sheds with capacity for up to 600 vessels), 47. 7. Whatever Diodorus' immediate source, this information probably derives from Philistus, who wrote a celebrated ἔκφρασις dealing with Dionysius' preparations of weapons, ships, and siege engines (*FGrH* 556 F 28).

port vessels.[60] The figures may be exaggerated in the literature, but it was literature available to Alexander and the nucleus of the tradition probably goes back to Philistus, whose
work the king knew and read.[61] To counter fleets of those
dimensions Alexander could be forgiven for making truly vast
preparations. Nor are the numbers beyond Alexander's capacity in 324. Demetrius' grandiose plans when he was king of
Macedon involved laying the keels of 500 ships (some of them
fifteens and sixteens),[62] and his resources then were a fraction
of Alexander's. The total, then, is credible; the efforts to
achieve it were prodigious. By the end of the reign the Cilician
and Phoenician coastline was a seething arsenal. Its master was
Craterus, who disposed of an army of 10,000 Macedonian
veterans and whose adherent, Philotas, was satrap of Cilicia
(Arr. *Succ.* F 24. 2). The combination of forces made him poten-
tially the most powerful man in the empire—after Alexander.

.By the time of the king's death the fleets for the invasion of
the west were well under construction. There were probably
new harbour installations, comparable with the great harbour
at Babylon with its capacity of 1,000 ships. The treasury of
Cyinda in Cilicia, so important in the period of the Successors,[63] probably owed its prominence to Alexander, who must
have transferred funds on an immense scale to finance the naval
preparations. Most of the projects recorded by Diodorus were
never completed and remained blueprints for the future. All of
them are a priori possible. Alexander, the city-founder *par excellence*, would have established cities wherever he went. Indeed
the foundation of cities is explicitly attested by Arrian (and
Aristobulus) as one of the prime objectives of the Arabian expedition.[64] These foundations would automatically ensure a

[60] Diod. xiv. 54. 5 (Ephorus, *FGrH* 70 F 204; Timaeus, *FGrH* 566 F 108).

[61] Plut. *Al.* 8. 3. Cf. T. S. Brown, *Historia* 16 (1967) 365–6, discounting Wilcken's
suggestion that Alexander read Philistus as preparation for his invasion of the west.
That may well be, but it is hard to think that the military descriptions left him un-
affected.

[62] Plut. *Demetr.* 43. 3. His father, Antigonus, also contemplated a fleet of 500 ships
during the siege of Tyre (315), exploiting the same areas of Lebanon that Alexander
had used for his ships' timber (Diod. xix. 58. 3–6). The first vessels were in commission
shortly after the siege ended, some 15 months later (Diod. xix. 62. 8, cf. 61. 5).

[63] Diod. xviii. 62. 2; xix. 56. 5; xx. 108. 2; Strabo xiv. 5. 10 (672); Athen. xi. 484c.
Cf. R. H. Simpson, *Historia* 6 (1957) 502–3; J. Bing, *Historia* 22 (1973) 344–50 (tracing
back the history of the fortress to the Assyrian period).

[64] Arr. vii. 19. 5, 20. 2.

transfer of population. If Alexander intended to populate his settlements in Arabia with manpower from the Phoenician coast,[65] there was no reason not to recruit colonists for north Africa from the eastern satrapies. Ever since his campaign in Bactria and Sogdiana he had made it a feature of his policy to enlist the prime of the military population of the eastern provinces to fight in his army far from their home satrapies. If Alexander had turned westwards, the Bactrians, Arachosians, Parthyaeans, Medes, and Persians might have performed the same functions as the Greek mercenaries in the far east, to be settled on alien territory as a permanent garrison community.

The actual plans of population transfer from Asia to Europe and vice versa are exactly what we should expect from Alexander. But the explanation given, the creation of concord and international friendship through mixed marriages (Diod. xviii. 4. 4), is strongly idealistic and inconsistent with the actual transfers of population accomplished during Alexander's lifetime. He introduced many foreign enclaves, superimposing them on indigenous populations, but there is no evidence that he ever attempted an ethnic blend.[66] Now the explanation is an accretion to the text, and it is the sole attempt to provide a motive for any of the plans. It is generally agreed to be a parenthetical remark either by Diodorus or his source.[67] The former is the more probable. Diodorus has some interest in the phenomenon of blended populations. He includes two excursuses, on the Celtiberians and the Libyphoenicians, and in both cases he comments on the virtues of intermarriage and the consequent creation of unity·and prosperity.[68] The thought is identical to that underlying the explanation of the Last Plans. In all probability Diodorus added a comment of his own, assuming that the attested plans for new foundations and population transfer

[65] The mission of Miccalus of Clazomenae was to enlist suitable colonists from the slave and free population of Syria and Phoenicia (Arr. vii. 19. 5).

[66] See particularly Briant, *Rois, Tributs et paysans* 240–52; Bosworth, *JHS* 100 (1980) 10–11, 101 (1981) 26.

[67] Cf. Badian (above, n. 6) 194 n. 41. Andreotti, *Saeculum* 8 (1957) 134, considered that the passage is evidence for an almost pacifist ideology in Hieronymus.

[68] Diod. v. 33. 1; xx. 55. 4. The context of the first passage comes from Poseidonius (*FGrH* 87 F 117), the second from a Sicilian source. In neither case can Hieronymus be at issue. Diodorus' terminology at xviii. 4. 4 is typically bland. Tarn himself (*JHS* 41 [1921] 11) noted that κοινὴ ὁμόνοια is a favourite catchword, attested in several other contexts (Diod. xvi. 20. 6, 60. 3).

were designed to produce racial unity. His assumption could conceivably have some truth, but it remains an assumption, irrelevant to the problem of the historicity of the plans.

The one remaining provision which concerns the military project is the building of a road across the coast of north Africa. As is well known, Tarn attempted to subvert this detail, maintaining that neither Alexander nor any of his Successors is known to have built a major road.[69] His argument has rightly been rejected on general grounds; once Alexander left the road system of the Persian empire, he would be forced to create new arteries of communication. That is undoubtedly true, and we may press the argument further. Alexander did construct military roads, and they are well attested in what even Tarn would accept as the best of sources. In the winter of 334/3 Thracian pioneers had built a road through the Climax range, to circumvent the arduous coastal route to Pamphylia.[70] That road was not of enormous length, but it was a new construction. On a lárger scale the army constructed a road to the Indus early in 326, building as it advanced through country that was otherwise impassable.[71] That is exactly the procedure that seems envisaged in the Last Plans. If a land army with adequate supplies were to cross the desert country of north Africa, it would need a proper road system. That must have been obvious to Alexander—and to his men, who would have had the privilege of the spadework. It is not surprising that they found the prospect unpalatable.

### THE BUILDING PROGRAMME

Nothing in the plan of conquest is implausible. Much of it was in motion by the time of Alexander's death and it is amply attested in the historical tradition. The same applies to the building-projects. The six temples for the international centres

[69] Tarn, *Alexander the Great* ii. 391–2, characterized by Schachermeyr as 'ein . . . recht seltsamer Einwurf'.

[70] Arr. i. 26. 1; Plut. *Al.* 17. 8. Tarn (i. 21) writes of 'rock-steps cut in the hill'. That is an imposition on the text, inspired by Polyaenus' description of the turning of Tempe— a totally different incident (Polyaen. iv. 3. 23).

[71] Arr. iv. 30. 7: καὶ ἡ στρατιὰ αὐτῷ ὡδοποίει τὸ πρόσω ἰοῦσα ἄπορα ἄλλως ὄντα τὰ ταύτῃ χωρία. See also Diod. xviii. 28. 2 (Alexander's funeral car was escorted by a battalion of road-builders).

of Greece and Macedon were blueprints for the future, and there is no evidence which can be adduced to confirm or refute Diodorus.[72] The proposed temple for Athene Ilias is a different matter. Strabo refers to a royal letter, despatched some time after Gaugamela, in which the king promised to expand the city of Ilium and make its temple a notable attraction.[73] That may be fiction, based on the tradition of the Last Plans, but we have no reason to assume so. Alexander had paid the sanctuary of Athene very considerable respect ever since his first visit in 334, and it must have been very high on the list of cult centres that he wished to embellish. There is nothing apart from general probability in favour of the great pyramid tomb projected for Philip (Diod. xviii. 4. 5). Whatever Alexander's views, public or private, about his divine parentage,[74] the recognition of his human father was obviously expedient in Macedon and a popular move with his troops, who had become increasingly restive at slights against the memory of Philip. The architect of Macedonian greatness could now be honoured with a memorial commensurate with his achievement, the equal of the most impressive royal monuments yet constructed. It was not in a form traditional or paralleled in Macedon, but it did embody the concept of kingly glory and Alexander presumably thought it appropriate for his predecessor (the mind boggles at the arrangements he might have made for his own obsequies!). Indeed there is a curious parallel. The pyramid was equally remote from Roman tradition, yet one of the more familiar landmarks on the line of the Aurelian

---

[72] See the comments of Schachermeyr, *JÖAI* 41 (1954) 130. It may be of significance that Pericles' building-project was reported to have entailed costs of 1,000 talents for each temple (Plut. *Per.* 12. 2). The figure is apocryphal (A. Andrewes, *JHS* 98 [1978] 2), but perhaps based on fourth-century tradition. If so, it perhaps gave Alexander an ideal to surpass.

[73] Strabo xiii. 1. 26 (593). Alexander had a perpetual reminder of the sanctuary in the sacred shield which he borrowed in 334 and had carried before him in every battle (Arr. i. 11. 7; cf. vi. 9. 3).

[74] See Badian (above, n. 6) 195 emphasizing (against Hampl [above, n. 5] 821–5) that the wording is Diodorus' and that the original document may not have explicitly described Philip as Alexander's father. In any case, however sincerely Alexander believed himself to be the son of Zeus Ammon, that did not entail disowning his earthly father. Like Heracles he enjoyed dual paternity (cf. *Greece & the E. Mediterranean* 70–1) and could still recognize Philip when it suited his purposes to do so. Equally, when he wished to circumvent Philip's rulings, he might question the relationship (Plut. *Al.* 28. 2).

Wall is a perfectly preserved pyramid tomb, some thirty-six metres high. It is the burial-place of C. Cestius, a notable of the Augustan era.[75] If such a man, a relatively humble senator, could strive after immortality by imitating the greatness of Egypt, Alexander could certainly commemorate his father on a scale that rivalled the original.

All that remains is the completion of Hephaestion's pyre. Quite unnecessary difficulties have been raised by this item, because of a general conviction that Hephaestion's corpse was burned and interred long before Alexander's death.[76] That, I think, cannot have been the case. Diodorus writes as though the funeral had been celebrated,[77] but, as we shall see, his detailed narrative refutes the general statement. Apart from a compressed note in Justin, only Aelian hints at a completed funeral,[78] but even he records a variant tradition that Hephaestion's funerary preparations served for Alexander himself—in other words the obsequies were incomplete. The rest of the sources are virtually unanimous. Hephaestion died at Ecbatana, passionately mourned by the king, and his body was transferred to Babylon. Like Alexander's, his corpse must have been embalmed to prevent decay, and the funeral proper might have been delayed indefinitely. Now Arrian claims that Alexander ordered a pyre to be built at Babylon at a cost of 10,000 talents. It is one of the details which, he says, were attested by all sources.[79] Plutarch records essentially the same details, agreeing on the projected cost and adding that Alexander desired his favourite architect, Deinocrates, to work on the monument.[80] That is largely the story of the vulgate. Justin

[75] *ILS* 917; *PIR*² C 686. For descriptions of the monument see E. Nash, *Pictorial Dictionary of Ancient Rome* ii. 321–3; J. M. C. Toynbee, *Death and Burial in the Roman World* (London, 1971) 127–8.

[76] See (e.g.) Schachermeyr, *JÖAI* 41 (1954) 127–38, enlarged upon by F. R. Wüst, 'Zu den Hypomnemata Alexanders des Grossen: Das Grabmal des Hephaistion', *JÖAI* 44 (1959) 147–57. Both scholars unnecessarily stress the distinction between pyre and tomb. Obviously the great monument was not designed to be consigned to the flames, but it could have formed the base of a pyre and, after the cremation, a permanent *heroon* for Hephaestion.

[77] Diod. xvii. 114. 1, 116. 1 (μετὰ δὲ τὴν ἐκφοράν).

[78] Aelian *VH* vii. 8 (Alexander threw weapons on the pyre and melted gold and silver over the body; compare Arr. vii. 14. 9); cf. Justin xii. 12. 12 (*tumulumque . . . fecit*).

[79] Arr. vii. 14. 8 (πρὸς πάντων ξυμφωνούμενα). Some sources, he claims, gave a higher figure.

[80] Plut. *Al.* 72. 5, on which see Hamilton's commentary.

(xii. 12. 12) records a cost of 12,000 talents, a figure which re-curs in the more detailed account of Diodorus (xvii. 115. 5). According to that author, Alexander amassed an army of architects and craftsmen, demolished ten stades of the walls of Babylon and built a vast rectangular structure, a stade in each direction. Its walls were decorated with elaborate friezes of gold, and around the base were the gold prows of quin-queremes, sporting life-size warriors chased in gold. The whole edifice rose to more than 130 cubits in height. Diodorus expresses himself in uncompromising indicatives, stating that the monument was actually completed.[81] That, as is usually admitted, is impossible. There is no trace of such a gigantic memorial in the ruins of Babylon, and even on Diodorus' account the accumulation of raw material and the mustering of craftsmen would have taken many months. The basic construction work can hardly have begun before Alexander's death.[82] Diodorus, then, is misleading. He reported a project which was merely anticipated as completely finished, a blunder only too characteristic of his work, but no worse than the repeated state-ment that Philip and Athens made peace in 340/39 (they actually went to war).[83]

The funeral of Hephaestion, then, was planned as an unsur-passably grandiose affair. Alexander's own inclinations were compounded by his officers. Eumenes was particularly eager to expiate his hatred of the living favourite and surpassed himself in the invention of elaborate funeral honours.[84] He and his brother officers had a material interest in ensuring that the ceremonies would be no slight to Hephaestion, and it is no sur-prise that their scale was too grand for completion before Alex-ander's own death. We know from Arrian (vii. 14. 10) that

---

[81] e.g. 115. 1: ᾠκοδόμησε τετράπλευρον πυράν. There are a dozen indicatives in the description.

[82] Badian (above, n. 6) 201 (also 196, n. 44) goes too far when he describes the build-ing as visibly under construction, 'an eyesore and a very present irritation'. Given the scale, very little of it can have taken place in eight months. Alexander's funeral car, a much more modest undertaking, required two years to complete. There may also have been some resistance from the Babylonian priesthood. Their well attested attempt to keep Alexander from the city (cf. Arr. vii. 17. 1 ff) could have had less to do with their proprietary rights over the revenues of Esagila than with the new monstrosity planned for the capital. They would hardly relish the loss of ten stades of circuit wall to honour a foreigner.

[83] Diod. xvi. 77. 3, 84. 2. Cf. Griffith, *History of Macedonia* ii. 579–80.

[84] Plut. *Eum.* 2. 10; Arr. vii. 14. 9. See above, p. 177.

3,000 competitors were enlisted for a gymnastic and musical
festival to surpass all previous celebrations. It was never held,
but the performers were in Babylon to compete at the king's demise. In the same way the preparations for the great monument
to Hephaestion, the huge brick cube[85] which would support
his pyre and ultimately his tomb, were under way in the first
months of 323. Craftsmen and architects were engaged, raw
material collected and bullion amassed from contributions by
court and empire, but the basic work still remained. The pyre,
then, comes in the same category as the plans of Mediterranean
conquest. It was a project conceived in Alexander's lifetime but
incomplete at his death.

There is clearly a close relationship between Diodorus'
account of the monument and his version of the Last Plans. He
stresses the unsurpassable magnitude of the project in words
that echo his commentary on the proposed temple at Ilium.[86]
Both exemplified the king's penchant for Homeric excellence,
to outstrip all rivalry, actual or potential. There is every likelihood that Diodorus' description of Hephaestion's pyre reflects
the actual plans published by Perdiccas. The scale of the work
is colossal, the outlay in gold and silver alone prodigious, beyond even the maximum figure of 12,000 talents which is said
to have been earmarked for it. 'Involving great expense' (Diod.
xviii. 4. 2) is an understatement. Now it has often been suggested that the two passages of Diodorus are interrelated. Jane
Hornblower airs the idea that the Last Plans in Book xviii come
from the same source as the description of the pyre.[87] Others
have argued for an anticipation of material from Hieronymus
in Book xvii. Fritz Wüst conceded that the accounts were independent but argued that the description of the pyre was an
insertion from an unknown secondary source.[88]

I do not see that the situation is so complicated. Provided

[85] See Wüst (above, n. 76), arguing against interpretations of the monument as a
step pyramid.

[86] xvii. 115. 1 (ὥστε . . . τοῖς ἐσομένοις μηδεμίαν ὑπέρθεσιν καταλιπεῖν; xviii. 4. 5 (ναὸν
ὑπερβολὴν ἑτέρῳ μὴ καταλείποντα). The verbal echoes mean very little. The language is
Diodorus' own, closely paralleled by his description of the Egyptian tombs (i. 46. 6, 66.
3 and 6; cf. iv. 45. 3). It may, however, have been inspired by similar sentiments in his
sources.

[87] *Hieronymus of Cardia* 94 (both passages from Cleitarchus).

[88] Wüst (above, n. 76) 154, stressing variants (one tradition that the building was
complete, the other that it is incomplete).

that we make the single assumption that Diodorus was in error to hold that the funeral preparations were completed, his account flows in a sensible, unitary stream. Alexander gives instructions for contributions to the funeral and imposes official mourning (xvii. 114. 4). His officers make elaborate donations (115. 1), while he himself arranges for the construction of a monument of unsurpassable greatness (115. 1–5). The total of contributions comes to 12,000 talents (115. 5). The narrative sequence is smooth and logical marred only by the repeated assumption that the funeral actually took place. That misapprehension makes it impossible that the narrative is an anticipatory extract from Hieronymus. In xviii. 4 Diodorus has no illusion that the work was finished, and he is unlikely to have made an error while grafting the material on to his earlier chapters. The same dilemma occurs if we assume repetition of earlier material in Book xviii. It is best to conclude that there are two separate descriptions. The first, in Book xvii, was taken from his main narrative source, Cleitarchus,[89] and the second clearly came from a different provenance, presumably the dominant source for Book xviii. What seems to me undeniable is that the plans for Hephaestion's monument were well known in the historical tradition, as was the projected campaign against Carthage and the west. The items which Perdiccas presented to the army clearly did not come as a bolt from the blue. They were on the whole familiar projects, which the regent skilfully juxtaposed, in order to underscore their cumulative expense. By now it is evident that these alleged plans do indeed represent Alexander's intentions at the time of his death. It looks very much as though we are dealing with actual posthumous papers, which Perdiccas had no need to forge or falsify. The unvarnished truth would suit his purposes eminently well.

### THE POLITICAL BACKGROUND

Why did Perdiccas consider it necessary to have the plans quashed? According to Diodorus, there was a direct connection with the activities of Craterus. That marshal had been sent to Cilicia with written instructions from the king, which were sub-

---

[89] I can see no merit in Hammond's suggestion (*Three Historians* 75) that Diodorus' description (like that of Alexander's funeral cortège) was derived from Ephippus.

sequently annulled by the Successors along with the rest of the
Last Plans.[90] The context of Perdiccas' strategem does admittedly have its problems, as Jane Hornblower has recently
emphasized, but they do not, in my opinion, justify her conclusion that the entire chapter is a collage by Diodorus, cobbled
together from a number of different sources.[91] There is some
chronological dislocation, to be sure. The execution of the
phalanx mutineers (xviii. 4. 7) is placed sensibly later than it is
in other sources,[92] but it is clearly a resumptive note, introducing the elimination of Meleager, which all authorities agree
in placing after definitive settlement.[93] Nor is the use of the term
'Successors' (διάδοχοι) at all conclusive. Diodorus only uses it
once elsewhere to describe the Successors as a corporate group
(contrasting with the Epigoni),[94] and it probably was not a
recurrent expression of Hieronymus. But the very rarity of the
term is a problem. Diodorus does not use it regularly as a label,
and the people designated at xviii. 4. 1 are not the Successors
conventionally understood as such. They are the marshals at
Babylon, the men who were the immediate, albeit temporary,
heirs to Alexander's power. I see no reason why Diodorus
should not be clumsily echoing the wording of his original.[95] But
the crux of the argument rests on the mission of Craterus. As is
well known and amply attested, he was sent out from Opis in
the summer of 324 to succeed Antipater as regent in Macedon.[96]
Diodorus, however, speaks as though his mission was Cilicia
and attaches the notice to the Last Plans. That was enough for

[90] Diod. xviii. 4. 1. The connection is explicit. Craterus' written instructions had
been given by Alexander, but the Successors decided not to complete the king's plans.
The decision is then enlarged upon (Diodorus uses the particle γάρ at 4. 2) with the
story of Perdiccas' approach to the army.

[91] *Hieronymus of Cardia* 94–6, esp. 94 'the more austere history of Hieronymus was
enriched by supplements from the Alexander vulgate'. The case, as she acknowledges,
had been argued by Rosen (above, n. 3).

[92] This was already noted by Badian (above, n. 6) 201 f. For other references to the
executions see Arr. *Succ.* F. 1. 4; Curt x. 9. 16–18; Justin xiii. 4. 7–8.

[93] Arr. *Succ.* F. 1. 4 (οὐ πολλῷ ὕστερον); Curt. x. 9. 21. In both cases the death of
Meleager is anticipated. Diodorus places it at the correct place and mentions its logical
prelude, the execution of the mutineers.

[94] Diod. i. 3. 3.

[95] Cf. xviii. 9. 1: 'Αλεξάνδρου καὶ τῆς βασιλείας υἱοὺς διαδόχους οὐκ ἔχοντος. Here
Hieronymus must have spoken of the succession to the Empire. He may well have (once
at least) described the marshals as the *de facto* successors. Compare Plut. *Demetr.* 14. 2
(perhaps based on Hieronymus), where Craterus is named as one of the διάδοχοι.

[96] Arr. vii. 12. 4; Justin xii. 12. 9; Curt. x. 10. 15; *Metz Epit.* 87.

Tarn to dismiss the passage as distorted, and Hornblower is inclined to follow him.[97]

Further analysis may be salutary. Diodorus clearly took his note about Craterus' mission in Cilicia from his main narrative source. The information recurs a few chapters later, where it is emphasized that Craterus had been sent to Cilicia and was about to bring his 10,000 veterans back to Macedon. That combines the two spheres of interest: Craterus had a prior commission in Cilicia to discharge before returning home. We may go further. Diodorus' wording is significant, repeated in both passages. Craterus was not merely sent; he was *sent in advance*.[98] The verb is a favourite with Diodorus, used on some twenty occasions. In every case it refers to a group or individual sent as a forerunner of a greater enterprise. In particular it is used three times with reference to the Macedonian advance force sent to Asia Minor in 336.[99] Craterus, then, was sent to Cilicia in advance of Alexander. He was to prepare the way for his lord and master. The connection with the Last Plans now becomes crystal clear. Alexander's main project was the Mediterranean war, and the centre of the preparations was the Cilician and Phoenician coast. Craterus was to superintend the naval build-up and ensure that there was no interruption of the construction work. His 10,000 veterans were an invaluable security force which could deter any attacks on the lumbering parties, such as hindered Alexander's own siege operations at Tyre.[100] They would also ensure that the coastal communities co-operated in the supply of munitions with alacrity (if not enthusiasm).[101] In due course Alexander would arrive to assume command and begin his move to the west. Against this background Craterus' apparent delay in Cilicia was not suspect but the fulfilment of Alexander's orders. He had not gone beyond the Levant at the time of Alexander's death because he was not intended to go further *in the first instance*. Ultimately he would

---

[97] Tarn, *JHS* 41 (1921) 8; Hornblower 95–6.

[98] ἔτυχε προεσταλμένος εἰς Κιλικίαν (4. 1); οὗτος γὰρ προεσταλμένος εἰς Κιλικίαν (12. 1).

[99] xvi. 91. 2, 93. 9; xvii. 2. 4. For other examples see J. I. McDougall's invaluable *Lexicon in Diodorum Siculum* (Hildesheim, 1983).

[100] Curt. iv. 2. 24; Arr. ii. 20. 4–5.

[101] He would be in a position to persuade the Cypriot kings to meet their obligations of copper, ropes, and sails (Curt. x. 1. 19).

proceed to Macedon to take up the regency, at a time when (on Alexander's reckoning) Antipater had left the Balkans with his new army of young Macedonian recruits. Whether this scenario had any hope of ultimate success we may well doubt;[102] but the fact remains that Craterus' first operational base was the Cilician coast. His presence there virtually confirms that the plans of western conquest were a reality, probably Alexander's highest priority in the last year of his life.

The annulment of the plans now requires little explanation. Craterus, as we have seen, was at the centre of a great arsenal and could command naval and land forces unmatched in quantity and quality. His men might have been unfit for war in Alexander's eyes (they had become disturbingly insubordinate), but they went on to win the Lamian War for Antipater and fuel the armies of the Successors.[103] While Craterus was in Cilicia, with the moral backing of Alexander's written instructions, he could simply do as he pleased. Given his popularity with the rank and file,[104] it was dangerous for the marshals at Babylon singly or collectively to take any action that might undermine his position. Not surprisingly Perdiccas turned to the Macedonian commons. The army, confronted with the accumulated expense and labour of Alexander's projects, had no hesitation in voting for their abandonment. The grandiose architectural monuments were consigned to limbo, as, more importantly, was the entire project of western conquest. There was to be no massive war in the west, no preparations for Craterus to complete. His presence in Cilicia was otiose, and he should move on to face his destiny in Macedonia, discharging the functions that the marshals at Babylon had defined for him.[105] It would be wrong, as has been forcefully argued by

---

[102] On the political tensions involved see Badian, *JHS* 81 (1961) 36–7; Bosworth, *CQ* 21 (1971) 125–6; Schachermeyr, *Alexander der Grosse* 516–19; *contra* Griffith, *PACA* 8 (1965) 12 ff.; Hammond, *KCS* 257.

[103] For the details see now *JHS* 106 (1986) 9.

[104] See particularly Plut. *Eum.* 6. 3; *Demetr.* 14.2; 'Suda' *s.v.* Κρατερός ( = Arr. *Succ.* F 19).

[105] Craterus' position in the Babylon settlement is a notorious crux, bedevilled by source divergences, real and apparent. I basically accept the views of Schwahn (*Klio* 24 [1931] 325) and Badian (*Studies in Greek and Roman History* 266) that his ultimate destination was Macedonia, where Alexander had originally intended him to be. Even if one accepts the traditional German theory of a *prostasia* in Asia (see, most fully, Schachermeyr, *Alexander in Babylon* 163–84), it remains true that Craterus was meant to be transferred from Cilicia as soon as possible.

Badian and Errington,[106] to interpret the army vote as a con-
stitutionally binding enactment. At most it had moral force,
but that moral force should not be discounted. The basis for
Craterus' position in Cilicia had been repudiated by the very
Macedonians whose support he needed in any contest for
power. As it happened, the Lamian War was a godsend. It en-
abled him to move west at a time when his presence was desperately needed. Even more importantly, he had the perfect
pretext for taking a great fleet with him.[107] That certainly was
not foreseen by Perdiccas when he had the plans quashed at
Babylon.

The ramifications cannot be taken further without being
engulfed in the morass of the politics of the Succession. Fortunately the implications for the evaluation of Diodorus are clear
enough. His report of the Last Plans is a unitary extract from
his main source (which I am sure was Hieronymus). We may
regret the omissions, which may be considerable, but he has at
least provided us with an intelligible narrative. The publication
of the document was indeed a political manœuvre, explicable
in terms of the balance of power at Alexander's death, but there
is no need to suspect chicanery or forgery. As regards the plans
themselves there is a surprising unanimity in the ancient tradition. Alexander did have enormous ambitions of conquest. Of
that there is agreement in general outline and in detail. We
need not doubt that in his last years his concept of his own
greatness had become obsessive. His intention was not merely
to surpass what had gone before but to leave posterity no hope
of equalling him. Whether architectural or military, his
achievements were to be a perpetual frustration for all succeeding dynasts. The Last Plans in Diodorus are the detritus of
those aspirations, surviving to bemuse later ages like Shelley's
monument of Ozymandias. Fragmentary and tantalizing they
may be, but they are reliably reported and historically invaluable.

---

[106] Badian (above, n. 6) 197–8; Errington, *Chiron* 8 (1978) 115–17.
[107] Diod. xviii. 16. 4 (cf. 12. 1); Arr. *Succ.* F 1. 4; Plut. *Phoc.* 26. 1. On the fleet see
above, p. 198.

# BIBLIOGRAPHY

What follows is a compromise. The footnotes give full coverage of the literature. I have extracted what seem to me the most significant contributions, arranged according to the interests of potential readers. Standard works of reference are excluded, as is specialist literature of peripheral importance.

I have used throughout the text established by A. G. Roos: (i) *Alexandri Anabasis*; (ii) *Scripta Minora et Fragmenta* (Teubner; 1967, 1968: second editions, revised by G. Wirth). This is a fundamental re-evaluation of the manuscript tradition, accepted as the basis of recent editions and translations:

BRUNT, P. A. *Arrian*: History of Alexander *and* Indica i–ii (Loeb Classical Library; Cambridge, Mass., 1976–83).

ARRIEN, *Histoire d'Alexandre*, trans. P. Savinel; postlude by P. Vidal-Naquet (Paris, 1984).

ARRIAN, *Der Alexanderzug: Indische Geschichte* (Greek and German), trans. and ed. G. Wirth, O. von Hinüber (Munich/Zürich, 1985).

## (i) BOOKS AND ARTICLES RELEVANT TO ARRIAN AND HIS HISTORIOGRAPHICAL MILIEU

AMELING, W., 'L. Flavius Arrianus Neos Xenophon', *Epigraphica Anatolica* 4 (1984) 119–22.
—— 'Cassius Dio und Bithynien', *Epigraphica Anatolica* 4 (1984) 123–38.

ANDREI, O., *A. Claudio Charax di Pergamo* (Bologna, 1984).

AVENARIUS, G., *Lukians Schrift zur Geschichtsschreibung* (Meisenheim/Glan, 1956).

BODEFELD, H., *Untersuchungen zur Datierung des Q. Curtius Rufus* (Düsseldorf, 1982).

BOSWORTH, A. B., 'Arrian's Literary Development', *CQ* 22 (1972) 163–85.
—— 'Arrian and the Alani', *HSCP* 81 (1977) 217–55.
—— *A Historical Commentary on Arrian's History of Alexander* i (Oxford, 1980).
—— 'Arrian at the Caspian Gates: A Study in Methodology', *CQ* 33 (1983) 265–76.

BOWERSOCK, G. W., 'A New Inscription of Arrian', *GRBS* 8 (1967) 279–80.
—— *Greek Sophists in the Roman Empire* (Oxford, 1969).

BREEBART, A. B., *Enige historiografische Aspekten van Arrianus' Anabasis Alexandri* (Leiden, 1960).

BRUNT, P. A., 'Stoicism and the Principate', *PBSR* 30 (1975) 7–35.
—— 'From Epictetus to Arrian', *Athenaeum* 55 (1977) 19–48.
—— 'On historical Fragments and Epitomes', *CQ* 30 (1980) 477–94.

DOSSON, S., *Étude critique sur Quinte-Curce* (Paris, 1887).

ECK, W., Jahres- und Provinzialfasten der senatorischen Statthalter von 69/
70 bis 138/39', *Chiron* 12 (1982) 281–362, 13 (1983) 147–237.

FOLLET, S., *Athènes aux II⁴ et III⁴ siècles* (Paris, 1976).

GRASSL, H., 'Arrian im Donauraum', *Chiron* 12 (1982) 245–52.

GUTSCHMID, A. VON, 'Zu den Fragmenten aus Arrians parthischer Geschichte', *Philologus* 8 (1853) 435–9 ( = *Kleine Schriften* iii. 125–30).

HABICHT, C., 'Zwei neue Inschriften aus Pergamon', *Instanbuler Mitteilungen* 9–10 (1959–60) 109–25.

—— "Zwei römische Senatoren aus Kleinasien', *ZPE* 13 (1974) 1–6.

HALFMANN, H., *Die Senatoren aus dem östlichen Teil des Imperium Romanum bis zum Ende des 2 Jh. n. Chr.* (Hypomnemata 58; Göttingen, 1979).

HAMMOND, N. G. L., 'Some Passages in Arrian Concerning Alexander', *CQ* 30 (1980) 455–76.

KIECHLE, F., 'Die Taktik des Flavius Arrianus', *Bericht der römisch-germanischen Kommission* 45 (1964) 87–129.

MILLAR, F., *Cassius Dio* (Oxford, 1964).

—— 'Epictetus and the Imperial Court', *JRS* 55 (1965) 141–8.

MOLES, J. L., 'The Date and Purpose of the Fourth Kingship Oration of Dio Chrysostom', *Classical Antiquity* 2 (1983) 251–78.

—— 'The Interpretation of the "Second Preface" in Arrian's *Anabasis*', *JRS* 105 (1985) 162–8.

NORET, J., 'Un fragment du dixième livre de la *Succession d'Alexandre* par Arrien retrouvé dans un palimpseste de Gothenbourg', *AC* 52 (1983) 235–42.

OLIVER, J. H., *The Civic Tradition and Roman Athens* (Baltimore, 1983).

PRITCHETT, W. K., *Dionysius of Halicarnassus: On Thucydides* (Berkeley, 1975).

REUSS, F., 'Arrian und Appian', *Rh. Mus.* 54 (1899) 446–65.

RUTZ, W., 'Zur Erzählungskunst des Q. Curtius Rufus', *Hermes* 93 (1965) 370–82.

SCHEPENS, G., 'Arrian's View of his Task as Alexander–historian', *Ancient Society* 2 (1971) 254–68.

—— 'Geschiedenis als drama in Arrianus' Anabasis Alexandri', *Koninklijke Zuidnederlandse Maatschappij voor Taal- en Letterkunde en Geschiedenis: Handelingen* 36 (1982) 153–68.

SCHWARZ, F. F., 'Arrian's *Indike* on India: Intention and Reality', *East & West* 25 (1974) 181–200.

STADTER, P. A., 'Flavius Arrianus: the new Xenophon', *GRBS* 8 (1967) 155–61.

—— 'Xenophon in Arrian's *Cynegeticus*', *GRBS* 17 (1976) 157–67.

—— 'The *Ars Tactica* of Arrian: Tradition and Originality', *CP* 73 (1978) 117–28.

—— *Arrian of Nicomedia* (Chapel Hill, 1980).

—— 'Arrian's Extended Preface', *Illinois Classical Studies* 6 (1981) 157–71.

SYME, R., *Tacitus* (Oxford, 1958).

—— *Roman Papers* (Oxford, 1979–84).

—— 'The Career of Arrian', *HSCP* 86 (1982) 181–211.

WHEELER, E. L., 'Flavius Arrianus: A Political and Military Biography' (diss., Duke University, 1977).
—— 'The Occasion of Arrian's *Tactica*', *GRBS* 19 (1978) 351–65.
WIRTH, G., 'Zur Tigrisfahrt des Kaisers Traianus', *Philologus* 107 (1963) 288–300.
—— 'Helikonios der Sophist', *Historia* 13 (1964) 506–9.
—— *Studien zur Alexandergeschichte* (Darmstadt, 1985).
ZECCHINI, G., 'Modelli e problemi teoretici della storiografia nell'età degli Antonini', *Critica Storica* 20 (1983) 3–31.


(ii) BOOKS AND ARTICLES RELEVANT TO ALEXANDER AND THE HISTORIOGRAPHY OF HIS REIGN.

ANDREOTTI, R., 'Die Weltmonarchie Alexanders des Grossen in Überlieferung und geschichtlicher Wirklichkeit', *Saeculum* 8 (1957) 120–66.
ATKINSON, J. E., *A Commentary on Q. Curtius Rufus' Historiae Alexandri Magni Books 3 & 4* (London Studies in Classical Philology 4; Amsterdam/Uithoorn 1980).
BADIAN, E., 'The Eunuch Bagoas: A Study in Method', *CQ* 8 (1958) 144–57.
—— 'Harpalus', *JHS* 81 (1961) 16–43.
—— 'The Date of Clitarchus', *PACA* 8 (1965) 5–11.
—— 'A King's Notebooks', *HSCP* 72 (1968) 183–204.
—— 'Nearchus the Cretan', *YCS* 24 (1975) 147–70.
—— 'The Deification of Alexander the Great', *Ancient Macedonian Studies in Honor of Charles F. Edson*, ed. H. J. Dell (Thessaloniki, 1981) 27–71.
—— 'Greeks and Macedonians', *Macedonia and Greece in Late Classical and Early Hellenistic Times* (Studies in the History of Art 10; Washington, 1982) 33–51.
BALSDON, J. P. V. D., 'The "Divinity" of Alexander', *Historia* 1 (1950) 363–88.
BERGER, H., *Die geographischen Fragmente des Eratosthenes* (2nd edn., Leipzig, 1903).
BERVE, H., *Das Alexanderreich auf prosopographischer Grundlage* i–ii (Munich, 1926).
BOSWORTH, A. B., 'The Death of Alexander the Great: Rumour and Propaganda', *CQ* 21 (1971) 112–36.
—— 'Arrian and the Alexander Vulgate', *Entretiens Hardt* 22 (1976) 1–46.
—— 'Alexander and Ammon', *Greece and the Ancient Mediterranean in History and Prehistory*, ed. K. Kinzl (Berlin 1977) 51–75.
—— 'Alexander and the Iranians', *JHS* 100 (1980) 1–21.
BRIANT, P., *État et pasteurs au Moyen-Orient ancien* (Cambridge/Paris, 1982).
—— *Rois, Tributs et Paysans* (Centre de Recherches d'Histoire Ancienne 43; Paris, 1982).
BROWN, T. S., *Onesicritus: A Study in Hellenistic Historiography* (Berkeley, 1949).
—— 'Callisthenes and Alexander', *AJP* 70 (1949) 225–48.

BROWN, T. S., 'Alexander's Book Order (Plut. Alex. 8)', *Historia* 16 (1967) 359–68.

DAFFINÀ, P., 'Aral, Caspio, Tanais', *Rivista degli Studi Orientali* 43 (1969) 363–78.

DIHLE, A., *Studien zur griechischen Biographie* (Abh. der Ak. der Wissenschaften in Göttingen Phil.-Hist, Kl., Dritte Folge, nr. 37; Göttingen 1970).

EDMUNDS, L., 'The Religiosity of Alexander', *GRBS* 12 (1971) 363–91.

FEARS, J. R., 'The Stoic View of the Career and Character of Alexander the Great', *Philologus* 118 (1974) 113–30.

FORNARA, C. W., *The Nature of History in Ancient Greece and Rome* (Berkeley, 1983).

FRASER, P. M., 'Current Problems concerning the Early History of the Cult of Sarapis', *Opuscula Atheniensia* 7 (1967) 23–45.
—— *Ptolemaic Alexandria* i–iii (Oxford, 1972).

FRAUSTADT, G., *Encomiorum in litteris Graecis usque ad Romanam aetatem historia* (diss., Leipzig, 1909).

GOUKOWSKY, P., *Essai sur les origines du mythe d'Alexandre* i–ii (Nancy, 1978–81).

GREEN, P., 'Caesar and Alexander: *Aemulatio, Imitatio, Comparatio*', *AJAH* 3 (1978) 1–26.

GUNDERSON, L. L., 'Quintus Curtius Rufus', *Philip II, Alexander the Great and the Macedonian Heritage*, eds. W. L. Adams, E. N. Borza (Washington, 1982) 177–96.

HABICHT, C., *Gottmenschentum und griechische Städte* (Zetemata 14, 2nd edn.; Munich, 1970).

HAMILTON, J. R., 'Cleitarchus and Aristobulus', *Historia* 10 (1961) 448–58.
—— *Plutarch Alexander: A Commentary* (Oxford, 1969).
—— 'Alexander and the Aral', *CQ* 21 (1971) 106–11.
—— 'Cleitarchus and Diodorus 17', *Greece and the Ancient Mediterranean in History and Prehistory*, ed. K. Kinzl (Berlin, 1977) 126–46.

HAMMOND, N. G. L. and GRIFFITH, G. T., *A History of Macedonia* ii (Oxford, 1979).

HAMMOND, N. G. L., *Alexander the Great: King, Commander and Statesman* (Park Ridge, NJ., 1980).
—— *Three Historians of Alexander the Great* (Cambridge, 1983).

HAMPL, F., 'Alexanders des Grossen Hypomnemata und letzte Pläne', *Studies Presented to D. M. Robinson* ii (St Louis, 1953) 816–29.
—— 'Alexander der Grosse und die Beurteilung geschichtlicher Persönlichkeiten', *La Nouvelle Clio* 6 (1954) 115–24.

HANSEN, G. C., 'Alexander und die Brahmanen', *Klio* 43/45 (1965) 351–80.

HAUBEN, H., 'The Expansion of Macedonian Sea-power under Alexander the Great', *Ancient Society* 7 (1976) 79–105.

HEUSS, A., 'Alexander der Grosse und die politische Ideologie des Altertums', *Antike und Abendland* 4 (1954) 65–104.

HÖGEMANN, P., *Alexander der Grosse und Arabien* (Zetemata 82; Munich, 1985).

HOFFMANN, W., *Der literarische Porträt Alexanders des Grossen im griechischen und römischen Altertum* (diss., Leipzig, 1907).

HORNBLOWER, J., *Hieronymus of Cardia* (Oxford, 1981).

JACOBY, F., *Die Fragmente der griechischen Historiker* (Berlin/Leiden, 1923–).

—— *Griechische Historiker* (Stuttgart, 1956; articles reprinted from Pauly–Wissowa).

KORNEMANN, E., *Die Alexandergeschichte des Königs Ptolemaios I von Aegypten* (Leipzig, 1934).

MARTIN, V., 'Un recueil de diatribes cyniques: Pap. Genev. inv. 271', *MH* 16 (1959) 77–115.

MENSCHING, E., 'Peripatetiker über Alexander', *Historia* 12 (1963) 274–82.

MERKELBACH, R., *Die Quellen des griechischen Alexanderromans* (Zetemata 9, 2nd edn.; Munich, 1977).

MOMIGLIANO, A., 'Terra marique', *JRS* 32 (1942) 53–64 ( = *Secundo Contributo alla storia degli studi classici* [Rome, 1960], 431–46).

NOCK, A. D., *Essays on Religion and the Ancient World*, ed.. Z. Stewart (Oxford, 1972).

PEARSON, L., 'The Diary and the Letters of Alexander the Great', *Historia* 3 (1954/5) 429–39.

—— *The Lost Histories of Alexander the Great* (Philological Monographs 20; New York, 1960).

PÉDECH, P., 'Strabon historien d'Alexandre', *Grazer Beiträge* 2 (1974) 129–45.

—— *Historiens compagnons d'Alexandre* (Paris 1984).

PRICE, S. R. F., *Rituals and Power* (Cambridge, 1984).

RICE, E. E., *The Grand Procession of Ptolemy Philadelphus* (Oxford, 1983).

ROISMAN, J., 'Ptolemy and his Rivals in his History of Alexander the Great', *CQ* 34 (1984) 373–85.

ROSEN, K., 'Political Documents in Hieronymus of Cardia', *Acta Classica* 10 (1967) 41–94.

SAMUEL, A. E., 'Alexander's Royal Journals', *Historia* 14 (1965) 1–12.

SCHACHERMEYR, F., 'Die letzte Pläne Alexanders', *JÖAI* 41 (1954) 118–40.

—— 'Alexander und die Ganges-Länder', *Innsbrücker Beiträge zur Kulturgeschichte* 3 (1955) 123–35.

—— *Alexander in Babylon und die Reichsordnung nach seinem Tode* (SB. Wien 268. 3; Vienna, 1970).

—— *Alexander der Grosse: Das Problem seiner Persönlichkeit und seines Wirkens* (SB. Wien 285; Vienna, 1973).

SCHWARTZ, E., *Griechische Geschichtsschreiber* (Leipzig, 1959; articles reprinted from Pauly–Wissowa).

SEIBERT, J., *Alexander der Grosse* (Erträge der Forschung 10; Darmstadt, 1972).

—— *Das Zeitalter der Diadochen* (Erträge der Forschung 185; Darmstadt, 1983).

SORDI, M., 'Alessandro e i Romani', *Rendiconti dell' Istituto Lombardo* 99 (1965) 445–52.

SORDI, M., (ed.), *Alessandro Magno tra storia e mito* (Milan, 1984).

STRASBURGER, H., *Studien zur Alten Geschichte*, eds. W. Schmitthenner, R. Zoepffel (Hildesheim, 1982).

TARN, W. W., 'Alexander's Hypomnemata and the World Kingdom', *JHS* 41 (1921) 3–17.

—— *Alexander the Great* i–ii (Cambridge, 1948).

WEBER, F., *Alexander der Grosse im Urteil der Griechen und Römer bis in die konstantinische Zeit* (diss. Giessen, 1909).

WEIPPERT, O., *Alexander-imitatio und römische Politik in republikanischer Zeit* (Augsburg, 1972).

WELLES, C. B., 'The Discovery of Sarapis and the Foundation of Alexandria', *Historia* 11 (1962) 271–98.

WILCKEN, U., 'Hypomnematismoi', *Philologus* 53 (1894) 84–126.

—— *Berliner Akademieschriften zur alten Geschichte und Papyruskunde, 1883–1942* (Leipzig, 1970).

WILL, E., *Histoire politique du monde hellénistique i–ii* (Nancy, 1966–7).

WILL, W., *Athen und Alexander* (Münchener Beiträge zur Papyrusforschung und Rechtsgeschichte 77; Munich, 1983).

WÜST, F. R., 'Die Rede Alexanders des Grossen in Opis', *Historia* 2 (1953/4) 177–88.

—— 'Zu den Hypomnematen Alexanders: das Grabmal Hephaistions', *JÖAI* 44 (1959) 147–57.

# GENERAL INDEX

Abdera, 109
Abii, Scythian tribe, 123
Abreas, 79
Achilles, 32, 75
Acuphis, Indian prince, 71
Aeacus, 119, 143
Aelian (Claudius Aelianus), of Praeneste, 7, 44, 170–3, 177
Aelius Aristeides, 34; on Amazons, 66; on Athenian imperialism, 143
Aemilius Paulus, L., 155 n.
Africa, 22, 85, 132, 185, 193; Al.'s proposed circumnavigation of, 190, 194
Agatharchides, of Cnidus, 9 n., 41 n.
Agesilaus II, Spartan king, 26, 139, 153
Agis, of Argos, poet, 113
Alani, 23, 31
Albani, 32
Alcetas, brother of Perdiccas, 199 n.
alcohol, ancient attitudes to, 178
Alexander I, of Macedon, 'the Philhellene', 109 n.
ALEXANDER III, of Macedon, 'the Great': eulogy of, by Callisthenes, 5–7; by Ptolemy, 137; by Arrian, 34–5, 135–45; Aristobulus' treatment of, 140–1, 147, 183, 192; in Tacitus, 153–5; in rhetorical tradition, 127–8, 144–5; Arrian's attitude to, 16, 32–3, 34–8, 70–1, 86, 145–52; in Cynic theory, 73–4, 148
    resources at accession, 102; at the Granicus, 12; and alleged relations with Amazons, 65–7; with Chorasmian king, 66–7, 192; murder of Cleitus, 63, 115, 146–7, 150; *proskynesis*, 63–4, 113–16; at Nysa, 69–72; at the Hyphasis, 123–7; at Malli town, 76–7, 78–82, 151; with Indian ascetics, 72–4, 190–1; in Carmania, 67–9; and Cyrus' tomb, 49–55; at Opis, 101–2, 126–7; reaction to Hephaestion's death, 65, 171–2, 177–8, 204–7; and Roman embassy, 83–93; on the Euphrates, 57–9, 62–3, 187–8, 191; Arabian expedition of, 56–9, 163–6, 187–90; 195–7; proposed circumnavigation of Africa, 129–32,

190–5; preparations in Levant, 197–200, 209–11; Last Plans of, 129–33, 185–211; last illness of, 157–70; tradition of poisoning, 175–9, 182–4, 191–2; treatment of Darius' family, 136–7; drinking habits, 140, 147, 158–9, 170–5, 183–4; attitude to divinity, 5–6, 113–15, 141–3
Alexander's surveyors, *see* bematists
Amazons, 65–7, 91 n.
Ammon, 6, 101, 141, 203 n.
Amorgos, 198
Amphipolis, 110
Anaxarchus, of Abdera, philosopher, 113, 123, 134, 150
Anaximenes, of Lampsacus, historian, 2, 109
Androsthenes, of Thasos, 60, 189 n.
Anicius Cerealis, C., 117
Antigonus (Monophthalmos), son of Philippus, 117, 120, 200 n.
Antimachus, of Colophon, poet, 68
Antipater, son of Iolaus, 175, 176 n., 182, 197–8, 199 n., 208, 210
Antiphon, Athenian politician, 138
Antium, 91
Antoninus Pius, 29
Antony, M., Cicero's attack upon, 96–9
Aornus, 128
Apameia, in Bithynia, 35 n., 36
Apis bull, 169
Apollo, 141, 168 n.
Appian: his use of Arrian, 32, 59 n., 62 n.; on the debate of Jan. 43 BC, 96, 97–9
Arabia, Arabs, 56, 63, 166, 189 n., 193, 195 n., 196
Arachosians, 106
Araxes, R., in Armenia, 31
Arbela, 78
Archias, son of Anaxidotus, of Pella, 60
Ariaspians, 87
Aristobulus, of Cassandreia, historian, 2, 3, 13, 30, 39, 61, 62, 77, 87, 102, 115, 140, 141, 158, 159, 167, 177 n., 183, 189, 191 n., 192, 195 n., 196; omissions in, 65, 69, 83; on Cyrus' tomb, 47–55; on Euphrates canals, 56; on death of Cleitus, 64; on naval preparations, 187